TWENTIETH - CENTURY
ORNAMENT

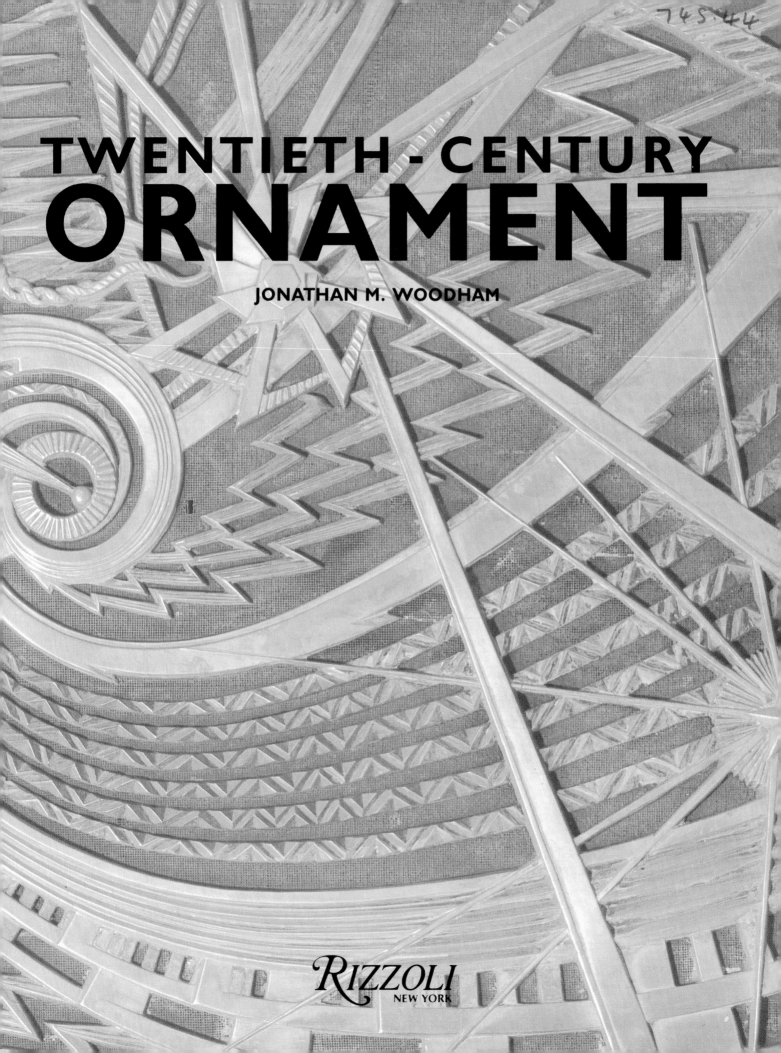

TWENTIETH - CENTURY
ORNAMENT

JONATHAN M. WOODHAM

RIZZOLI
NEW YORK

First published in 1990 in the United States
of America by
Rizzoli International Publications, Inc.
300 Park Avenue South, New York,
New York 10010

**Library of Congress Cataloging-in-
Publication Data**
Woodham, Jonathan M.
    Twentieth-century ornament.
    Jonathan Woodham.
        p.   cm.
    Includes bibliographical references.
    ISBN 0–8478–1221–9
    1. Decoration and ornament—History—
20th century.   I. Title.
NK 1390, WG 1990
745.4′442—dc20   89–49452 CIP

This book was conceived and produced by
JOHN CALMANN AND KING LTD, London

Designed by Richard Foenander
Picture research by Susan Bolsom-Morris

Typeset by Fakenham Photosetting Ltd
Printed in Singapore by Toppan Ltd

ACKNOWLEDGEMENTS

I would like to thank my wife Mandy for her
help and support at a time when she has had
so much else to preoccupy her; also friends,
colleagues and students at Brighton
Polytechnic, especially those connected with
the BA (Hons) History of Design degree from
whom I have learnt so much. Gratitude is also
due to the staff of the many libraries and
museums I have consulted, but above all to
Susan Bolsom-Morris who has performed the
difficult task of locating many of the more
unusual images in this publication with such
apparent good humour and tolerance.
                                Jonathan M. Woodham

For my Parents

Contents

LEFT **Warner fabric**, *Webster Vine* (originally called *Jacobean*). This was first produced between 1913 and 1918. Despite its strong flavour of that period, its decorative elements also contributed to its enduring success in the marketplace. It was still a good selling design in the 1950s and has recently been re-released. Such designs reveal the problems in considering ornament in terms of specific historical periods or design movements. Across the design spectrum there are many patterns which have been highly successful in commercial terms over many decades. In domestic decorative schemes these tend to reflect traditional values.

BELOW **Wedgwood**, *Edme Plain* in *Queen's Ware* on *Edme* shape, first introduced in 1908 and still in production. It was very popular in the 1920s, either plain or decorated with various print and enamel patterns. It is ornamented by a raised ribbing effect.

Foreword

In any comprehensive study of the varying ways in which ornament has been used in consumer society, it soon becomes evident that its adoption is not restricted to the output of progressive designers and their fashion-conscious clients, prominent as these have been in the majority of histories of design. Nor is it something which is merely confined to the decorative arts with their slight undertones of cultural élitism. Advances in mass-production technologies, increased levels of affluence, greater sophistication in marketing and retailing strategies and ready access to fashionable trends through the mass media have all contributed to the appeal and importance of ornament in numerous fields of design: automobiles, domestic appliances, buildings and packaging are no less significant bearers of ornament in the twentieth century than interiors, furniture, furnishings, wallpapers and ceramics. Ornament has been, and is likely to remain, an essential and meaningful part of almost every aspect of everyday life.

Ornament may be imbued with a multiplicity of meanings. It can convey ideas and expectations of warmth and security in the domestic environment through the adoption of traditional patterns and motifs in furniture, furnishings and fitments; it can promote an image of financial security for banks through the use of established classical forms and details in buildings and decoration; it can give rise to notions of luxury and opulence in the elaborate decorative schemes of hotel foyers, theatre auditoriums, public spaces in civic buildings and other places of leisure, entertainment and work. Furthermore, ornamentation may be deployed or purchased in order to indicate power, wealth, refinement, education, exoticism, contemporaneity, individuality or even social conformity. It provides a means of expression which, in one form or another, has been exercised by people from all sectors of society, irrespective of wealth, race, class or gender, and is an important aspect of the material culture of the twentieth century.

The wider public dimension of ornament is of great significance in this context. While the symbolic and aesthetic function of domestic ornament is obviously fundamental to many people's private lives, its more widely accessible counterpart also has an important role to play in the shaping of patterns of taste. Widely disseminated in the everyday architectural environment of shops and shopping centres, offices, factories or places of entertainment and leisure, it is a vital ingredient in the provision of visual stimulus for the general public. Cinema and television, having emerged as major determinants of twentieth-century visual and material culture, have also been key elements in this wider climate of ornamental design. The screen has exerted a powerful shaping force in the lives and expectations of millions, promoting images of affluence and aspiration dressed up in a wide range of styles—historical, modernist, futuristic and exotic. Such widespread currency for all kinds of ornamental and decorative fashions has been enhanced further by the rapid growth and increasing sophistication of the advertising industry. This has utilized all kinds of graphic ephemera, as well as the moving image, as a means of inducing people to consume any number of products which reflect notions of taste, status and lifestyle. Graphic ephemera, including style magazines, Do-It-Yourself manuals, comic strips, trade catalogues and billboards, have also become an accepted part of contemporary life, and cannot be ignored as major communicators of all kinds of ornamental expression.

Throughout the century ornament and decoration have been used by manufacturers and designers as tools to boost the sales of many mass-produced consumer products—for example, in the field of domestic appliances. An increasingly wide range of these domestic aids has been taken for granted as part of consumer life; as their functional benefits have been absorbed into the everyday routine, so their ornamental and decorative features have become increasingly important considerations in their purchase. These features may simply be applied to a two-dimensional surface, as with bucolic motifs of agricultural workers harvesting sheaves of corn on the sides of electric toasters, or realized in three dimensions, as in neo-Classical ornamental forms and motifs applied to electric fire design.

Ornament has been applied with no less vigour, and often with far greater dramatic effect, to the automobile, one of the major consumer status symbols of the twentieth century. Although commonplace for decades in the industrialized world, it has exerted an increasingly significant social impact since the turn of the century. After the First World War, styling played an increasingly important part in its mass appeal, with radiator grilles, dashboards, manufacturers' marques and other key features providing rich opportunities for ornamental expression. This reached a high point in the neo-Baroque exuberance of the chromium-plated fantasies of automobile design in the United States in the 1950s.

Thus it may be seen that ornament is a feature of almost all aspects of life in the industrialized world. However, in this survey of twentieth-century ornament it is clearly impossible to embrace fully all dimensions of the subject. It has been necessary to restrict this survey largely to the countries of Europe and North America, together with those contexts in which Western industrial culture has been a dominant force. This is less problematic than might at first appear, since cultural hegemony largely rested with European countries until the late 1930s, whether transmitted via the social mores and economic mechanisms of empires or through the artistic activities of the avant garde. After the Second World War, American cultural and economic values exerted an increasingly significant global influence: the consumer affluence and commodity fetishism so alluringly depicted in Hollywood films came to symbolize for many peoples across the world the visible trappings of "a better way of life." Although this influence has subsequently diminished with the emergence of other major economic forces such as Japan, the values of Western consumerism and styling have remained at the forefront of international trade. It is only over the past fifteen years that a far richer diet of cultural influences has emerged as a potent force in the market-place, ranging from the "alternative"

values of craft production to the minimalist aesthetic of Japanese-inspired retailing interiors. The advent of Flexible Manufacturing Systems (FMS), which have introduced the possibility of limited, yet economic, production runs of products for specific markets, has enlarged further the possible ornamental variations of mass-produced consumer goods.

Just as it is impossible to chart exhaustively the use of ornament across the globe within a limited space, so it is problematic to attempt any comprehensive analysis of the visual and ornamental culture of the majority. Indeed, many ornamental trends have been relatively constant throughout the decades of the twentieth century: manufacturers of textiles and ceramics in particular have had many, generally traditional, patterns in production for long periods. Furniture, fitments and fittings have followed a similar path. Such ornamental expressions of domestic stability and felicity, while they are important in terms of volume sales in any given period, do not characterize most forcefully the particular fashions and tastes of the times. This survey is concerned with many of the major shifts in aesthetic outlook which have subsequently been seen to characterize particular periods and trends across a wide range of design media; none the less, it is hoped that it will cast light on a number of the broader concerns, both from the point of view of design consciousness and the visual culture of everyday life.

In an examination of ornamental trends in the leading industrial countries, it is evident that many different and distinct fashions live alongside each other. For example, the 1920s and 1930s are often associated with the output of Art Deco and its legacy, whether in the decorative inlays of furniture, or the brightly coloured geometric patterning of tableware, cigarette cases, carpets and interior design. But it is also a period characterized by the streamlined ornamentation and styling of a wide range of consumer goods in the United States, which was stimulated by a public appetite voracious for symbols of progressive technology and a widespread interest in the futuristic visions of science fiction. The Modern Movement, associated with the legacy of the avant-garde designers of Weimar Germany, post-Revolutionary Russian Constructivism and De Stijl, also came to the fore in the interwar years; although theoretically opposed to ornament for its own sake it had, none the less, particular traits which contributed an identifiable design aesthetic, particularly in the fields of textiles, wallpapers and graphics. Widespread references to past historical epochs also abounded and were widely disseminated in the suburban housing boom in Britain: "Stockbroker Tudor" houses with inglenook fireplaces, half-timbering and stained glass representations of Elizabethan sailing ships set in heavily panelled front doors were typical of the period. Parallels may be made with many other European countries as well as the United States where Spanish Colonial, Queen Anne and other architectural styles provided an appropriate setting for furniture and furnishings which drew on the past for inspiration.

A similar co-existence of styles pervades all other periods throughout this century, culminating most recently in the cult of Post-Modernism, where references to styles and ornamental motifs drawn from a variety of cultures and epochs abound alongside each other, often entirely divorced from their original meanings or associations. Initially conceived as a means of enhancing the supposedly restricted language of Modernism which had largely dominated the architectural and design output of the design establishment until the 1960s, Post-Modernism has itself become generally little more than a stylistic game which provides a ready outlet for marketing ornament and decoration and making profit.

Ornament is an important tool in the communication of social and cultural values, and is often seen as an emblem that symbolizes a commitment to a particular lifestyle or belief. But by its very nature, it is also a highly marketable commodity, able to be controlled and exploited by commercial interests and market forces. As goods become more widely available they generally lose the conviction of their original message and content, becoming instead routes to profitability rather than conveyors of ideology.

BELOW **Wedgwood**, *Queen's Ware*, dating from the early years of this century. The "revived" late eighteenth- and early nineteenth-century freehand enamelled border patterns were popular at this time. Another form of historicism is evident in the Chinoiserie-inspired plate in the centre, reproducing the *Japan* pattern first introduced by the Wedgwood company in the early nineteenth century.

RIGHT **Warner fabric**, *Munster*, by Marianne Straub, 1957. An enduring line, this design relied on textural surface for variety and interest. Ordered by clients as varied as the British Government's Ministry of Works and Heals Fabrics Ltd, it outlived many rapidly changing vogues in textile pattern design.

FAR RIGHT **Warner fabric**, *Peony Gardens*, designed by Richard Hanley (USA) for Warner Greeff in 1969. Such designs show the continued interest throughout the century in traditional floral motifs and subject matter as suitable for furnishings as well as other design media.

BELOW ***Old Country Roses*** tableware in bone china by Royal Albert (Royal Doulton), first introduced in 1962. This is the world's best-selling tableware design and since its launch has achieved sales of over 90 million pieces in many different countries. It shows the enduring attraction of patterns which explore traditional notions of the "country garden", a theme which Royal Albert first introduced in 1893. The *Old Country Roses* pattern was designed by Harold Holdcroft and had achieved such popularity by 1975 that the range was extended from dinner, tea, coffee and breakfast sets to include ornaments such as vases, candlesticks and trinket boxes. More recently other manufacturers have taken up the pattern for tablecloths, tablemats, napkins and aprons. Such a history over almost thirty years underlines the shortcomings of attempting to categorize ornamental styles into tight historical compartments, for many traditional patterns of taste live on through countless changes in fashion.

1
Progressive Design and Historical Inspiration 1900 to 1914

Nineteenth-century Roots and the Arts and Crafts Legacy

The nineteenth century is generally associated with widespread industrialization and the development of new technologies for the mass-production of a wide variety of goods. New processes and techniques made the large-scale manufacture and application of ornament and decorative motifs a reality, while the development of transport and communication networks increasingly allowed the transmission and absorption of a wide variety of styles and cultures. The growth of museums and the mounting of major international exhibitions in Europe and the United States, commencing with the 1851 Crystal Palace exhibition in Hyde Park, London, furthered this process. Attracting millions of visitors to experience the national pavilions and products of countless nations, the exhibition introduced manufacturers to a seemingly endless supply of sources with which to embellish their products. As a result, the Victorian householder was able to draw on an encyclopaedic range of ornamental motifs to decorate the home. Unfortunately, such goods were often of less than the highest quality and attracted the contempt of many design reformers in Europe and the United States, in terms of both the low value placed on the creativity of the individual designer and the social consequences brought by industrialization to the majority of those who worked under its shadow.

Hoping to remedy this situation, William Morris and his Arts and Crafts followers pursued a critique of this design and lifestyle in the second half of the nineteenth century, but their writings, ideology and aesthetic doctrines were only given material form in the houses and furnishings of an "enlightened" upper-middle-class clientèle. Such a restricted market clearly affected the realization of the more socially-orientated Arts and Crafts aspirations for the provision of a better living and working environment for society as a whole. None the less, the movement provided a significant catalyst for progressive developments in design in the early years of the twentieth century, especially in continental Europe.

A fervent dislike of the reliance on historicism by members of the academic establishment in the fields of fine arts, architecture and design had already found fresh and vigorous expression in the work of a new generation of designers in the closing years of the old century. This was, perhaps, epitomized in the organic arabesques of the Art Nouveau style. This had taken root in variable conditions: the cold, wet soil of Charles Rennie Mackin-

FOLLOWING PAGES **Inlay** by Koloman Moser, 1903, exhibiting a typically strong sense of geometric linearity in this ornamental detail from a chest, using inlays of rare woods and other expensive materials to rich decorative effect.

LEFT **Apollo Theatre**, London, designed by Lewen Sharp, 1901. This rich essay in a heavily ornate Baroque style was typical of theatre design of the period.

Austria and the Wiener Werkstätte

An important design group of the new century was the Wiener Werkstätte (the Vienna Workshops), founded in 1903 by the designers Josef Hoffmann and Koloman Moser, together with their financial backer Fritz Wärndorfer. Like a number of other contemporary ventures in Germany and elsewhere, its roots were in the Secessionist, anti-establishment spirit of the late 1890s and its leading practitioners looked northwards to certain aspects of British Arts and Crafts practice and outlook for an indication of ways to develop. Indeed, as with a number of other European groups, the Wiener Werkstätte provided an important link between forward-looking ideas of the late nineteenth century and more radical strands of twentieth-century development.

Across Europe the Secessionists had placed significant stress on the advancement of the applied arts, and Wiener Werkstätte activities similarly embraced a wide variety of design fields, including fashion, textiles, furniture, wallpaper, graphics, ceramics, jewellery and architecture. Their attitude accorded with the prevalent nineteenth-century notion of the *Gesamtkunstwerk* ("the total work of art"), whereby all aspects of design were integrated into a unified whole, a philosophical and aesthetic premise that firmly underpinned the group's activities. This ideal was perhaps most fully realized in the architecture, interiors and furnishings of the highly influential Palais Stoclet in Brussels, designed by Josef Hoffmann and executed by the Wiener Werkstätte.

Initially the group's products, particularly those of Moser and Hoffmann, revealed a sense of structure and geometry suggesting links with the work of Mackintosh and the Glasgow School, which was well known in Austria.[2] After the departure of Moser from the group in 1907, an altogether more florid and decorative style developed, under the impetus of artists such as Carl Otto Czeschka and Berthold Löffler; the tendency gained further licence with the appointment of Dagobert Peche as manager of the Artists' Workshops in 1915. Furthermore, despite its increasing emphasis on retailing outlets in the years leading up to the First World War, the Wiener Werkstätte was concerned ultimately with aesthetic rather than social and egalitarian inclinations, since the majority of its products catered for the wealthy upper echelons of fashionable Austrian society. Although important links were forged with the manufac-

tosh's Glasgow, the more temperate environment of Antonio Gaudí's Barcelona and the Turin of Raimondo d'Aronco, the windy lake-shores of Louis Sullivan's Chicago, the flatlands of Holland or the more fertile regions of Austria, Belgium, France and Germany.[1]

ABOVE **Printed silk design** by Charles Rennie Mackintosh, *c.* 1900. The strong flowing lines and forms of this watercolour design show Mackintosh's affinity for the organic forms of Art Nouveau at this time, albeit manifest in aspects of the Celtic Revival in Scotland. The pronounced graphic linearity in many of the details can be found in much of Mackintosh's contemporary work in other fields, including stencilwork, furniture decoration and glass.

RIGHT **Fabric design** in watercolour, *c.* 1910, by the Wiener Werkstätte textile workshop which was set up in 1905.

turing industry, particularly in the fields of wallpaper and textiles, this élitist tendency was compounded by the Wiener Werkstätte's unwillingness to address whole-heartedly the implications of industrial production, which were felt by many of its participants to run contrary to the central and dominant role envisaged for the artist-craftsman or woman. Parallels may be drawn with debates about the respective merits of individual artistic expression and standardization among members of the more industrially orientated Deutscher Werkbund, particularly in the years immediately prior to 1914.

Before the Wiener Werkstätte's liquidation in 1932 it experienced a succession of financial problems and structural re-organizations. Its design output came under increasing attack from critics such as Julius Klinger and Adolph Loos, an architect-designer and author of an important essay of 1908 entitled "Ornament und Verbrechen" ("Ornament and Crime"). At this period the group was dominated by women, many of whom had completed their training at the Vienna Kunstgewerbeschule (School of Arts and Crafts) during the War years. Their extravagantly ornate work afforded male detractors an opportunity for criticism, and blame for the organization's demise was placed firmly at their door.

France in the early 1900s

In France the final flowering of Art Nouveau was seen at the large-scale International Exhibition held in Paris in 1900, and the style lingered only comparatively briefly in the early years of the new century, in spite of efforts to produce cheap Art Nouveau furniture for department stores and a certain fashionability of the trend among a number of architects who blended it with elements of the neo-Baroque. However, in general, most of the more progressive tendencies in early twentieth-century French design were not closely allied to mass-production or the pockets (and tastes) of the everyday consumer. They

LEFT **Mathilde Flöge**, wearing a costume designed by herself, *c.* 1905, which shows the close relationship between fashion and the applied arts and concern for the importance of design as a unifying element in all aspects of life. Ms Flöge is standing before a cabinet designed by Koloman Moser and is wearing jewellery by Josef Hoffmann. She and her sister ran a leading Viennese fashion salon and many of their gowns were close in style and spirit to the art of Gustav Klimt.

inclined rather more towards the fine arts, high fashion, individuality and the whims of a wealthy clientèle. Organizations such as, for example, the Société des Artistes Décorateurs, founded in 1901, helped bring the decorative and applied arts to the art-conscious public in a series of annual exhibitions from 1907 onwards. Likewise the Salon d'Automne, which was founded in 1903 largely to promote the fine arts, held a series of annual exhibitions that included a section on the decorative arts from 1906 onwards.

Despite a predilection for eighteenth-century design and ornament as a promising source for modern French design, particularly among furniture designers, there had also been a growth of interest in a wide range of non-European sources, including African, Persian and Eastern. This preoccupation with the exotic was furthered by the impact of Diaghilev's Ballets Russes which first performed in Paris in 1909, although it was not until the following year that it exerted a particularly strong oriental influence on the dress and décor of fashionable society. The 1910 production of *Schéhérazade* designed by Léon Bakst, rich in striking colour combinations and a spirit of oriental decadence, made its mark.

Parisian Taste:
Paul Poiret and Raoul Dufy

Lucien Vogel's fashion magazine the *Gazette du Bon Ton*, published in Paris from 1912 to 1914 (and again from 1920 to 1925), was given imaginative expression by a number of highly talented fashion illustrators who vividly conveyed something of the fashionable taste of the time. Another patron of such work was the Parisian couturier and arbiter of taste, Paul Poiret, who published *Les Robes de Paul Poiret raconté par Paul Iribe* in 1908 and *Les Choses de Paul Poiret vues par Georges Lepape* in 1911. In the latter year he also set up a school of decorative art in Paris, named after his second daughter, Martine. It was attended by a number of talented working-class children who were encouraged to develop their ideas without the formal training and inhibitions resulting from the curricula of official schools of art and design.[3] The pupils worked on bold, brightly coloured patterns for textiles, wallpapers, ceramics, furniture and murals, and often found inspiration in visits to the zoo, botanical gardens

and the countryside. So successful was the venture that in the following year Poiret was able to persuade the Salon d'Automne to devote two rooms to the pupils' sketches and patterns. He also opened an interior decoration business, L'Atelier Martine, selling a whole range of designs by the "Martines" as well as offering related consultancy work for the decoration of hotels, cafés, restaurants, offices and private houses.[4] Although not without its critics, the enterprise flourished to such an extent that orders came in from a number of countries, including the United States, and a London branch was opened in 1924.

Poiret's projects were largely inspired by his acquaintance with Austrian and German developments in art and design education and practice. Significantly, he had met Josef Hoffmann on a visit to Austria in 1910 and was well acquainted with the work of the Wiener Werkstätte, an interest which he consolidated in succeeding years. Although he was not an admirer of all aspects of the Wiener Werkstätte's output, he approved of the flower-pattern textiles derived from folk art, which shared many characteristics with those executed by the "Martines".[5]

During the same years Raoul Dufy had begun to influence a number of designers in textile printing. He had collaborated with Poiret and the "Martines" before joining the firm of Bianchini and Férier in 1912. Textile design was a field in which fine artists were often commissioned by interior designers to contribute to their decorative schemes for wealthy patrons; yet again this tended to echo the aura of artistic élitism associated with fashionable designers in many other media at the time.

The Salon d'Automne of 1910 included designs produced by progressive German designers. These were comparatively simple in form and decoration, exhibiting a restrained use of ornament and emphasizing the design co-ordination of complete rooms. Awareness of this new approach, together with comparisons made between the French and the less blatantly craft-orientated contributions of several other national displays at the Exposition Universelle et Internationale held at Brussels in the same year, led to calls to re-establish the international prestige of French design.

LEFT **Raoul Dufy,** fabric design for L'Atelier Martine, produced by Bianchini-Férier, Lyon. This audacious, almost naive, but highly decorative design shows Dufy's close affinities with the Martine aesthetic.

Germany: Standardization and Individual Expression

Germany was the source of the most significant and advanced ideas on design in the early twentieth century, culminating in the foundation of the Deutscher Werkbund in Munich in 1907, an organization which sought to forge a collaboration between industry and the applied arts and to re-establish the dignity of labour in the context of machine production. This progressive spirit, it was hoped, would overcome not only the poor quality apparent in most mass-produced German design together with the more anti-industrial and romantic strains of the Arts and Crafts movement, but would also establish modern German design as an important economic force in the international market-place.

In parallel with other countries this modern approach had as its background Germany's own Secession movement of the 1890s and the more radical elements of the German Arts and Crafts movement. Karl Schmidt had founded the Dresdener Werkstätten für Handwerkskunst (the Dresden Workshops for the Arts and Crafts) in 1898, the same year in which the Vereinigte Werkstätten für Kunst im Handwerk (the United Workshops for Art in the Crafts) was established in Munich; both became major commercial enterprises involved in a variety of design fields, including furniture, textiles, ceramics and lighting. Such moves towards the establishment of concerns promoting high-quality artistic craftsmanship and furthering exploration of the implications of machine production were consolidated by the establishment of the Werkstätten für Deutschen Hausrat (Workshops for German Furnishings) and the Münchener Werkstätten für Wohnungs-Einrichtung (Munich Workshops for Domestic Furnishings). There was a move towards a simpler, more functional-looking aesthetic with a more restrained use of ornament than that of the flowing, curvilinear forms associated with Jugendstil, the German Art Nouveau movement also popular in the 1890s. Growing recognition of these new trends in German applied art was aided by the critical attention afforded them at the International Exhibitions held in Paris in 1900, Turin in 1902 and St Louis in 1904, but the solid achievements of this design reform movement prior to the foundation of the Deutscher Werkbund can most usefully be gauged by the success of the Third German Applied Arts Exhibition, mounted in Dresden in 1906.[6]

The Deutscher Werkbund

As a direct result of this exhibition, Friedrich Naumann, an artistically aware liberal politician convinced of the vital role of machine production in the regeneration of German culture, collaborated with Karl Schmidt of the Dresdener Werkstätte. Together they sought to establish the basis for a national organization which would further consolidate progressive tendencies in German design— the Deutscher Werkbund. Another key figure behind the foundation of this new body was Hermann Muthesius, who had reviewed the 1906 Dresden exhibition favourably and pointed to the Dresdener Werkstätte as proof that progressive design was commercially viable, morally responsible and reconcilable with industrial production.

He shared the enthusiasm of a number of his contemporaries for many of the underlying principles of the Arts and Crafts movement, as had been revealed in his important publication *Das Englische Haus* (*The English House*) of 1904, based on studies of contemporary British architecture and design. In Berlin in the early 1900s, Muthesius found himself a key figure at the centre of the debate concerning reform of arts and crafts education, and used his influence to appoint progressive designers to key academic posts. Through his enthusiastic espousal of reform in the applied arts, he aroused the considerable antagonism of many conservative industrialists con-

BELOW **Hermann Muthesius**, fireplace, executed by Bergner and Franke *c.* 1912. The metalwork detailing in the rear reveals Muthesius' close links to the English Arts and Crafts movement.

nected with the Fachverband für die Wirtschaftlichen Interesse des Kunstgewerbes (Trade Association for the Economic Interests of Applied Art).

It was in the resulting atmosphere of dispute and controversy that the Deutscher Werkbund was founded in Munich in October 1907, with about a hundred artists, industrialists and other interested parties present. Part of the wider movement for German cultural reform,[7] its aim was to bring together artists, craftsworkers and manufacturers to improve the design, quality and reputation of German consumer products, overshadowed as they had been by foreign competitors, particularly the French. The Werkbund was soon organized on a national basis and, especially after the move of the head office to Berlin in 1912, membership grew significantly in the years leading up to the outbreak of the First World War.[8] However, despite considerable efforts through propaganda, exhibitions and publications,[9] the organization's success was comparatively limited in the face of a conservative industrial sector which saw design largely in terms of an encyclopaedic use of historic ornamentation. In order to demonstrate more forcefully the outlook and achievements of the Werkbund it was decided to mount a major exhibition in Cologne in 1914. This massive enterprise consisted of almost a hundred buildings, with a huge range of both crafts-based and industrially produced design on display within. Although a number of the more vociferous members of the Werkbund had argued for a style which was compatible with efficient mass-production technologies, and thus one which exhibited ornamental restraint, many of the exhibits drew on a wide variety of ornamental styles. The heavy, historicizing ornamentation generally associated with mid-nineteenth-century furniture and furnishings, the sinuous arabesques of *fin-de-siècle* Jugendstil and the greater austerity of neo-Classicism were among the many kinds of ornamental motifs evident in much of the furniture, furnishings and interiors on show. However, the exhibition has been remembered by design historians more for the progressive, functional contributions of the avant garde and the fierce arguments concerning the relative merits of standardization (Typisierung) and individual artistic expression.[10] These were put forward by Muthesius and Henry Van de Velde respectively, although the issue had been simmering on and off since the Werkbund's foundation.

Van de Velde, a Belgian by birth, played an important role in the early years of the century in the development of German design theory and practice, and maintained in his autobiography (written over fifty years later) that he was a key contributor to the ethos which gave rise to the Deutscher Werkbund. Through his involvement with the more progressive tendencies in German art and design education as Principal of the Weimar School of Arts and Crafts, he had sought to develop links between students, craftsworkers and local industry. In this respect, he shared a number of the wider aims of the Werkbund, which he joined in 1908. But by the time of the 1914 Cologne Exhibition he had become concerned that the balance of the organization had clearly swung in favour of industry rather than art, feeling that Muthesius' emphasis on the need to create forms compatible with mass-production technology amounted to the surrender of artistic integrity to economic interests. This ideological confrontation demonstrated the Werkbund's lack of aesthetic cohesion, something that was borne out in several of the exhibition displays.

Despite the inclusion of many products revealing a predominantly functional aesthetic, where ornament played a role subordinate to form, visitors could take in a wide variety of styles and ornamental motifs. These included elements of the neo-Baroque in Paul Ludwig Troost's dining-room in the Bremen-Oldenburg House, nineteenth-century undertones in interior design by Walter Gropius, heavy neo-Classical furnishings by Peter Behrens, elements of organic Jugendstil in Van de Velde's Theatre and furniture, Expressionism in Bruno Taut's Glass Pavilion and élitism in the luxury goods on display in the Austrian Werkbund Pavilion. Both the diversity of approach and the fact that the designs shown were beyond the price range of the majority revealed that the goal of a modern German style of quality, the desired outcome of a marriage between art and mass-production technology, was still in the throes of conception. It was not until the 1920s that a real change became evident.

By the First World War, however, the standardization lobby in the industrial sector could point to some successes. Most widely known was the design work of Peter Behrens for the rapidly growing electricity supply and production company, the Allgemeine Elektrizitäts Gesellschaft (AEG). Appointed as design consultant in 1907, Behrens had responsibility for design across the spectrum, whether consumer or capital goods, architecture or publicity material. Ornament and decoration were much restrained in designs which conveyed the clean lines, forms and spirit of modern technology.

"Ornament and Crime"

In the context of such debates it is important to consider the position of the Austrian Adolf Loos who, like a number of progressive designers associated with the Werkbund, has been seen as a contributor to a truly twentieth-century vocabulary of design. An important theorist and apostle for a functionalist aesthetic, he was as much opposed to the Deutscher Werkbund as he had been to the ornamental decadence of the Wiener Werkstätte and the Wiener Sezession, which he had attacked in his essay "Ornament und Verbrechen" ("Ornament and Crime") in 1908. There he pronounced that "the evolution of culture marches with the elimination of ornament from useful objects." He felt that the Werkbund was furthering the cause of the artist, and thus the notion of applied art, in the design process. In his opinion ornament was largely an irrelevance in modern life, as was any self-conscious quest for modernity, since the form of articles of use should derive naturally from their function. For him "the modern ornamentalist" was "either a cultural laggard or a pathological case."

Ornament, Status and Transatlantic Travel

Loos's aesthetic outlook was not necessarily what the majority wanted, whether wealthy or otherwise. Ornament and decorative motifs were felt to give clear indications of the status of the owner or user and related to traditional contexts or expectations. Something of this conflict of outlook could be seen in the interior decoration and ornamentation of the great transatlantic liners of the early years of the century. These ships, the majority of which were German or British, were seen very much in terms of national prestige. They attracted considerable interest in this era of fierce competition in the transatlantic passenger trade (greatly stimulated by unrestricted immigration to the United States).[11] All kinds of historically derived styles were utilized to convey an aura of luxury: plasterwork, furniture, lighting, wall and floor coverings and other surfaces drew on sources from Louis

XIV to North Africa as a means of creating the desired effect of opulence. The rather austere leanings of the design reformers found expression in a number of German liners, but ultimately did little to curb the wealthier passengers' appetite for luxurious, highly ornamented surroundings. For example, the North German Lloyd Line's *Kronprinzessen Cecilie*, which went into transatlantic service in 1907, included a number of first-class cabins designed by progressive designers such as Richard Riemerschmid and Bruno Paul and executed by the Vereinigte and Dresdener Werkstätte.[12] These rather neat and restrained interiors contrasted strongly with the extravagant ornamentation and historic eclecticism found elsewhere in the more prestigious public areas of the ship, as in the Viennese café and Renaissance dining room. Although the proto-Modernist design lobby were offered other, more significant, commissions for interior design on contemporary liners these met with limited approval as their aesthetic restraint did not epitomize the glamour with which the richer transatlantic passengers expected to be surrounded.

Germany's great competitor in transatlantic passenger trade before the First World War was Britain. The Cunard Line's highly successful *Mauretania* went into service in the same year as the *Kronprinzessen Cecilie* and reflected a wide range of historicizing European styles in its interior design. Similarly, the White Star Line's *Olympic*[13] had first-class cabins with eleven different decorative styles as well as an Arabian indoor swimming pool, with marble drinking fountain and bronze lamps.

Early Twentieth-century Britain: Arts, Crafts and Industry

Such predilections were a fair reflection of the contemporary aesthetic climate in early twentieth-century Britain. Despite the foundation in London of the promisingly entitled Design and Industries Association (DIA) in 1915, there was little by way of genuine sustenance for the spirit of progressive design allied to the realities of mass-production, although Britain was not only a dominant international force in terms of industrialization, but also the original home of the Arts and Crafts movement and the source of inspiration for a number of significant continental developments in design.

The Ornament of Edwardian Opulence

Ornament in the Edwardian era drew on a wide range of styles. One of the more insistent, particularly in an urban context, was the Beaux-Arts classicism often associated with the period and exemplified by many of the luxury hotels built during this time. One such building was the London Ritz of 1903–6, with its opulent, spacious and ornate interiors, designed by one of the most successful architectural design partnerships to specialize in such work, that of Arthur J. Davis and Charles Mewes, whose output epitomized the apparent affluence of the age. Other London examples revealing similar tendencies included A. G. R. Mackenzie's Waldorf Hotel, with its luxurious Palm Court of 1906–8 replete with elaborate plasterwork ornamentation and potted plants, and Davis's exuberant Royal Automobile Club of 1908–11.

Theatre design provided another rich forum for the exploration of the hugely diverse ornamentation that typified the age. The music hall, so much a feature of late Victorian and Edwardian life, plundered an almost encyclopaedic variety of sources, ranging from the Middle East and the Orient to European Baroque. Rich and elaborate Indian décor, for example, dominated the auditorium of the huge Olympia Theatre in Liverpool. Built as a music hall for Moss Empires in 1905, it was designed by Frank Matcham, one of the leading architects specializing in the field. Similarly, variations on a Chinese theme enlivened the interior of the Grand Theatre in Clapham, London, complete with pagoda boxes and ornamental dragons. Designed by E. A. Woodrow in 1900, the contents rather contradicted the Baroque flavour of the exterior.

Theatre-going was a fashionable Edwardian pastime, and a considerable number of theatres opened in London's West End during the period, complementing the extravagances of contemporary hotels. Several theatres were designed by the highly successful W. G. R. Sprague, including the Albany (1903), the Aldwych and the Strand (both 1905), the Globe (1906), the Queen's (1907) and the Ambassador's (1913). Although Sprague favoured Baroque ornament and decoration, he occasionally drew on Italian Renaissance, Georgian and other sources. The Edwardian period also gave rise to another vogue in theatre architecture, the large-scale lavish extravaganza. One of the most celebrated of these mammoth enterprises was the London Opera house, which opened in 1911. Designed by Bertie Crewe for the American, Oscar Hammerstein I, the façade was modelled on Perrault's seventeenth-century Louvre, with the gargantuan gilded sculptural and decorated interior drawing on the French Renaissance and other European styles.

Although in its infancy before the First World War, cinema design also began to reflect the spirit of the age, with elaborate plasterwork detailing and other ornamental features, although it was not until the inter-war years, when the cinema became a major social force, that ornament and decoration began to display rather more extravagant features.

Edwardian public houses, particularly in metropolitan areas, provided another rich opportunity for ornamentation. They were often filled with mirrored glass, decorative tilework, elaborate cabinetwork and plaster

BELOW **Walter Thomas**, *The Vines* public house, Lime Street, Liverpool, England, 1907. This interior, with its lavish plasterwork and exuberant detail, is a rich excursion in the Edwardian Baroque reminiscent of contemporary theatre design.

detailing, all of which drew on the past for inspiration. Much of the decoration, such as embossed wallpapers and ceiling coverings, could be bought by the roll, and there were also readily available substitutes for fibrous plasterwork. Craftsworkers specialized in decorative glass techniques such as embossing, sandblasting and silvering which featured in so many town halls, libraries and other public buildings of the period.

The Omega Workshops

One avant-garde organization which involved many of the leading British artists of the day was that of the Omega Workshops Ltd, established in 1913 with the critic Roger Fry and artists Vanessa Bell and Duncan Grant as co-

directors. Fry was an important proselytizer for progressive Continental artistic developments in the rather academically stifling climate of early twentieth-century London. As well as clearly admiring the fine art of late-nineteenth-century France he had been impressed by the activities and output of the Wiener Werkstätte. Though by no means as important as its Austrian counterpart in terms of scale, influence or talent, the Omega Workshops also explored the concept of the *Gesamtkunstwerk* through involvement with a wide range of design media,

BELOW **Interior** of the Cadena Café, 49 Westbourne Grove, London, executed by the Omega Workshops in 1914. The Workshops were responsible for the waitresses' uniforms as well as the mural designs, floor rugs and lamps. The stress on the production of a co-ordinated, aesthetically charged environment, surface decoration and an "artistic" ambience brings to mind the decorative schemes of the Wiener Werkstätte in Austria or the Atelier Martine in France.

including furniture, textiles, ceramics and other fields relating to co-ordinated interior design. The designers themselves often used bold, brightly coloured, abstracted forms which showed a knowledge of the paintings of Matisse, the Fauves and the Cubists on the Continent. The Omega Workshops also shared the Wiener Werkstätte's ambivalence about purpose, clientèle and mass-production; despite carrying out a number of commissions for public interiors such as the Cadena Café in London's Westbourne Grove and a Post-Impressionist Room for the widely visited and publicized *Daily Mail* Ideal Home Exhibition,[14] Fry placed much reliance on his contacts with fashionable and wealthy London society as a means of enhancing the Workshops' reputation. This, together with his antagonism to critics, undoubtedly restricted the success of the enterprise, which closed down in June 1919.

Ornament in Early Twentieth-century USA

The remarkable increases in production capacity which had been taking place in the United States in the later nineteenth and early twentieth centuries were not generally accompanied by innovative design. As in many European countries, contemporary ornamentation drew on an extensive selection of sources, with variations on traditional styles playing a dominant part. Such an outlook, spurred on by the wide-ranging classicism permeating the architecture of the World's Fair Columbian Exhibition held in Chicago in 1893, drew criticism from both Frank Lloyd Wright and Louis Sullivan, two of the country's most progressive architects, who decried this tendency to celebrate the styles of past, generally European, cultural epochs instead of expressing the spirit of American democracy. The massive Columbian Exhibition also gave many Americans a taste of the grand, elaborate, decorative interiors which dominated the public spaces of large buildings—such as stations, libraries, hotels, theatres, apartment blocks and offices—for the first thirty years or so of the new century.

As in Europe, Beaux-Arts classicism, with its ponderous sculptural detail, had become a common feature of many American cities by the early 1900s. However, exploration of other stylistic themes continued apace, whether the Flemish Gothic of the exterior detailing of Cass Gilbert's 1913 Woolworth Building in New York or the Georgian, Italian Renaissance, French eighteenth-century, Elizabethan, Beaux-Arts Baroque and other styles which inspired the exterior form and interior decoration of many houses for the wealthy. Similar tastes in domestic furnishing and decoration were furthered by the abundance of contemporary magazines devoted to such concerns as this.

Hotel architecture on a grand scale, catering for the upper and middle classes, flourished in the early years of the century, encouraged by the economic recovery. New York, in particular, boasted a large number of hotel buildings proffering many varieties of ornament and decoration. The rampant eclecticism of the period could be seen in Clinton and Russell's Astor Hotel on Broadway, of 1904–9, which featured among its interiors a Pompeiian billiards room, a Flemish smoking room, a German Renaissance hunt room, an American Indian grill room and an Oriental room, as well as several Art Nouveau rooms. Hotel design of a rather more restrained type was to be found at Warren and Wetmore's Ritz-Carlton on Madison Avenue of 1910; their use of Adam neo-Classicism became widely known as Ritz Hotel Adam. *Habitués* of such metropolitan haunts of the wealthy also welcomed echoes of the opulent ethos and lifestyle associated with the fashionable hotels of Edwardian England, especially when taking tea in the Palm Courts that had become almost *de rigueur* for the grand hotels of the time. One of the most splendid of these, modelled on the Carlton Tea Room in London, was the glass-domed Tea Room of Henry J. Hardenbergh's New York Plaza Hotel of 1907, with its marbled columns, mirrors and classical detailing.

American theatre design similarly reflected the many ways in which ornamental styles were deployed prior to the outbreak of the First World War. Among the most successful architects in this genre were Herts and Tallent, both graduates of the Ecole des Beaux Arts. A strong Art Nouveau flavour pervaded their designs for the New Amsterdam Theater of 1903 and the renowned German Theater of 1908, both in New York. The interior of the latter was a collaboration with the celebrated Art Nouveau designer, Alphonse Mucha, who contributed murals and decorative stencilwork. In 1911, Herts and Tallent were equally able to draw on Moorish inspiration for the façade of their New York Folies Bergère dinner-theatre, ornately patterned in ivory, turquoise and gold terracotta.

Theme-restaurants were also popular at the time and allowed a great deal of ornamental freedom. One of the best known was Murray's Roman Gardens, designed by Henry Erkins in 1907.[15] The main dining room conjured up the atmosphere of a Pompeiian atrium, with all kinds of Roman statuary and architectural features as well as a variety of plants under an artificially lit fictive evening sky. Any diners not content with a single theme could enjoy their meal in an environment drawn from an older civilization in the Egyptian Dining Room. Such "ornament for effect," though somewhat cruder in its directness, was seen by a wider public in the stylistic pot-pourri of kiosks and features at Coney Island's Luna Park and Dreamland which opened in 1903 and 1904 respectively. There, Venetian, Tudor, Japanese, Indian and Classical styles all vied for the attention of visitors.

In many areas of the decorative arts there was a plentiful supply of craftsworkers who were familiar with all aspects of ornamental detailing. Many of them had arrived in America as part of the large-scale emigration from Europe, especially Italy, which continued until after the First World War. Ornament of all kinds and periods could be designed to order as well as bought in ready-made form from a wide range of catalogues. These offered stylistic confections fashioned from fibrous plaster, terracotta and pressed wood, as well as all varieties of decorative brickwork and tiling.[16] Wallpaper design, though scorned by progressive architects and designers such as Frank Lloyd Wright, similarly reflected a number of styles and ornamental motifs. Friezes on the upper parts of the wall were popular, as were wallpaper borders, used both as surrounds to doors, windows and fireplaces and as a means of creating panels on wall surfaces, which were useful for pictures, mirrors or simply for general decorative effect. Such patterns were also often matched with those of curtains, upholstery and bedspreads.

It is clear that, despite the reforming zeal of a number of avant-garde theorists and practitioners of design, the early years of the century witnessed a wide variety of ornamental and decorative styles in Europe and the United States. Attempts by the Austrian Adolf Loos, the German Hermann Muthesius and others to stifle the ornamental excesses associated with much mass-produced nineteenth-century design were more than countered by the fashionable, colourful and seductive decorative motifs bought by many of the design-conscious wealthier classes.

On a more everyday level, the plethora of styles which was to be found in the furniture, furnishings, fittings and fitments of people's homes and leisure environment provides firm evidence that no particular style dominated the period, despite a number of fashionable trends. Public houses, restaurants, theatres and cinemas on both sides of the Atlantic drew on all kinds of sources for their ornamentation, embracing a wide range of historical, geographical and cultural references. Ornament was used to convey feelings of exoticism and novelty, status and stability, refinement and opulence, sophistication and education, according to the context in which it was displayed. The fact that it was increasingly mass-produced, was highly visible on the pages of mass-circulation magazines and could be purchased by the yard from the pages of all kinds of catalogues consolidated its position at the core of everyday life.

LEFT **Henry Janeway Hardenbergh**, the Tea Room at the Plaza Hotel, New York, modelled on the Carlton Tea Room in London. The marbled columns and other classical ornamental motifs, the rich floral swags seen on the carpet in the foreground, and the mottled lighting effects lent by the coloured glass in the roofing all contribute to the atmosphere of refined elegance and luxury expected in the best hotels of the period.

LEFT **Entrance hall** to Hill House, Helensburgh, Scotland, designed by Charles Rennie Mackintosh, 1902–3. The geometric patterning on the carpet and furniture again shows links with the Wiener Werkstätte. To the right of the picture one can see delicate stencilwork which was carried out in rose and green and was repeated right round the hall. Hill House was built for W. W. Blackie and is among the largest and most successful of Mackintosh's domestic designs.

RIGHT **Ebony and erinoid clock** designed by Charles Rennie Mackintosh for a terraced house at 78 Derngate, Northampton, England, owned by the engineer W. W. Bassett Lowke. One of many minor pieces he designed for the house in about 1917, the geometric decorative motifs are reminiscent of both earlier Wiener Werkstätte work and certain characteristics which were to be readily associated with Art Deco.

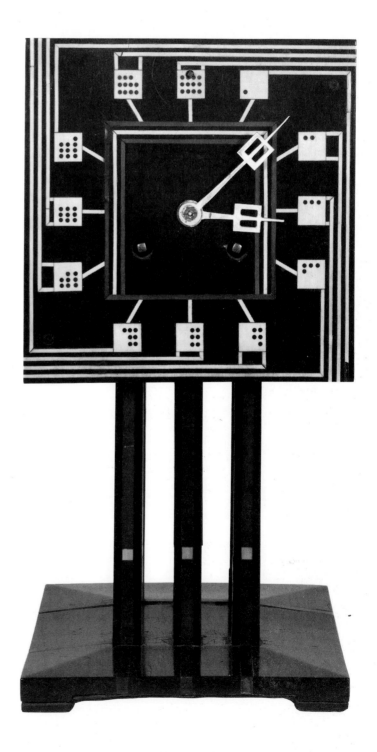

FAR LEFT **Fabric design**, Wiener Werkstätte, c. 1910. This fabric reveals close links with decorative motifs in contemporary printing by Gustav Klimt.

FAR LEFT BELOW **Printed silks** by the Wiener Werkstätte, designed by Edward Wimmer and Lotte Froemmel-Fochler, c. 1912. They reveal a move away from the more structured designs of Moser and Hoffmann in the early years of the century towards the more florid ornamentation of Dagobert Peche who was linked with the Werkstätte from 1915.

LEFT **Josef Hoffmann**, the large dining-room of the Palais Stoclet, Brussels, 1905–11. Employed by the wealthy Adolphe Stoclet, Hoffmann used the finest talents available from the Wiener Werkstätte and deployed the most luxurious materials: sideboards of Portovenere marble and macassar wood; marbled walls with mosaics by Gustav Klimt, executed by Leopold Forstner. The co-ordination of all the ornamental elements within a clear architectonic framework typifies the desire of many of the Austrian avant garde to produce a unified aesthetic.

BELOW **Women's shoes** in coloured silk and leather, executed by the Wiener Werkstätte, c. 1914. Such highly decorative footwear shows the attention paid by Werkstätte designers to all aspects of design in daily life, ranging from architectural interiors to items of personal adornment.

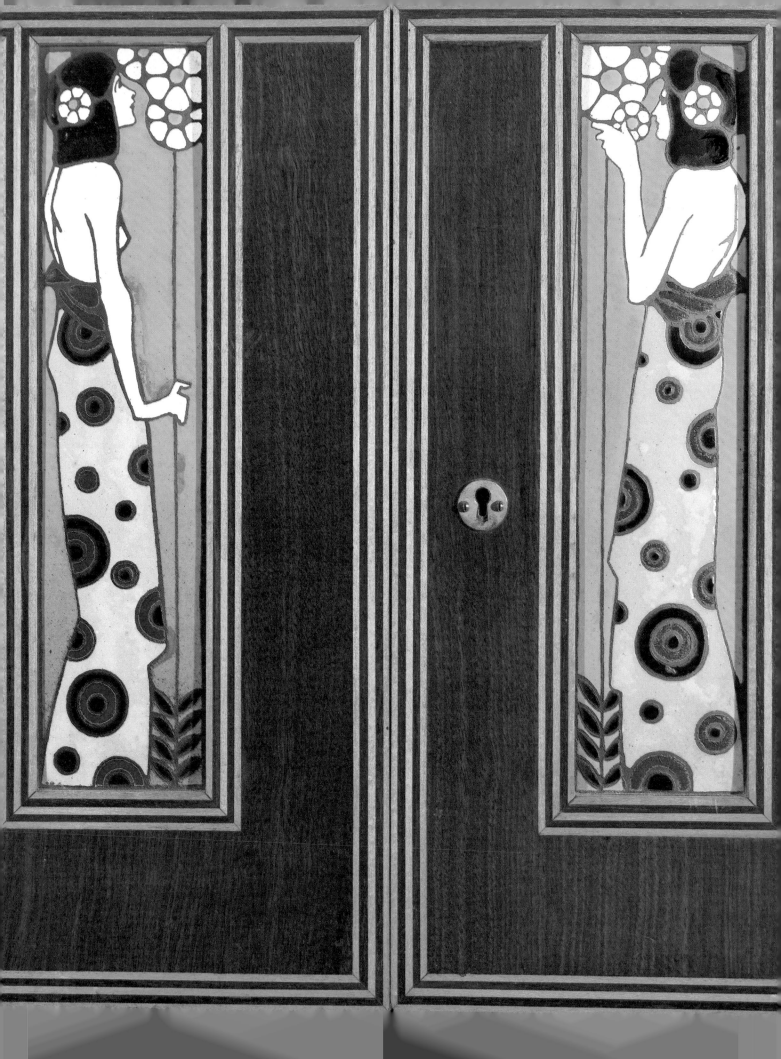

LEFT **Johanna Maria Holman**, macassar sideboard with inlaid ebony veneer and ivory handles, *c*. 1905. The inset paintings of young girls with flowers and their flowing curvilinear arabesques show affinities with the Jugendstil, while the construction and form of the sideboard relate closely to the geometrical tendencies of progressive Viennese designers in the early years of the twentieth century.

RIGHT **Gertrud Kleinhempel**, bedroom design for the Dresdener Werkstätte at Hellerau, *c*. 1902. She was one of a number of women designers who achieved recognition in the early years of this century. This interior was characterized by restraint in terms of ornamental detailing, with an emphasis on utility and simplicity of form common to many crafts-based organizations.

RIGHT **"Villa Mucki"**, executed by the Dresdener Werkstätte, *c*. 1904. This was a kind of playhouse/hinged screen with windows, for storing toys in the corner of rooms after the end of the day. The geometric decorative details were typical of the time.

ABOVE **Turkish bath** on the Olympic Ocean
Liner, White Star Line, 1911. Like the
Moroccan Room on the *SS France*, this essay
into Middle-Eastern exoticism showed the
extent to which First Class passengers
expected to have their appetite for all manner
of ornamental styles indulged.

ABOVE RIGHT **Moroccan Room** of the *SS
France*, 1910, which shows the wide variety
of styles deployed in a single ocean liner. A
Moroccan aesthetic not only reflected the
international competition to win a major share
of transatlantic passenger trade through an
emphasis on exotic styles, but also reflected
the particular contemporary competition
between Germany and France for control of
that country.

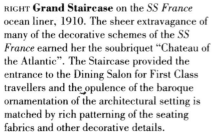

RIGHT **Grand Staircase** on the *SS France*
ocean liner, 1910. The sheer extravagance of
many of the decorative schemes of the *SS
France* earned her the soubriquet "Chateau of
the Atlantic". The Staircase provided the
entrance to the Dining Salon for First Class
travellers and the opulence of the baroque
ornamentation of the architectural setting is
matched by rich patterning of the seating
fabrics and other decorative details.

GREAT BRITAIN

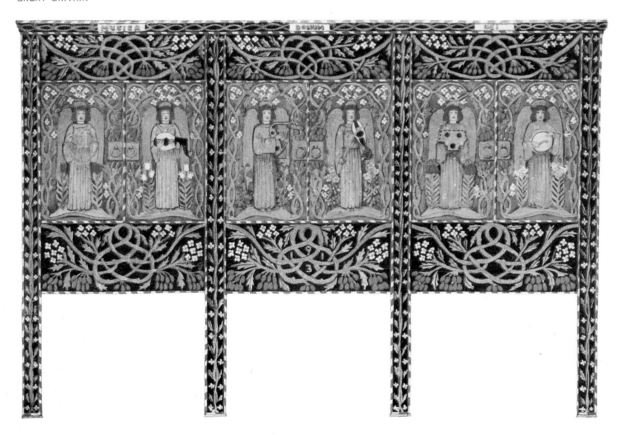

(Drawn by Allen Chandler)   DESIGN FOR A MUSIC CABINET BY M. H. BAILLIE SCOTT

ABOVE **M. H. Baillie Scott**, design for a music cabinet, *c.* 1914. This highly decorative piece was designed for a music room at Marvel Hill, Witley, England. The medievalizing panels, executed in gesso by Allen Chandler from Baillie Scott designs, reveals a strong influence of the Arts and Crafts movement. The carving in the frames around the door panels was executed by J. C. Pocock.

RIGHT **Ceramic stove**, Gmundner Ceramic School, Germany, 1910. The richly coloured foliage designs reveal a debt to Jugendstil.

LEFT *Jacobean* **wallpaper** manufactured by C. Knowles & Co. Ltd, *c*. 1910. This design, with its formalized floral motifs, typified the contemporary taste for historicizing styles.

BELOW LEFT **Owen W. Davis**, ceiling decoration by the Anaglypta Company, *c*. 1910. Such mass-produced means of applying ornamentation with the appearance of "craft" skills were widespread at this time when an extensive range of period styles were deployed.

RIGHT **Plasterwork Shop** of G. Jackson & Sons Ltd, 49 Rathbone Place, London W1, *c*. 1928. A large variety of ornamental plasterwork detailing could be bought off the peg or designed for specific commissions. Interiors were, as a result, able to be clothed in whatever historical dress the customer desired.

ABOVE **Peter Behrens**, plate with blue striped rim decoration, *c*. 1905. It shows Behrens' links with the flowing forms of Jugendstil, which he explored in a wide variety of design media, most notably in the furnishings and equipment of his house in the artistic colony of Darmstadt in 1901.

LEFT **Henry Van de Velde**, Chocolate Service, Meissen, 1900–5. The strong, organic quality of the forms and applied decoration reveal Van de Velde's roots in Art Nouveau.

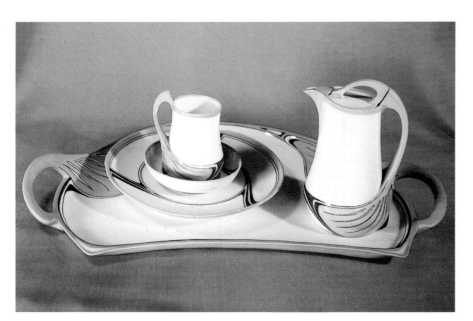

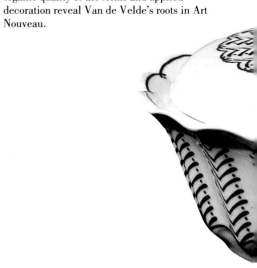

LEFT **Walter Gropius**, hall for Hermann Gerson of Berlin, exhibited at the 1914 Werkbund Exhibition at Cologne. The Cologne exhibition was associated generally with Gropius' progressive functional design, but this illustration of one of three suites reveals the fact that his interiors and furnishings looked back to the nineteenth century.

BELOW **Peter Behrens**, large porcelain soup terrine and dish, 1912. This design, despite its slightly fussy fluted forms, reveals a greater affinity with an abstract machine aesthetic than the flowing curvilinear decorative motif seen in the earlier plate design.

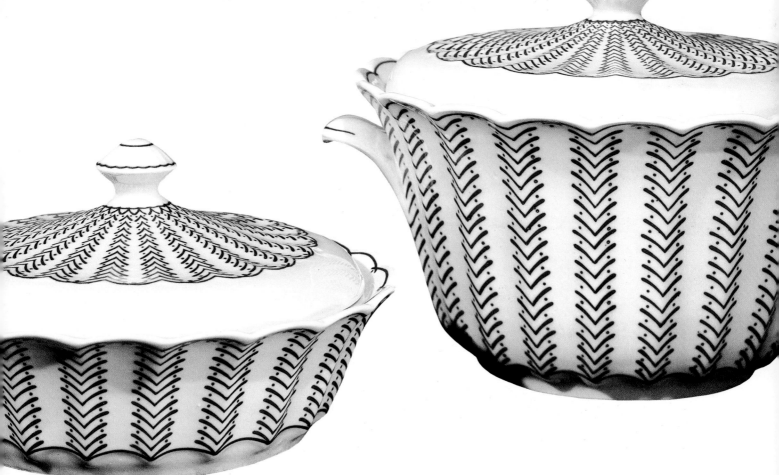

LEFT **Bathroom** decorated by L'Atelier Martine, *c.* 1914. The strong, emphatically two-dimensional decorative plant forms on the walls typify early Martine interest in stylized floral motifs and bright, Fauve-like colours.

BELOW LEFT **Bedroom** decorated by L'Atelier Martine for Poiret, Exposition des Arts Décoratifs at Paris, 1925. Poiret decorated all three barges moored on the Seine near to the Exposition entrance. This illustration of the interior of the barge *Amour* shows, among other details, a number of bold Martine fabric designs and a Martine chair in the foreground.

RIGHT **Poiret**, cape with designs by Raoul Dufy against an Atelier Martine background, 1926.

BELOW **Chest** decorated by Atelier Martine, in silver-leafed wood with incised decorations in black with handles of silk tassels, after designs by Mario Simon, 1923. Although this piece relies on large floral motifs for a major part of the decorative effect, the overall feeling is far more sophisticated than the rather bold, at times almost naive, forms of Martine work ten years earlier.

TOP LEFT **Vanessa Bell**, *White* printed linen, Omega Workshops, 1913.

ABOVE LEFT **Roger Fry**, *Amenophis* printed linen, Omega Workshops, 1913. The faceted construction underlying this design showed a number of links with the late work of Cézanne and that of the Cubists in France. As can be seen from these illustrations there was a considerable variety of stylistic approach among the group.

ABOVE **Omega Workshops**, Winifred Gill and Nina Hamnet modelling dresses. The textiles hanging in the background include *White* and *Amenophis*, while the painted screen, like the dresses, reveals links with the bold forms and colours of the early twentieth-century avant-garde French art so admired by Roger Fry and his circle.

RIGHT **Vase** thrown by Phyllis Keyes and decorated by Duncan Grant in the 1930s, on a tiled table made for Leonard and Virginia Woolf in the 1920s. Such painterly decorations reflected the ornamental ideals of the Omega Workshops in their concentration on surface rather than structure.

ABOVE **Bachelor's Wall Paper** design,
manufactured by the M. H. Birge Company,
Buffalo, New York, in 1902. This novelty
paper featured the heads of Charles Dana
Gibson's "Gibson Girls" and was widely
promoted in many American newspapers. The
faces were printed in black and the hair in
blue over light blue areas of colour.

RIGHT *The American Perfumer*, January
1910. This illustration of an embossed and
lithographed perfume package shows that the
flowing organic arabesques associated with
the Art Nouveau style lingered on well into
the twentieth century.

THE AMERICAN PERFUMER

AND ESSENTIAL OIL REVIEW.

JANUARY 1910

PERFUMER PUBLISHING CO
100 WILLIAM ST. NEW YORK

Triple Extract

The Mutual Manufacturing Co. Canton Ohio.

Designed Embossed and Lithographed by The BUEDINGEN BOX & LABEL CO.

~OFFICES~
BROWN & STATE STS.
ROCHESTER, N.Y.
AND
395 BROADWAY,
NEW YORK.

SEE PAGE VIII

Reproduced by courtesy of the Mutual Manufacturing Co.

BELOW **Henry Erkins**, the Egyptian Dining Room, *Murray's Roman Gardens* at 228–232 West 42nd Street, New York, built in 1907. This almost stage-like setting on the mezzanine floor with loose references to Egypt reveals an encyclopaedic range of ornamental styles with which many were acquainted. The entrance to the building was remodelled to represent the ancient residence of Cardinal Rohan in Paris.

BOTTOM **Henry Erkins**, the Main Dining Room, *Murray's Roman Gardens*. The Main Dining Room, with its artificially lit atrium, was intended to be like a Pompeian garden, and contained classicizing and other historical motifs.

BELOW RIGHT **Night view** of Coney Island Luna Park, Brooklyn, USA. Frederick Thompson, an entrepreneur, completed his exotically picturesque scheme in 1903, with its juxtapositions of Indian, Classical, Renaissance and other decorative styles. Another similarly extravagant enterprise, Dreamland, included a miniature Doge's Palace set in Venetian canals, a Tudor hospital, Old Nuremberg and other attractions. Like cinema designs in the 1920s, theme parks offered the public an experience of all kinds of ornamental styles.

RIGHT *Savon de Ramses* label, 1910s. Highly colourful patterns and decorative motifs reflect the widespread interest in exotic styles. The Egyptian theme would have proved an alluring one to potential consumers of *Ramses* soap.

2
From Historicism to Art Deco
1910 to 1940

The dominant trend in ornament of the inter-war years is often characterized by the geometric stylization of Art Deco, which proliferated widely in the wake of the Exposition des Arts Décoratifs et Industriels held in Paris in 1925. One end of the market, both European and American, was unashamedly orientated towards luxury, the other towards the mass market in which the art industries catered for the new middle-class home-owners of the 1920s and 1930s. However, many other ornamental trends played a popular and highly significant part during the period. The enthusiastic tastes of the 1920s embraced all manner of ornamental variations from Colonial to Chippendale, and encouraged the widespread plundering of form and decoration from diverse cultures and distant corners of the globe.

The American Cinema:
Stylistic Pluralism

A much more exuberant, fantasy-laden and indulgent counterpart to domestic ornamentation was evident in contemporary American cinema design. The cinema, the most powerful form of mass entertainment of the age, provided decorative opportunities not only in the settings of many of the films themselves but also in the buildings

and interiors to which audiences flocked in their millions to indulge their celluloid fantasies. The rapid development of the film industry and the formation of studio chains led to a tremendous upsurge of cinema theatre construction in the 1920s. The designs of many of these picture palaces were ornamental *tours de forces*, drawing on a wide range of decorative motifs and ornamental styles as a means of creating an awe-inspiring environment which would entice the audience. Deriving from cultures as far-flung as Aztec, Mayan, Persian, Egyptian and Chinese, they can be seen as the more exuberant successors to theme-restaurants and Coney Island diversions. Amongst the leading orchestrators of such cinema fantasies were Thomas W. Lamb, Rapp and Rapp, John Eberson and C. Howard Crane. Lamb could draw on French Rococo and Baroque motifs in his extravagant scheme for the Loew Midland Theater of 1927 in Kansas City, Rapp and Rapp on Mansart's Chapelle Royale for Louis XIV for the grandiose foyer of their Chicago Tivoli Theater of 1921, and Crane on the Far East for the Detroit Fox Theater of 1928.

It was John Eberson's "atmospheric" theatres, however, that were perhaps the most striking innovations in this highly competitive market. His first essay in this *genre* was the auditorium for the Houston Majestic of 1923, which sought to convey the impression of sitting in an Italianate garden in the open air under an evening sky. The walls on either side of the auditorium were fictive, shallow, three-dimensional architectural settings which heightened the sense of illusion. Such fantasy set the fashion for "atmospheric" cinemas of all kinds, including Spanish, Dutch, Chinese and Moorish. In order to facilitate the production of appropriate plaster ornament and applied decoration for these outlets, Eberson established a workshop, the Michelangelo Studios.

The Hollywood showman Sid Grauman helped to popularize a wide range of exotic styles in a number of Los Angeles cinemas, providing a "real life" counterpoint to many of the extravagant film sets that could be viewed on their screens. The Churrigueresque Spanish Baroque of eighteenth-century Mexican churches provided the source for Grauman's Million Dollar Theater of 1918, designed by William Lee Woollet. Egyptian Revival forms and ornament in Grauman's Egyptian Theater of 1922, by Meyer and Holler, established a vogue which spread to apartment blocks and other buildings. Grauman's 1927 Chinese Theater, also by Meyer and Holler, boasted Chinese Chippendale motifs which covered all available surfaces and fitments.

Cinema Design in Britain

After the First World War, as in the United States, the architecture and interior design of British cinema theatres were tremendously varied. The ingredient of fantasy was a necessary asset in the eyes of the cinema-going public and the buildings explored a wide spectrum of ornamental variations, both historical and contemporary, which were also characteristic of many products of everyday life. For example, the contemporary vogue for chinoiserie in interior design and decoration found popular expression in a number of cinemas, such as the exterior and interior of the 1929 Palace in Southall, London, designed by George Coles. Very much in tune with the prevailing eclecticism of the age, Coles proved himself to be equally versatile in the Egyptian style, as in his impressive Carlton cinema exterior of 1930 in Islington, London.

The late 1920s also saw the appearance in Britain of the "atmospheric" cinema interiors as developed by Eberson in the United States. Among the best known of these were the London Astoria cinemas designed by Edward Stone for Paramount. The interiors were created by T. R. Somerford and Ewen Barr and provided evocative fantasies on Italianate, Egyptian and Moorish as well as Deco themes. Another designer who drew on a wide range of styles was Theodore Komisarjevsky, commis-

BELOW **John Eberson**, Majestic Theater, Houston, Texas, 1923. One of Eberson's earliest "atmospherics", this interior design conveyed the effect of sitting in the garden of a late Renaissance palazzo.

sioned by Sydney Bernstein in 1930 to work on the interior designs of the new Granada circuit. The most spectacular of his creations was the 3,500-seat Granada cinema in Tooting of 1931, which drew on fifteenth-century Venetian Gothic sources, evoking a distant culture the moment cinema patrons entered the foyer.

Other Design Trends in Britain after the First World War

From the 1830s through to the present day, times of economic difficulty have given rise to design initiatives. The period immediately following the end of the War was no exception and saw government departments and others placing a greater emphasis on better quality design in everyday life. In 1919 the Ministry of Reconstruction published a paper entitled *Art and Industry*, which optimistically sought to improve the contemporary state of design production and consumption, defined in the paper as "making cheaply and selling dearly, an exploitation of the materials and means of manufacture which has led to monotony and drudgery, to loss of interest and thought, to loss of art."[1] Manufacturers were encouraged to place a greater emphasis on good quality than on purely commercial products, which were felt to offer a less secure economic base from which to rebuild Britain's trade at home and abroad. The British Institute of Industrial Art was incorporated in 1920 with government funding, and the stage looked set for a number of interesting developments in design practice and propaganda in both the industrial and public arenas. Unfortunately, in the troubled economic climate of the early 1920s, Treasury grants ceased, making the work of the Institute hard to continue effectively. The ambitiously named Design and Industries Association (DIA), founded in London in 1915, was also active at this time. Like many design-reform pressure groups of the inter-war years, its actual impact on manufacturing industry as a whole was extremely modest. However, its effect on *post facto* design history has been disproportionately greater by far. Individuals involved at the time gave a distorted view of its contemporary relevance, relying on organizational publications and records rather than on more informed and dispassionate evaluations.

The DIA advocated an aesthetic that was characterized by restraint in ornament and decoration. This was not something to which consumers readily warmed and they continued to be fascinated by historicizing ornament for many aspects of home decoration: Queen Anne, Tudor, Jacobean, Georgian and other styles with connotations of heritage were all readily available and eagerly purchased, whether in the form of furniture, textiles, wallpaper or other types of domestic design. Ceramic and flatware manufacturers also drew heavily on traditional sources for pattern, shape and decoration.

Floral ornamentation continued to be popular, as it had been earlier in the century. As an article of the mid-1920s in the *Manchester Weekly Guardian* commented:

> Everywhere the wretched *hortus siccus* flourishes. It lurks in knobs and handles, it is blatant in bath mats, lampshades illuminate it, "toilet ware" revels in it, and the most modest objects are conspicuously garlanded; it sits at the bottom of soup plates and is uncovered slowly by spoonfuls, on pots and vases intended to hold the real flowers it blandly invites comparison, it is engraved on glass, it is carved in wood, it is painted, woven, embroidered.[2]

Although such traditional tendencies dominated the period there were also companies with a more adventurous outlook. In the field of textiles, for example, W. Foxton Ltd commissioned designers of the calibre of Claude Lovat Fraser, who often used a geometrical pattern with small repeats, an unusual feature at this time. Other individual designers whose work reflected similar progressive qualities included Phyllis Barron, Enid Marx and Dorothy Larcher.

There were similar initiatives by designers in other fields, although these were supported by a very limited number of companies. Among these were Carter, Stabler, Adams of Poole who sought to promote ceramic designs which were generally characterized by clean shapes and flat, simple decorative motifs applied to their surfaces, and were thus more modern in inspiration than the often florid creations of their competitors. In furniture, Gordon Russell's company reflected a similar move towards a lighter, elegant modern style, with simple forms and a restrained use of ornament. Other fields of everyday design, from wallpapers to typography, saw similar developments but their impact in the marketplace was comparatively limited since most manufacturers, buyers, retailers and consumers appeared to endorse more decorative and ornamental trends, both traditional and fashionable.

The Aesthetics of British Suburbia

The inter-war period saw a tremendous increase in housebuilding in Britain, which produced about four million houses of which around 2,700,000 were built in the 1930s. Almost two-thirds of these were privately owned, many of them located in the suburban developments which sprang up along the rapidly evolving transportation networks linking them to the city centres. This growth of suburbia brought with it a set of values which reinforced the notions of stability, tradition, domestic comfort and tranquillity sought by the growing class of home-owners. Speculative builders sought to cater for the widespread predilection for imagery that embraced popular ideas of wholesome traditional values: timbered gable ends (applied for ornamental rather than functional purposes), heavy panelled front doors with iron hinges and stained glass embellishments. Such "period" features were not restricted to the exteriors, since "Tudor" and "Elizabethan" wood-panelled halls and din-

LEFT **Arthur Sanderson & Sons** (Eton Rural Cretonnes), printed textile, 1921, shown at the Ideal Home Exhibition at Olympia, London, 1920. Produced in eleven colourways, the pattern displays characteristics of the "Jazz" idiom.

BELOW **Half-timbered** Nissen hut, 1930s. Much of the speculatively built British housing in the interwar years looked to the heritage of the past for many of its stylistic features, with half-timbering playing a highly visible part. This predilection for historicism spread through all aspects of domestic furnishings; the extent to which it predominated can be seen in its inappropriate reconciliation with the aesthetically unrelated form of the hut.

ing rooms, so often described in contemporary advertisements, were important selling features. Needless to say, this essentially retrospective aspect of taste did not endear itself to the British propagandists for modern architecture and design.

In 1932 Paul Nash, a ceaseless proselytizer of the Modernist cause, estimated that a taste for the antique was preferred by 80 per cent of the population, or at least by builders and furniture makers. In his often wry and amusing volume *Room and Book* he characterized the suburban "dream home":

> A gabled house with bogus beams and lattice windows. And Mr Drage's idea of what the city man likes to come back to in the evenings? A sham ingle nook and a gas log fire. With what sort of curtains and rugs does the city man's wife brighten up the drawing room? Old English chintzes and Persian carpets. What is it that his mother-in-law is irritably working on her tambour? A tea cosy of Jacobean design. And so it goes on. An endless dance of ancient masks like a fearful fancy dress ball composed of nothing but travesties of the Jacobeans and poor Queen Anne. It is time we woke up and took interest in our time.[3]

The British Empire and Design: the Wembley Exhibition of 1924

The cosy domesticity of suburbia and the DIA's attempts to reform modern taste were not the only elements affecting design in post-war Britain. As was the case with the empires of other European countries, the future economic and political role of the British Empire was reassessed after the war. Much effort was made to promote the Empire through state organizations such as the Government-funded Empire Marketing Board (1926–33) as well as through film, posters, packaging and other ephemera, popular literature, educational propaganda and exhibitions. Of the latter, by far the most significant was the large-scale British Empire Exhibition mounted at Wembley in 1924, attracting almost seventeen and a half million visitors in its first season.[4] The conservative ornamental tastes of the British consumer could be seen in many of the displays, especially in the Palace of Arts which contained, according to the Prince of Wales, "the first show of British art of a truly imperialist nature."[5]

The predilection for historical styles was reinforced by the sequence of rooms furnished in the styles of 1750, the 1820s, 1852, 1888 and 1924. Other influences of a more exotic nature could be seen in exhibits such as the Waring and Gillow Chinese Lacquer Room in the Palace of Industry. Chinoiserie was fashionable throughout the 1920s, whether in gramophone cabinets or wallpapers, and was commercially available in such places as the Oriental Departments of both Liberty and Whiteley's Universal Stores.

Egyptian themes were also popular for a while, with ornamental motifs providing a rich vocabulary for the styling and decoration of a wide range of articles, from jewellery and biscuit tins to cinemas and furniture. This vogue for Egyptiana was much stimulated by archaeological finds of the period, particularly Tutankhamen's Tomb which had been discovered by Lord Caernavon in November 1922 and widely heralded in the media. The Wembley exhibition celebrated this event in the full-scale reproduction of the Tomb, which attracted a great deal of interest and attention. The arts and crafts of the British dominions and colonies also made an impact, displayed in the many exotic pavilions such as those of India, East Africa and West Africa. In several instances native workers lived on site in reconstructed villages and could be seen involved in a wide variety of craft activities such as weaving, metalworking and carving. Many of their products could be bought at the exhibition or in a number of leading London stores, a factor which further helped to promote an interest in non-European arts, culture and ornament.

French Design: the Resurgence of National Prestige

After the end of the First World War there was considerable awakening of activity in the decorative arts in France. Design promotion received a fillip in 1919 with the forming of two organizations: La Compagnie des Arts Français and Décoration Intérieur Moderne (DIM), founded by Louis Süe and André Mare and by René Joubert respectively. The major Parisian department stores also played an influential part in helping to revive national design prestige through the establishment of their own studios, which were geared to the provision of a design service for their clientèle. The studios for Au

Printemps, Le Louvre, Au Bon Marché and Les Galeries Lafayette were entitled, respectively, "Primavera," "Studium Louvre," "Pomone" and "La Maîtrise," and all took a prominent role at the 1925 Exposition des Arts Décoratifs et Industriels in Paris, which was to be a major showpiece of French (and other national) design.

As with the earlier years of the century, the 1920s saw the launching of many luxury liners. Reflecting national status in the battle for transatlantic trade during the economically competitive post-war years, a number of these majestic ships were sponsored and subsidized by the French government. They provided golden opportunities for the re-establishment of French dominance in design since, through the Société de l'Art Français Moderne, many leading French artistes-décorateurs were involved in the design of interiors such as that of the *Paris*, launched in 1921. The *Ile de France* of 1927 promoted equally high standards and involved designers of such merit as Jacques-Emile Ruhlmann, Raymond Subes, René Lalique, Süe et Mare, and Paul Poiret's Atelier Martine. These liners were generally in the lavish, opulent style associated with Art Deco, drawing on a wide range of flat, decorative motifs and stylized abstractions from nature. Lacquerwork, exotic woods and other expensive materials further contributed to the overall extravagant atmosphere. Similar preoccupations with such expressions of national design prestige continued into the 1930s, and were fully realized in the 1935 liner *Normandie*, which again provided a potent vehicle for contemporary French decorative arts. Although the extravagant tenor of the decorative schemes owed much to her Art Deco-dominated predecessors, a wider and more eclectic range of designs was deployed.

Non-European influences

The fine arts, particularly the work of the Cubists, Fauves and Expressionists, which revealed a specific concern with non-European and "primitive" artworks, also exerted a considerable influence on design of the period, particularly in the fields of textiles and other forms of surface decoration. A heightened interest in anthropology, ethnography and archaeology was a further spur to such tendencies and, in addition, the arts and cultures of the French colonies in Africa, Indochina and Guinea made a noticeable impact on the prevailing design aesthetic. Colonial possessions assumed a political and economic importance for several European countries in the troubled years after the First World War. French appetite was further stimulated by the Colonial Exhibition mounted at Marseilles in 1922, where artefacts from the colonies could be viewed at first hand. Exotic materials, such as mother-of-pearl and ivory, were incorporated into many decorative objects and the importation of a rich variety of woods was reflected in contemporary furniture production. A wide range of exotic motifs, such as tropical flora and fauna, provided an exciting diversity of ornamental detail. Similar tastes continued to be aroused by subsequent colonial exhibitions, the most significant being the Exposition Coloniale Internationale, held in Paris in 1931 and visited by more than thirty-three million people.

Something of the almost indiscriminate yet widespread fashionability of non-European cultures was seen in the popularity of the packaged "primitivism" exemplified by Josephine Baker, the American black singer and dancer. Emerging as an idol in Paris in the 1920s and 1930s after featuring in *La Revue Nègre*, which had opened at the Théatre des Champs Elysées in 1925, she became part of the current African vogue, complete with her infamous banana costume and other exotic outfits. The culture of oppressed black America was able to provide a popular musical and terpsichorean counterpart to the fashionable ethnographic interests of progressive artists such as Picasso and Matisse.

The Exposition des Arts Décoratifs et Industriels, Paris 1925

This exhibition attracted almost six million visitors and did much to popularize the style which subsequently became known as Art Deco. The roots of this style had been established before the First World War:[6] the geometric tendencies of the architects and designers of the Wiener Werkstätte, the art of Cubism, the strident colours of the Fauves, the strikingly colourful exoticism of the designs for Diaghilev's Ballets Russes and the work of Paul Poiret's Atelier Martine can all be seen to presage much of the ornamental stylization which permeated the Paris Exposition. Even the idea of mounting a large-scale exhibition in Paris had originally been proposed before

the war. As a projection of the continuance of the great French cultural traditions it assumed an added importance in the post-war era of reconstruction, with the aim of promoting contemporary French design. Ironically, particularly in the light of the official stipulation that exhibits should embody "modern aspiration and real originality," Modernism and innovation were largely overpowered by the surging tide of Art Deco ornamentation and styling. Significantly, Le Corbusier's genuinely original contribution, the Pavillon de l'Esprit Nouveau, was looked on very unfavourably by the exhibition authorities who placed a high fence around it, which was only removed just before the opening of the exhibition after the intervention of Charles Monzie, the French Minister of Fine Arts. Furthermore, the international jury's wish to award Le Corbusier the first prize was vetoed. That the Pavilion should have been such a *cause célèbre* is not entirely surprising since the functional aesthetic of the interior rather undermined the need for decorative art; its furnishings and equipment were largely drawn from standard mass-production items rather than from the more luxurious ornamental products that were so pervasive throughout the rest of the exhibition. As one historian has remarked, "even the paintings on the walls were of the type then supposed to be capable of mass-production."[7] Konstantin Melnikov's Constructivist Russian Pavilion also made a considerable impact on account of its innovative form and structure which used wood, glass, colour, lettering and emblems to telling effect. Alexander Rodchenko's Workers' Club, with its utilitarian aesthetic, typified a new Russian category of public architectural design in the 1920s, although its austerity and progressive nature, like Melnikov's and Le Corbusier's contributions, set it apart from the sumptuous, indulgent, "Jazz Age" styling which characterized design and architectural offerings elsewhere.

Nowhere was this gulf more strikingly seen than by comparison of Le Corbusier's and Melnikov's pavilions with Jean-Jacques Ruhlmann's Hôtel d'un Collectionneur. Involving many of France's leading decorative artists, the latter contained furniture and décor which was luxurious, expensive and incompatible with economic mass-production. Although he had exhibited since before the First World War, it was this display that brought Ruhlmann to a much wider audience, one which was astounded at the sumptuousness of the work on show. Süe et Mare attracted almost as much notice with their Musée de l'Art Contemporain. Its aura of richness and

bright colour was also sustained by the contributions of many other French artists and designers. The Ambassade Française, which comprised twenty-five rooms situated around a three-sided courtyard, occupied the most prominent site in the Esplanade des Invalides and provided another major opportunity for the demonstration of French decorative skill.

The pavilions of the earlier mentioned studios of the major Parisian department stores were especially effective in helping to disseminate a taste for decorative arts as well as embodying in their architecture the stylistic qualities associated with Art Deco. Many of the other, particularly French, pavilions also exhibited Deco styling and ornamentation, ranging from the extravagant, geometric, organically derived detailing of the urns outside the Sèvres Factory Pavilion to the domed Pavillon de Nancy et l'Est, which explored the decorative possibilities of steel and metal in its striking entrance hall. Overall, despite the Exhibition's impact on the media,

related ephemera and exhibition visitors, contemporary opinion tended to share the view of two British critics who remarked that many of the rooms on display "were mere testimonials to the ingenuity of the designer and the wealth of the purchaser."[8]

Among the many French designers whose work attracted a great deal of attention at the Paris exhibition was Edgar Brandt, who had emerged as a *ferronnier* of distinction. In addition to the work displayed on his own stand, his designs in wrought iron and bronze could be seen in the gates and grilles at the imposing entrance to the exhibition, the Porte d'Honneur, as well as the Hôtel d'un Collectionneur and several other pavilions and sites throughout the exhibition. Many of his stylistic abstractions of natural forms were influential in the USA and elsewhere.

American Design after 1925: European Influence

The Exposition des Arts Décoratifs et Industriels provided an important source of inspiration for the establishment of a modern, essentially non-historicist, style in America. The United States did not participate in the Exhibition,[9] and it seems likely that economic considerations were conditioning factors in the decision to abstain. None the less, an investigative commission of over one hundred representatives, drawn from a wide range of institutions and industries connected with the decorative arts, was appointed by the American Secretary of Commerce, Herbert Hoover. Headed by Professor Charles Richards, Director of the American Association of Museums, its purpose was to report on the state of contemporary European design.

Not surprisingly, French design made a strong impression on many of the visitors. As a result, in 1926, Richards organized a touring exhibition of textiles, furniture, ceramics, glass and other goods drawn from the 1925 Paris show. Aiming to introduce contemporary French design in the decorative arts to a wider American audience, it was shown at the Metropolitan Museum, New York, and at eight other museums across the United States. Boosted by such exposure, as well as by a number of conferences on the theme of "Modern Decorative Art," the French decorative aesthetic soon became a fashionable style which was actively promoted by many leading stores throughout the country. This culminated in two important department-store exhibitions in 1928: Macy's, with fifteen rooms designed by both American and foreign designers, and Lord and Taylor's, whose New York Exposition of Modern French Decorative Art included five modern rooms designed by in-house staff alongside their French counterparts. However, such goods were generally expensive and not geared to the "democracy," as Lewis Mumford termed it, of mass-production processes.

On the whole, American textile manufacturers were conservative in their design outlook, despite their technical proficiency. Like their counterparts in the furniture industry, they responded to public demand by marketing the full gamut of period styles, and left it to individual artist-designers to develop a Modernist vocabulary. However, by the early 1930s, there was a significant European flavour in certain quarters of the American textile industry. At its best, there were artists of the calibre of Erté and Raoul Dufy designing for the Amalgamated Silk and Onondaga Companies of New York. At its weakest, the output merely reflected a loose awareness of European trends in a series of poor imitations. American rug design was also largely inspired by German and French examples, the latter including the bold, floral patterns of the "Martines" as well as similar work marketed by the large French stores from studios such as Pomone and Primavera. To many American manufacturers and retailers these appeared to bridge the gap between traditional and modern idioms more successfully than the highly abstract designs of artists such as Léger or Lurçat.

None the less, by the early 1930s a more progressive outlook among American designers began to make itself felt with the emergence of textile designers such as Ruth Reeves, also known for her wallpaper and carpet designs. She became a design consultant for the New York furnishing firm of W. and J. Sloane for whom she worked throughout the decade. She had studied under Fernand Léger in Paris in the 1920s and her work showed a marked Cubist influence.

American Deco: Architecture and Ornament in New York

The geometric forms, patterns and ornamental motifs of Art Deco featured right across the design spectrum in the United States; leaping gazelles, flat stylized garlands of flowers and abstractions based on plant forms and fountains appeared in a great many different capacities throughout the country. The style was closely linked with architecture during the second half of the 1920s, particularly in the decoration applied to the exterior detailing and public interior spaces of skyscrapers in New York. The metalwork of elevator grilles in the public lobbies, the flat geometric patterning of marble floors, lettering, clocks, lights and other fixtures and fitments all betrayed their French sources.

William Van Alen's Chrysler Building of 1930, for a while the world's tallest building, is one of the most celebrated American monuments to Art Deco ornament and detail. The geometric detailing of the stainless steel cladding of the roof of the building, with its low-relief arches topped by a spire, has been a distinctive feature of the New York skyline ever since its erection. Large

ABOVE **William Van Alen**, stainless steel gargoyles and decorative brickwork frieze on the 31st floor, Chrysler Building, New York, 1928–31. The frieze, which is formed with grey and white bricks, conveys a feeling of movement, blended with the sense of geometry associated with contemporary Deco. Metal hubcaps have been placed at centre of the roundels, while the abstracted eagles on the corners relate to contemporary Chrysler car radiator ornaments.

stainless steel gargoyles, modelled on the 1929 Chrysler automobile bonnet ornamentation, together with the flat, stylized decorative brickwork frieze of automobile wheels and radiator caps which encircled the building, paid tribute to its patron, Walter P. Chrysler, the motor-manufacturing magnate. At ground-floor level there are many more ornamental Deco details including the geometric metalwork patterning of the entrance doors. The lobby is one of the most striking of American Art Deco interiors, featuring murals on the theme of transportation and human endeavour, buff and red marble veneers on the walls, and elevator doors and walls inlaid with African wood floral abstractions.

There are innumerable other buildings in New York that feature aspects of Art Deco ornament: Sloan and Robertson's Chanin Building of 1929 is a striking example, exhibiting a great deal of intricate work on both exterior and interior, particularly in the impressive lobby with its exploration of the ornamental possibilities of marble and bronze. In much contemporary ornament of this type, both internal and external, the French parentage of many decorative motifs was apparent, as in the fountains and sunbursts which featured widely, particularly in decorative metal grilles. The ornamental vocabulary was further enhanced by the widespread use of glazed terracotta tiles and mouldings, cast stone, decorative aluminium panels and coloured glass. These were all part of the decorative repertoire of the period and were readily available and extensively advertised in the trade and architectural press.

Deco in other American Centres

Art Deco also exerted a considerable impact in other parts of the United States including Washington DC, where it became fashionable as the city grew rapidly in the years of Roosevelt's New Deal. In addition to the style's widespread adoption in countless splendid apartment lobbies, its characteristics were also vividly displayed on Government buildings, particularly those in

the Federal Triangle. In the same period there was a tremendous building boom in the resort of Miami Beach, fast becoming a mecca for tourists and others seeking a healthy, glamorous environment more economically than was possible in the wealthier environs of nearby Palm Beach. Its significance as an important centre for Art Deco architecture has been recognized by its designation in the National Register in the 1980s. Much of the decorative imagery found on buildings and in their lobbies was derived from natural forms, with a widespread preponderance of flamingoes, pelicans and herons. The proliferation of nude figures in many decorative schemes has been attributed to the contemporary vogue for sun worship. Los Angeles too was a city which saw a wide range of Deco architecture and ornamentation, with extensive deployment of brightly glazed terracotta surfaces. Numerous ornamental schemes made overt references to speed, motion and transportation, developments

which caught the public imagination as they underwent a period of dramatic and rapid change in the 1920s and 1930s, evocatively expressed in Herman Sachs' mural, "The Spirit of Transportation," on the ceiling at the main entrance to Bullocks department store on Wilshire Boulevard. The iconography of travel embraced modern images such as aeroplanes, ocean liners, railway locomotives and airships, but also a winged Mercury, messenger of the gods.

References to speed and transportation played a much more prominent part in the following decade with the advent of streamlining, when aerodynamic forms provided the impetus for ornamentation on a great many products (see Chapter 3). In Los Angeles architecture this tendency was celebrated in the sleek, rounded, ocean-liner-derived forms of the Coca-Cola Bottling Plant at 1334 South Central Avenue, designed in 1936 by Robert V. Derrah.

The Rockefeller Center and Radio City Music Hall

A landmark of 1930s urban development in New York, the Rockefeller Center complex provided almost unprecedented scope for Art Deco design and ornament. Many of the external sculptural commissions reflected this opportunity, typified by Lee Lawrie's polychromed stone reliefs representing Wisdom, Sound and Light above the

BELOW **Robert V. Derrah**, Coca-Cola Bottling Plant at 1334 South Central Avenue, Los Angeles, California, 1936. The factory was converted into a streamlined ocean liner format, complete with "portholes" and "bridge". The transatlantic luxury liners were key images of the era; this was blended with the sweeping lines of the streamlining aesthetic, the visual embodiment of American material culture of the 1930s.

main entrance to the R.C.A. Building, Hildreth Meiere's highly decorative plaques on the themes of Song, Drama and Dance and Paul Manship's sculpture of Prometheus in the sunken plaza.

The Radio City Music Hall in the Rockefeller Center is possibly one of the most dazzling monuments to Art Deco. Donald Deskey, who had visited the 1925 Paris exhibition and subsequently set up a design practice in New York, won the competition for co-ordination of the interior design. Furniture, textiles, wallpaper, carpets, lighting and other designs all contributed to the luxurious atmosphere, and many of his interiors were striking essays in Art Deco-inspired Modernism. Several newly available materials were employed, such as Bakelite, Formica and even aluminium foil (in his printed wallpaper designs on the theme of "Nicotine" for one of the men's smoking rooms).

To work with him on the project Deskey commissioned several fellow members of the American Union of Decorative Artists and Craftsmen (AUDAC), an organization which had been set up in 1928 to promote modern design. Amongst them was Ruth Reeves who produced a Cubist-inspired carpet design with musical-instrument motifs for the grand foyer. Other leading artists and designers who worked on the interior included the painter Stuart Davis whose mural on the theme of "Men without Women" enlivened the basement-lounge smoking room, and Yasuo Kuniyoshi who produced a striking floral mural for one of the women's powder rooms. Further contributions were "The Spirit of the Dance," by the sculptor William Zorach, and a variety of ceramic pieces by Henry Varnum Poor.

Art Deco and its Legacy in Britain

As has been mentioned, the British artist and designer Paul Nash, like many of his contemporary practitioners and critics, had earlier attacked the aesthetics of nostalgia which found such blatant expression in the suburban housebuilding boom of the inter-war years. Equally vigorous was his condemnation of the most commonly available commercial alternatives promoted by manufacturers and retailers; their wares usually featured "Modernistic" or "Jazz" styling of the kind associated with the 1925 Paris exhibition and seen in the ubiquitous sunray motifs embodied in garden-gate and window construc-

tion, and the decorative detailing of cast-iron rainwater heads. Nash was equally scathing about the Deco-inspired contents of many suburban houses in the 1930s, whose fireplaces with their geometric, polychromatic, glazed-tile ornamentation, ceramic ornaments, radio cabinets and countless other domestic artefacts as well as furnishing fabrics and linoleum patterns all came under criticism.

Nash, like a number of his contemporaries who were aware of the efforts of European avant-garde designers to promote a machine aesthetic, campaigned for a greater recognition of the potential role of modern design in British industry. He studied production methods and produced designs for interiors, textiles, rugs, ceramics and glass, as well as a wide range of graphic media. However, although much of his output explored the decorative possibilities of geometrically based motifs in a sensitive and aesthetically pleasing manner, like most Modern Movement-inspired contemporary work it failed to make a significant impact on the taste of retailers, manufacturers and the general public.

A growing preoccupation with health and hygiene in the home also stimulated a move away from the period ornament which had previously characterized so much domestic furniture and fitments. Such dust-collecting surfaces, along with the coal fire, were seen as both potential health hazards and difficult to clean. The proliferation of flush doors with no mouldings and the boxing in of stair banisters and fireplaces left surfaces which were easier to clean. Similarly, many items of furniture, particularly the domestic sideboard, showed more rounded forms with less decoration, complementing the geometric patterns of the wallpapers and furnishing textiles which became popular from the late 1920s onwards. For a brief while also, in the early to mid-1930s, Modernistic styling affected the outward form of a number of speculative suburban developments, which boasted flat-roofed houses, smoothly finished white walls and steel-framed windows. This was, however, a short-lived vogue since the majority of the new property-owning classes preferred an aesthetic more reflective of traditional values of domesticity.

None the less, Deco styling and ornament proved to be a significant feature of British design and architecture in the late 1920s and 1930s. Its use of colour and often rich though abstract decoration made it much more widely acceptable as an expression of contemporaneity than the more purist characteristics of the avant-garde

Modernists such as Le Corbusier in France or Walter Gropius in Germany. Well-known examples of Deco ornamentation are those found on London buildings such as Raymond Hood's and Gordon Jeeves' Ideal House of 1928, Wallis, Gilbert and Partners' Hoover Factory of 1931–2 or Oliver Bernard's foyer for the Strand Palace Hotel of 1929–30. Zigzags, chevrons, sunrise motifs and other forms of decorative geometric abstraction provided the sources for countless other aspects of design, including shopfronts, cinema design, architectural detailing, lettering and typography, cocktail bars and domestic appliances. On a more personal level, handbag and cigarette lighter design, jewellery and other elements of adornment also reflected the trend.

The Art Deco Cinema in Britain

As mentioned earlier, the cinema was the dominant form of entertainment in the period. In the 1930s in particular, its architecture and interiors were often striking expressions of Art Deco form and ornament, as could be seen in the faience-tiled, rounded, sweeping forms of the external elevations, sculptural motifs and detailing as well as

BELOW **Entrance lobby** of the New Oxford Street Corner House, London, designed by Oliver Bernard for J. Lyons and Company Ltd, late 1920s. This bold scheme has a stage-set feel to it, drawing on the more exotic aspects of Art Deco styling, particularly in the geometric patterning on the "capitals" and round the doorways.

ABOVE **Ceiling** of the auditorium of the New Victoria Cinema, Wilton Road, Westminster, London, designed by E. Walmsley Lewis, 1930, influenced by Hans Poelzig's Berlin Grosses Schauspielhaus of 1919. Indirect lighting looks to Art Deco as a source of inspiration and adds to the "underwater palace" atmosphere.

in the internal décor, lighting, furniture and fitments. Even the elaborate decorative consoles of the highly popular Wurlitzer and Compton electric organs, which rose up from the floor for entertainment in the intervals between films, contributed to the effects of opulence and glitter so popular with the public.

The Deco cinema style in Britain is most closely associated with Oscar Deutsch's Odeon cinema chain of the 1930s. The competition between cinema chains to exact the most financially favourable deals with the Hollywood producers whose output dominated British screens was reflected in the attention given to architecture, in terms of both exterior and interior cinema detailing. The sumptuous Art Deco-inspired sets of many contemporary movies often echoed the evocative interiors in which they were being screened, the latter heavily permeated by the ornament and decorative styling

associated with the 1925 Paris exhibition. Among the most conspicuous examples of the genre were T. Cecil Howlett's design for the 1935 Odeon at Weston-super-Mare, the interior of George Coles' 1936 Odeon at Muswell Hill in London and Andrew Mather's black granite Odeon in Leicester Square. Another impressive essay in Deco-influenced style was the 1930 New Victoria in Westminster, London, designed by E. Walmsley Lewis. Showing a clear knowledge of Poelzig's Grosses Schauspielhaus of 1919, the blue and green interior provided a spectacular expression of Art Deco forms, motifs and lighting effects.

Other Ornamental Traits in Britain

Throughout the 1930s in Britain continuous efforts were made by an articulate but ultimately relatively ineffective body of campaigners to promote Modern Movement design as an appropriate contemporary aesthetic. Spurred on by the 1932 Gorell Report on Art and Industry a series of exhibitions was organized to promote this outlook, the most significant being the Dorland Hall Exhibitions of 1933 and 1934 and the large-scale British Art in Industry exhibition of 1935. Despite the inclusion of a number of striking designs by leading Modernist designers the shows were increasingly characterized by extravagant, expensive, showy and highly ornate products and ensembles. At Dorland Hall in 1933 were included such flights of fancy as Oliver Hill's boudoir with glass *chaise-longue*, silvered glass walls and glass floor, and Messrs Arundell Clarke's Study of a Ruling Prince which, according to one critic, would "add a touch of envy to the burdened taxpayer in a day of economic depression." This was perhaps capped by Oliver Hill's living room of 1934, with its snakeskin and fur-covered furniture complemented by a Surrealist painting by Frederick Burgess. Oliver Hill was one of the leading culprits singled out in reviews of the 1935 British Art in Industry Exhibition, especially for his garden dining room in which, as one commentator waspishly remarked, "it is impossible to visualize real people eating real food—pure Hollywood."

Decorators and Decoration: Britain, France and the United States

Such indulgence was not restricted to the realm of exhibitions. With the success of society designers such as Syrie Maugham and Sybil Colefax, the profession of interior decorator became fashionable in wealthy circles. Doyennes of the design world were wickedly satirized in Evelyn Waugh's portrayal of the archetypal mid-1930s decorator, Mrs Beaver, in his novel *A Handful of Dust*. Often found in the pages of magazines such as *Vogue* and *Harper's Bazaar*, Syrie Maugham's decorative schemes became widely known, especially those which played upon the use of white, off-white and mirrors. During the 1930s these settings gave way to ones in which there was a greater reliance on wallpapers and colour, at a time when there was a renewed interest in patterned wallpapers, Regency and even Victoriana.

A revival of several neglected styles was a feature of 1930s furnishings and fitments and gave scope for daring combinations of past and present, evident in the work of many decorators in Britain, the United States and France. It was seen at its most excessive in Louis Süe's scheme of the late 1930s for Helena Rubinstein's house on the Quai de Béthune in Paris, and in the Surrealistically tinged decorative exuberance of the mid-1930s Paris apartment of Carlos de Beistegui.

1930s Mural Decoration and the neo-Romantic Effect

Painted decorative schemes were also popular among the well-to-do. In France a group of artists known as the neo-Romantics were influential in this field, as well as in

BELOW **Advertisement** for Fortnum and Mason's Contemporary Decoration Department. Interior decoration, as typified by Evelyn Waugh's Mrs Beaver in *A Handful of Dust*, had become fashionable by this time; leading stores devoted whole departments to it. Fortnum and Mason commissioned work from leading artists and designers.

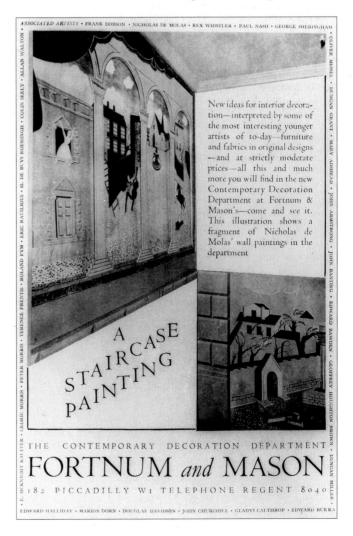

fashion illustration and theatre design. Included among such celebrated exponents were the artist-illustrator Christian Bérard and painters Eugène Berman and Pavel Tchelichew. Collected in France, the United States and Britain, Eugène Berman's work typified the genre and was characterized by his exploration of *trompe-l'oeil* scenes tinged with a strongly Surreal flavour. His compositions of architectural ruins and melancholic landscapes proved popular and were often incorporated into room settings.

British decorative painting was typified by the work of artists such as Frank Brangwyn, Clement Cowles, Duncan Grant and Rex Whistler, who painted the murals for the Tate Gallery Restaurant in London in 1926–7. As well as a great deal of work for revues and theatre productions, Whistler also produced numerous schemes for private houses.

Surrealism and Ornament

Surrealism, a movement both artistic and literary, was formalized by André Breton in the *Manifeste du Surréalisme* of 1924. Not only was it a radical force in literature and the fine arts, as has been widely recognized, but it also exerted a considerable impact on a variety of aspects of design and ornament during the 1930s, as in certain elements of the output of the French neo-Romantic decorators. Although Surrealism attracted considerable public attention and ridicule in a series of exhibitions mounted in the second half of the decade—in London in 1936, in New York in 1936–7 and in Paris in 1938— it had already made an impact in progressive design circles. Characterized by the unsettling juxtaposition of previously unrelated objects or ideas, its subject matter was often drawn from the realm of dream association. The couturier Elsa Schiaparelli was strongly influenced by the work of the Surrealist showman Salvador Dali who, in

1936, inspired her design of a hat in the form of a shoe. In the same year he also collaborated with Schiaparelli on the design of an evening dress with red lobster and green parsley motifs. The lobster appears to have been a favourite preoccupation: he had earlier used one as the incongruous covering for the handpiece of a telephone in the house of the English patron Edward James in Wimpole Street, London. Other Dali essays in the Surreal included a pink satin sofa inspired by the lips of the Hollywood actress, Mae West. Similar fantasies provided the basis for much furniture and interior decoration of the ultra-fashionable and wealthy.

It is clear that many varieties of ornament were popular in the years following the First World War. While there was a widespread admiration for historical styles, particularly with regard to domestic design which drew upon a wide range of motifs reinforcing ideas of homeliness and permanence, there was a growing acceptance of "Jazz Age" styling. This acceptable face of modern design derived from the colourful, geometric forms associated with Art Deco, and made a significant popular impact in the later 1920s and 1930s on both sides of the Atlantic. Its impact was not restricted to ornament and decoration in the home, but could be found in offices, factories, hotels, restaurants and, significantly, in cinema and film-set design—association with the entertainment world added glamour and lent all kinds of Deco-inspired ornament a fashionable aspect. The fine arts were also an important influence, whether on the ultimately widespread popularity of Art Deco (which looked to Cubism and the Fauves for flat, decorative forms and bright colours as well as visual forms inspired by primitive and ethnographic sources) or on the more esoteric and costly fantasies inspired by Surrealist painting and sculpture.

LEFT **Room interior** with a "surrealist" flavour, 1930s. Fantasy and whimsy are important elements in this fashion-conscious interior.

LEFT **Leroy Co.**, wallpaper design, France, *c.* 1925. This rich, stylized floral pattern was typical of well-to-do tastes of the period.

RIGHT **Marquetry panel** for Wagons Lits trains, *c.* 1920. This was one of a number of such decorative designs found in the Wagons Lits, incorporating flat abstractions from natural forms.

BELOW **Savon Charamy**, Paris, *c.* 1920. This striking packaging design, drawing upon the fashionable fan motif, looked to a blend of floral and geometric elements for its decorative effect.

ABOVE **Ann Doornan**, Africa Room of
Loew's Ohio Theater in Columbus, Ohio,
1928. A graduate of Columbia's School of
Architecture, Doornan was Chief Designer for
this cinema theatre. She was allocated a
budget of one million dollars and travelled
around the world collecting decorative
accessories, including these in the Africa
Room.

LEFT **Theodore Komisarjevsky**, interior of
the Granada Cinema, Tooting, London, 1931.
Having designed cinemas in the Hispano-
Moresque style, at Tooting Komisarjevsky
turned his attention to the Venetian Gothic.
As in Eberson's "atmospherics" in the United
States, some of the ceiling appears open to
the elements, adding to the theatricality of
the Gothic tracery and courtly paintings.

LEFT **The Mayan Theater** by Morgan, Wells and Clemens, 1040 South Hill, Los Angeles, California, 1927. Such Pre-Columbian sources of inspiration made fitting counterparts to other "primitivizing" styles and cultures which provided West Coast designers with diverse sources of inspiration.

RIGHT **The Cocoanut Grove** Ballroom at the Ambassador Hotel, Los Angeles, California, 1920s, blending exotic palm trees with almost Moorish painted architectural fantasies.

BELOW RIGHT **Meyer and Holler**, Grauman's Chinese Theater, 6925 Hollywood Boulevard, Los Angeles, California, 1927. Commissioned by the entrepreneurial showman Grauman, this Chinese fantasy was carried through from the dramatic pagoda-like entrance to the taps in the lavatories. In this illustration of the usherettes posing outside the cinema one can see the extent to which the fantasy was carried through almost to the last detail.

LEFT **Imitation leather wallpaper** in the Chinese Style, Arthur Sanderson & Co., mid 1920s. This was one of a number of Chinese-style designs produced by Sanderson. Embossed and stencilled with pagodas, trees and figures on a surface of gold leaf, this was very expensive to purchase, retailing at six shillings per yard. A cheaper variant was issued without gold leaf on a flat ground.

BELOW **Oliver P. Bernard**, decoration for a restaurant exterior at the British Empire Exhibition, Wembley, 1924. These decorative panels for the Lyons Restaurants reveal one facet of the stylistic pluralism seen on the 216-acre site, drawing on exotic, Persian-like sources.

RIGHT **Huntley & Palmer's** biscuit tins in the Egyptian style, *c.* 1924. These were probably produced in conjunction with the highly popular British Empire Exhibition at Wembley of 1924, in which the British discovery of Tutankhamen's Tomb was celebrated in a large-scale facsimile at which visitors could marvel.

BELOW RIGHT **Egyptian car mascot**, 1920s. The Egyptian style, always a popular source of stylistic inspiration, received a boost with the discovery of Tutankhamen's Tomb in 1922 and could be found in all spheres of ornamental design in the 1920s.

BELOW **Sonia Delaunay**, costume for Diaghilev's ballet revival of *Cleopatra* in London in 1918. The references to Egypt are loosely, rather than historically, derived. References to the colour theories in which the Delaunays were interested can be seen in the coloured circular bands emanating from Cleopatra's nipples, and repeated on a larger scale on the skirt.

RIGHT **International Building**, Rockefeller Center, New York, decorative screen by Lee Lawrie, *c.* 1935. This decorative screen symbolizes the internationalism of the building. The four figures on the bottom row represent the races of the world; above is a trading ship with three figures representing art, science and industry, together with Mercury, the messenger of commerce. The upper panels represent regions of the Earth, while the lower ones symbolize the old order and the new industrial age. The rather flat, hieratic, almost Assyrian style was fashionable at the time.

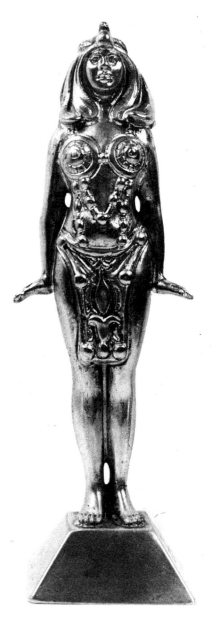

Fig. 12.—A Wooden Bracket.

Fig. 13.—A " Sunco " Bowl Fitting.

Fig. 14.—A Wood Shade Fitting.

Fig. 15.—An Imitation Vellum Shade.

Fig. 16.—A Hexagonal Shade Fitting.

Fig. 17.—A Selz Silk Shade.

Fig. 18.—The " Pearlite " Sphere.

Fig. 19.—A G.E.C. Two-light Bracket

Fig. 20.—A " Silk-Ray " Shade.

Fig. 21.—A " Supastone " Fitting.

Fig. 22.—A G.E.C. Table Standard.

Fig. 23.—A Piano and Bridge Lamp.

Fig. 24.—A " Sunco " Flambeau.

LEFT **Light fittings** from *The Electrical Review*, 1927. Such illustrations reveal the generally conservative ornamental taste associated with the homes of the majority in Britain at this time, even in such product areas as lighting.

RIGHT **Wrought iron** fire basket, Rowe Bros & Co. Ltd, early 1930s.

BELOW **Brookhill Public House**, Satley, England, *c*. 1930. The Tudor style was an enduring one in the interwar years in Britain and provided a dominant style in public houses such as this. The applied plasterwork on the cornice and beams, the leaded glass and dominant fireplace all provided the reassurance of traditional styles.

TOP LEFT **Frederick Suhr**, design of warriors from the *Safari* series for Belding Hemingway, USA, printed silk, late 1920s. This semi-abstract design of warriors, shields and spears reveals a widespread interest in exotic sources and a debt to the more decorative tendencies of late Cubism.

LEFT **The Totem Fountain** by Granet and Expert from the Colonial Exhibition, Paris, 1931.

ABOVE **"Jungle" fabrics** advertisement for Warner & Sons Ltd, 1936.

TOP RIGHT **Exotic perfume label**, *Belle des Bois*, Foulon, 1920s.

ABOVE RIGHT **Josephine Baker** in exotic costume at the Folies-Bergère, Paris.

These illustrations reveal the widespread range of applications for exotically inspired designs in the interwar years. International, colonial and imperial exhibitions all played a role in furthering such tastes and interests.

LEFT **Edouard Bénédictus**, decoration, Relais, 1930.

BELOW **Shop front**, Paris, 1920s.

The flat, abstract, geometric patterning which adds a fashionable interest to the façade of the shop is close in style to the Art Deco-inspired motifs by Bénédictus, especially that on the top right.

RIGHT **Robert Mallet Stevens**, *La Semaine à Paris* newspaper offices, detail of the glass by L. Barillet, 1928–9. The glass decoration portrays the days of the week and relies for its decorative effect on large geometrically based areas of glass of different textures and colours. The overall character is strongly Art Deco.

BELOW RIGHT **Jacques Henri** mannequins, modelling ensembles designed by Sonia Delaunay in front of a Citroen B12 painted to her designs, 1925. Delaunay collaborated with Heim on the Boutique Simultanée on the Pont Alexandre III at the 1925 Paris Exposition.

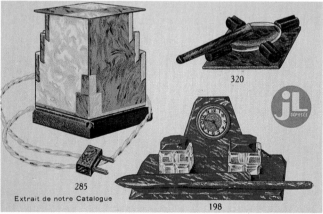

ABOVE **The main lounge** on the *Normandie* ocean liner, 1932–5, with etched and painted glass murals by Jean Dupas. The decoration and ornamental schemes associated with this ocean liner were intended to impress and act as an advertisement for the best of French design talent. The opulent settings follow the luxurious strain of Art Deco seen in the *Hotel d'un Collectionneur* by Ruhlmann at the 1925 Paris Exposition.

LEFT **Ashtray, clock, light** from a French catalogue, *c*. 1930. These designs show the ways in which plastics were used to decorative effect. The light, with its stepped geometric form, reflects contemporary trends.

RIGHT **Interior** of the *Pavillon de l'Esprit Nouveau* by Le Corbusier at the 1925 Paris Exposition.

BELOW **Interior** of the *Hotel d'un Collectionneur* by Ruhlmann at the 1925 Paris Exposition.

These two interiors reveal the sharp conflict of two aesthetic outlooks. Le Corbusier's Pavillon was the subject of fierce attacks by those supporting the highly ornate character of the majority of buildings and designs on show at the 1925 exhibition, epitomized by the oppressive sumptuosity and decorative intensity of the interior of Ruhlmann's *Hotel*.

LEFT **Pavillon de l'Intransigeant** by Henri Favier at the 1925 Paris Exposition. Curvilinear arabesques on the entrance gates were typical examples of decorative ironwork of the period.

RIGHT **Fountain scene** from the film "Our Blushing Brides", 1930, with Merrill Pye as Unit Art Director under Cedric Gibbons. The central fountain and ornamental screens can be traced directly to the 1925 Paris Exposition, which had been visited by Gibbons, the leading Hollywood Art Director of the day. The Exposition provided the inspiration for many MGM sets and did much to spread the influence of Art Deco.

ABOVE **Lamp** by Edgar Brandt, 1920s.

RIGHT **Girault Hairdressing Salon** by
Azema, Edrei & Hardy, 1923.

These two illustrations reveal the importance
of decorative ironwork in the period, whether
used architecturally or for individual items.
Brandt was the leading metalworker of his
day and his work was influential on both sides
of the Atlantic. He established a New York
outlet for his business, Ferrobrandt, which
provided ornamental metalwork for a number
of new buildings in Manhattan as well as film
sets.

LEFT **Ladies' Powder Room** at Radio City Music Hall, New York, by Yauo Kuniyoshi, early 1930s. This exotic decorative scheme was a counterpart to the "masculine" men's smoking room. Kuniyoshi painted this floral scheme in the space of a few weeks, after Georgia O'Keeffe's original painting peeled off. It illustrates the "fantasy" element associated with design in the leisure industry of the period.

BELOW ***Jazz* carpet** for the Grand Foyer of Radio City Music Hall, early 1930s, showing the influence of Synthetic Cubism in its decorative interpretations of musical instruments, referring to activities associated with the building.

BOTTOM ***Nicotine* wallpaper** designed by Donald Deskey for Radio City Music Hall, early 1930s. This design was executed on aluminium foil produced by the J. Reynolds Tobacco Company and shows a number of "masculine" pastimes.

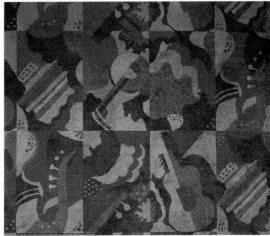

LEFT **Cast glass relief** by Lee Lawrie, produced by Steuben (Corning Glass) over the main entrance on the east façade of the RCA Building, Rockefeller Center, New York, early 1930s. Lawrie received the major sculptural commissions for the RCA Building and this piece appropriately symbolized cycles of light and sound. It is part of a dramatic, larger, painted sculptural design on the subject of *Genius, Which Interprets to the Human Race the Laws and Cycles of the Cosmic Forces of the Universe*.

BELOW **Chrysler Building**, New York, lobby mailbox, *c.* 1930. The flat, decorative, abstracted forms were typical of the attention to detail throughout the public spaces of Van Alen's renowned building. Eagles were used as Chrysler radiator ornaments and could be found as decorative devices elsewhere in the building, most notably on the exterior at the corners of the 31st and 63rd floors.

BELOW **Donald Deskey**, desk, chair and lamp, *c.* 1930, produced by Deskey-Vollmer in walnut, flat-banded copper and glass. There are close links with European Art Deco in the exploration of the ornamental impact of copper and glass. The decorative bands on the lampstand have a futuristic feel to them, sharing the science-fiction spirit of many of the exhibits seen at the New York World's Fair nine years later.

BOTTOM **Hanns Teichert**, murals in the main floor bar, Boulevard Bridge Restaurant, Chicago, 1933. The murals, Cubist pastiche in style, show the influence of European trends in much decorative work in America at this time. The sweeping stainless steel trim along the top and to the rear of the bar reveal both an awareness of the growing interest in streamlining as a decorative motif, and of the European-influenced moderne.

RIGHT **Ronald Atkinson**, foyer of The Daily Express Building, Fleet Street, London, 1932. This interior, with its indirect lighting and zig-zag detailing, is emphatically Art Deco in character. It draws on a wide range of stylistic sources, with allusions to the Gothic in the dramatic fan-vaulted ceiling, to Egypt in the central approach to the main staircase, and to contemporary cinema design in the overall sense of luxury. Monometal (an antecedent of aluminium) was used extensively to heighten the sense of excited intensity. On the wall, to the rear of the photograph, can be seen one of two murals in metal on imperial themes by Eric Aumontier.

RIGHT **Foyer** of the Odeon Cinema, Fortis
Green Road, Muswell Hill, London, designed
by George Coles, 1936. Although Deco in
feel, it is less intricate than many of its earlier
antecedents. Much of its detailing, such as
the rather idiosyncratic horizontal bandings
running off the middle and capitals of the
columns leading to the balcony, has traits in
common with the streamlined moderne.

FAR RIGHT **Whitehall Theatre**, London,
early 1930s, designed by Edward A. Stone.
The striking decorative bandings and inset
panel show the influence of Continental,
particularly French, design in England.

BELOW **Greta Garbo and Anders Randolf**
in an Art Deco setting from *The Kiss* of 1929,
under the art direction of Richard Day. Note
the metallic, geometric features and styling of
the table, together with the dramatic striped
lines of the reflective floor surface.

ABOVE LEFT **Evening slippers** manufactured by Bob, Inc., *c.* 1925. Made in leather with stones on the ankle straps, the rather fanciful, almost ethnic feel of the abstract decorative motifs in pink, blue and yellow on a silver ground is not unlike the effect of surface patterns found in work by the Memphis group almost six decades later.

ABOVE **A. M. Cassandre**, *Etoile du Nord* railway poster, 1927.

LEFT **Norman Bel Geddes**, window display for the Franklin Simon department store, New York, 1927.

Geddes' display was one of a number which were held in New York stores to promote modern design in the wake of the 1925 Paris Exposition. The European influence is apparent in the flat, decorative semicircles on the stand to the right of the mannequin. These derive from one of the classic Art Deco posters by Cassandre and reveal how an ethos of fashionability was thought to exude from things French.

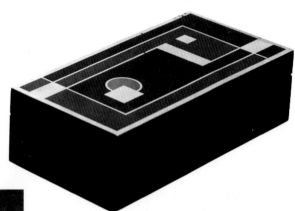

ABOVE **Walter Dorwin Teague**, Eastman Kodak Camera and Box (Model No. 1 A Gift Camera), 1930. Manufactured in chrome-plated and enamelled metal, leather and paper, this richly decorated camera draws on the more decorative traditions of European design in the 1920s as seen in the flat, geometric devices.

LEFT **Ilonka Karasz**, a rug for a child's room, from Macy's "International Exposition of Art in Industry" exhibition in 1928. This came from a show at the American Designers Gallery which subsequently travelled to department stores in ten cities throughout the United States. Its geometric simplicity reveals a debt to Eastern European craft traditions; Karasz was born in Hungary and emigrated to the United States shortly before the First World War.

LEFT **Silk** with batik decoration, designed by
Artur Lakatos, executed by Klara Roman,
c. 1914. There was a significant growth in arts
and crafts activity in Hungary in this period,
including the establishment of textile
workshops under Lakatos, Lajos Kozma and
Klara Roman, who specialized in batik
design. The workshops also collaborated with
textile manufacturers.

BELOW *Liljebla* (Blue Lily) tableware,
designed by Wilhelm Kage and produced by
Gustavsberg, 1917. An attempt to elevate
standards of taste in everyday design by
producing inexpensive products for working
people, it was admired by critics rather than
its projected clientele who preferred
traditional, more heavily decorated wares.
Nonetheless it was in production until 1940.

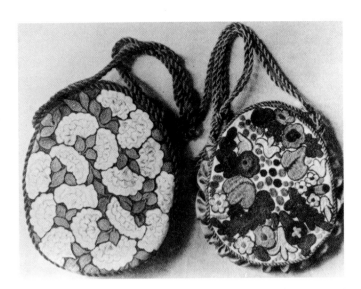

LEFT **Embroidered handbags**, designed by Anna Leznai, sewn by peasant women and girls employed by her to carry out her designs, *c.* 1914. Embroidery was used for personal and domestic decoration and was part of a strong national folk tradition in Hungary at the time.

BELOW **Sofia Stryjenska**, mural painting from the Polish Pavilion, Exposition des Arts Décoratifs, Paris, 1925. This detail, from one of a number of panels representing the months, drew on Polish folk traditions for its motifs. Stryjenska was a leading artist who exhibited tapestry designs and book illustrations at the Paris Exposition.

ABOVE FAR LEFT **Talcum bottle**, *c.* 1930.

ABOVE LEFT **Tile designs**, Maw & Company, 1930.

LEFT **China tea service**, Shelley Potteries, *c.* 1930.

RIGHT **Stained glass** shop transome from Rowe Brothers catalogue, 1930s.

The sunrise motif was commonplace in 1930s Britain and appeared in many contexts in addition to those illustrated here, ranging from garden gates and gable ends to packaging and fashion accessories. There was great contemporary interest in health, exercise and fresh air; the sun and its rays were popular symbols of this.

ROWE BROS. & COMPANY LIMITED

Shop Transomes.

R 30.

R 31.

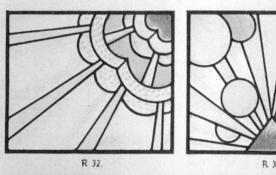

R 32.   R 33.

R 34.

Scale, 1 in. to 1 ft.

579

LEFT **Gregory Brown**, *Leaping Deer with Hillocks and Trees*, roller-printed linen produced by W. Foxton Ltd, 1931.

BELOW **Harold Holdway**, *Reindeer* tableware manufactured by Spode Ltd, 1936.

Deer, in many attitudes, were a highly popular decorative motif in the 1920s and 1930s and appeared in patterns in a wide range of design media both in Europe and the United States.

RIGHT **Wrought iron chandelier**, designed by Wilhelm Hunt Diederich, *c.* 1925, New York City. Diederich, a regular exhibitor at the Salon d'Automne in Paris in the 1910s and 1920s, believed in relating the fine arts to everyday objects. This piece, probably produced to his designs by Greenwich Village blacksmiths, emphasized the handcrafted quality of production. The composition of ibexes on either side of a fountain-like central motif have roots in the crafts of many ancient cultures but are close to the deer and fountain motifs found in Deco design of the period.

LEFT **Delamarre grille** in wrought iron and bronze, designed by Réné Chambellan for the Chanin Building, New York, 1928. There were many opportunities for decorative artists to embellish the skyscrapers of the late 1920s and 1930s, injecting a heavy European flavour. This *tour de force* represents ironwork at its most exhilarating, full of energy and displaying a number of geometric motifs—zig-zags, lightning flashes and starbursts—which are associated with Art Deco. The dynamic of speed and motion looks forward to the preoccupations of the following decade.

ABOVE RIGHT **Lounge** of the Carlton Hotel, Washington DC, 1930s. The furniture, with its bold decorative patterning and strong sense of geometry is typical of contemporary interiors. The neon flames of the fireplace provide something of a risqué, almost "post-modern", dimension.

RIGHT **Frank Lloyd Wright**, living room at Taliesin, Spring Green, Wisconsin, showing the changes which were made to the 1925 interior during the 1930s: the emphasis on flowing geometric shapes and forms, seen in the substitution of circular chairs for earlier rectilinear ones as well as the striking floor design, reveals links with wider decorative trends of the period.

3
Modernism and Opposition to Decoration 1918 to the late 1930s

The Modern Movement is often portrayed as being opposed to ornamentation, focusing instead on an aesthetic vocabulary that was concerned with notions of standardization, the exploration of new materials and abstract forms, and compatibility with the realities of modern mass-production technology. However, this self-conscious alignment with the *Zeitgeist* or "spirit of the age" was largely symbolic. Many Modern Movement products, seen through the eyes of subsequent generations, exude particular stylistic and ornamental traits. The movement was also at the root of a powerful tradition which for a long while dominated the tastes of the cultural establishment, whether seen in the Eurocentric aesthetic puritanism of the collections of the Museum of Modern Art in New York in the 1950s, the morally charged opposition to ornamental embellishment of the British state-sponsored Council of Industrial Design (COID) in the same period, the German Rat für Formgebung (Council for Design), founded in Darmstadt in 1951, or the Japan Industrial Design Promotion Organization (JIDPO), which was established in 1969.

The Netherlands: De Stijl

The Netherlands remained neutral during the First World War and, as a result, avant-garde ideas in design, architecture and the fine arts were able to develop without the intrusion of hostilities, unlike their counterparts in France or Germany. The most significant advances were those which centred on the De Stijl group. Officially launched by the artist Theo van Doesburg in 1917 in a magazine of the same title, the group became a powerful disseminator of progressive ideas which affected interior, typographic, textile and furniture design as well as the fine arts and architecture.

De Stijl, in its earlier phases, owed a great deal to the philosophical and artistic outlook of the painter Piet Mondrian, who, after his exposure to Cubist painting in Paris in the years immediately prior to the First World War, had moved away from representational art towards abstraction. Important also were the ideas of the Dutch architect H. P. Berlage and his interest in the American architect and designer Frank Lloyd Wright. The group aimed to explore a universal language of beauty, the syntax of which would provide a basis for creativity in all aspects of the man-made environment. Its aesthetic vocabulary consisted of straight horizontal and vertical lines, with an emphasis on right angles and a palette restricted to the primary colours of red, blue and yellow

LEFT **Theo van Doesburg**, *Composition IV* triptych in stained glass, executed by Vennootschap Crabeth, The Hague, for a private townhouse by Jan Wils in Alkmaar, 1917. These panels, over six feet in height, were a clear statement of the De Stijl aesthetic, exploring a harmonious balance between vertical and horizontal, as well as a more subtle counterpoint between the exploration of primary colours in the wings and the secondaries in the central panel. In the earlier phases of the De Stijl group's activities there was a commitment to collaborative environmental projects which culminated in the "total work of art".

with black, white and grey. These ideas affected the form and coloration of domestic interiors, the geometric patterns of tiled floors, the composition of stained glass windows, the lettering on shop fascias and many other aspects of design in daily life. Fresh aesthetic impetus was added later by De Stijl's chief propagandist van Doesburg, through the introduction of dynamic diagonal lines.

Van Doesburg developed links with other progressive European figures in the early 1920s: contact was made with Walter Gropius in Weimar, where van Doesburg offered courses in the close vicinity of the Bauhaus (see page 114); relationships were also forged with the Russian Constructivist artists El Lissitzky and László Moholy-Nagy in Berlin, resulting in issues of the *De Stijl* magazine in September of 1922 devoted to both Suprematism and El Lissitzky. In 1923 van Doesburg collaborated with Cornelis van Eesteren on models and architectural drawings for a De Stijl architecture exhibition at Léonce Rosenberg's Galerie l'Effort Moderne in Paris. This period marked the beginnings of the "international phase" of De Stijl, coinciding with a marked change in membership of the group which culminated in the withdrawal of Mondrian in 1925.[1]

As with the Russian Constructivists and Modern Movement designers associated with the Bauhaus in Germany, De Stijl exerted a strong influence across many aspects of design. For example, there were members of the group who were interested in textile design, continuing to explore the vocabulary of rectangles of primary colours balanced within a grid of vertical and horizontal lines. From 1919 Bart van der Leck experimented with printed textiles and worked in the medium until the late 1920s. Another leading member of the group, Vilmos Huszár, who had designed the first cover for the group's magazine in 1917, also applied De Stijl principles to interiors and textiles. Striking too were Gerrit Rietveld's ideas, affecting a wide range of furniture, architectural and interior designs, from his famous Red/Blue Chair of 1917–8 to the Schröder House in Utrecht of 1924 where both the exterior elevations and the whole interior layout followed the aesthetic principles of De Stijl. Van Doesburg's designs embraced a wide spectrum of media, including interiors and furnishings, graphics and architecture. Among the most striking of his achievements were his interiors for the restaurant-nightclub the Café Aubette in Strasbourg, on which he began work in 1926. The furnishing and decoration of ten public rooms gave van Doesburg an unprecedented opportunity to put his theories into practice in the context of interior design. The cinema-dance hall was his most striking contribution: rectilinear planes of flat colour set within white borders at 45 degrees from the angle of the walls, ceiling and windows created a unified environment. The influence of De Stijl in these and succeeding years was felt right across Europe.

The Amsterdam School

Much more expressive in form and content was the output of the Amsterdam School from about 1918 into the early 1920s, which centred around the thoroughly individualistic architectural and design work of Michel de Klerk and Piet Kramer. Its official mouthpiece was the magazine *Wendingen*, whose layout reveals many of the ornamental and decorative changes in Dutch design of the period. The overall style, with roots in Expressionist painting and carving, the handicrafts and the flowing, linear forms of the artist Jan Toorop, as well as in facets of the *œuvre* of Berlage and Frank Lloyd Wright, was characterized by highly expressive, almost organic, forms and detailing. These were visible in the distinctive profiles of buildings, the individual shapes of window-frames and doors, house numbers, lettering and applied metalwork, as well as in the rich textures and patterns of decorative brickwork, hung tiling and sculptural ornament. Perhaps the most complete expression of this style was the subsidized Sparndaam housing development in Amsterdam, integrating interior and exterior space, form and ornamental detail. The impact of the style was felt in many fields of the decorative arts, from light-fittings to carpets.

Modernism in Germany

The Modern Movement, though thoroughly international in outlook and practice, is perhaps most frequently associated with German design of the 1920s, and in particular with the Bauhaus in Weimar, established under the directorship of Walter Gropius from the end of the First World War until its final demise under the National Socialists in 1933.[2] To a significant degree the contemporary influence of the Bauhaus in the context of German design of the time has been distorted by the availability and accessibility of convenient documentation; the subsequent aesthetic influence of Bauhaus outlook and practice has been far more fertile than any contemporary impact it had on patterns of German manufacture and consumption of the 1920s and early 1930s. It is only more recently that the wider realities of design, consumption and production in Germany in those years have been seriously addressed in research and publication.[3]

BELOW **Hans Poelzig**, auditorium of the Grosses Schauspielhaus, Berlin, 1919. This *tour de force* of Expressionist design, with its dramatic lighting and overwhelming display of stalactites, reflects in dramatic form the German avant-garde post-War antipathy to the rational, standardizing tendencies prior to 1914.

The Establishment of the Bauhaus

Bound up as it was in the rapidly changing social, political and economic climate of the inter-war years, the history of the Bauhaus provides a useful model against which the course of Modernism in Germany can be evaluated.

There was considerable political and social upheaval in the wake of the First World War and many Germans were thoroughly disillusioned with the pre-1914 outlook of large-scale German industry, which they believed to have been a major contributory cause to the outbreak of hostilities. Among the avant garde there was a marked move away from the rational, standardization-orientated aesthetic, so visible in many buildings and products on show at the Deutscher Werkbund Exhibition at Cologne in 1914, towards a strongly spiritual and Expressionist

outlook. Expressionism, with its emphasis on primitivism and feeling, had surfaced in pre-war Germany in the activities of artistic groups such as Die Brücke, Der Sturm and Der Blaue Reiter (as well as in Bruno Taut's expressive use of metal and glass in the Glass Pavilion at the Cologne Exhibition of 1914). A number of artistic associations with Expressionist leanings were founded in the unsettled immediate post-war period, the most prominent being the Arbeitsrat für Kunst (Workers' Council for Art) and the Novembergruppe, established in the wake of the German Revolution late in 1918. With similarities in style, their output was charged with political meaning as well as being formally far removed from the rationalism associated with industrial products.

The school of architecture and applied arts known as the Bauhaus was established soon afterwards, in April 1919, with the publication of a four-page manifesto written by the Director, Walter Gropius, and carrying a title-page woodcut by Lionel Feininger. Portraying a cathedral, Feininger's work exhibited Expressionist characteristics and echoed the spiritual flavour of Gropius' text, which proclaimed:

> There is no essential difference between the artist
> and the craftsman. The artist is an exalted
> craftsman. In rare moments of inspiration,
> transcending the consciousness of his will, the
> grace of heaven may cause his work to blossom into
> art. But proficiency in a craft is essential to every
> artist. . . . Together let us desire, conceive and
> create the new structure of the future, which will
> embrace architecture and sculpture and painting in
> one unity and which will one day rise toward
> heaven from the hands of a million workers like the
> crystal symbol of a new faith.[4]

Such an outlook might seem odd in the light of Gropius' pre-war commitment to the tenets of standardization and an industrial aesthetic but, like others involved in the arts, he became opposed to forces associated with large-scale capitalism in the early post-war years. Indeed, in 1919, he became Chairman of the radical Arbeitsrat für Kunst, writing articles and speeches on its behalf. His support of handicraft reflected widespread opposition to the creative restrictions imposed by the division of labour in large-scale industry. Perhaps as a consequence, the Bauhaus was involved from the outset with political controversy, whether on account of staffing appointments or the political nature of radical causes espoused by students.

Early Bauhaus Output

The first few years of the Bauhaus curriculum were dominated by the activities of Johannes Itten, a member of the original staff, who placed considerable emphasis on the exploration of the senses and emotions in the pursuit of artistic goals. One of the most important early Bauhaus projects was the Sommerfeld House of 1920–1, usually read as an Expressionist building, although critics have pointed out its primitive and picturesque aspects, as well as making comparisons with the work of Frank Lloyd Wright in some features of the interior decoration, particularly the geometrically based woodcarvings by Joost Schmidt in the vestibule. The stained-glass window on the staircase by Josef Albers, with its patchwork of asymmetrical abstract geometric shapes, also enhanced the fanciful dimension. However, many of the "primitive" characteristics seen at the Sommerfeld House may also have had much to do with the dearth of appropriate conventional building materials, in this case replaced as a result of the availability of large quantities of teak planking. None the less, before the German economy stabilized and thoughts moved once more to the positive reconciliation of art and industry, an interest in folk art characterized some of the Bauhaus output of these early years, as in the tapestry workshops where such ideas were blended with themes drawn from contemporary painters.

A Change of Style

From about this time onwards, for a variety of reasons—organizational, economic and political—there was a noticeable shift in outlook, a fresh direction which gained impetus as the German economy began to stabilize in the mid-1920s. Progressive currents of avant-garde artistic developments outside Germany, particularly of De Stijl and Russian Constructivism, also began to exert an impact; in 1921 van Doesburg was in Weimar propagandizing the De Stijl cause, and in 1922 Wassily Kandinsky was appointed to the staff, joined the follow-

RIGHT **Joost Schmidt**, carved teak door in the Sommerfeld House, Berlin-Dahlem, 1921–2. Although there is an underlying strong, structured geometric feel to the design it exhibits expressive, primitivizing character in its decorative woodcarving motifs.

ing year by László Moholy-Nagy. Among the most fascinating products of the Bauhaus to reflect the new stylistic tendencies of the avant garde were Josef Hartwig's lacquered chess set, whose pieces were based on geometric solids, and brightly coloured toys by Alma Buscher and Ludwig Hirschfeld-Mack.

Craft activity began to be accepted as a basis for industrial prototypes. Experimentation with different materials and formal configurations provided a means of enhancing the industrial vocabulary. Design geared to industry was seen increasingly as a justification of the Bauhaus's activity on economic grounds. This was at the root of the 1923 Bauhaus Exhibition, mounted in the Haus am Horn, designed by Adolf Meyer and Georg Muche. Industrially prefabricated elements and new techniques were utilized wherever possible, and everything on display was geared towards notions of industrial production. For example, Theodore Bogler's earthenware containers for kitchen supplies were actually put into production by the Velten-Vordamm ceramic factory; sleek in form, they had as their only ornament, stencilled impersonally on the side, the names of the foodstuffs they were intended to contain—a 1920s precedent for the High-Tech motifs applied to many products of the late 1970s and 1980s. Even the typography for the posters announcing the 1923 Exhibition was largely conceived in a clean, modern, machine-age style.

Bauhaus GmbH

After considerable political upheaval the Bauhaus was forced to re-establish itself in Dessau in 1925–6. The new-found faith in the spirit of an industrial aesthetic, which had gathered strength as a result of the move, could be seen in the new buildings and furnishings of the School, reflecting a move away from crafts and towards architecture. Accompanying this re-orientation was an attempt to capitalize on the School's design output by setting up a limited company, Bauhaus GmbH, in 1926. Among items marketed as a result were a number of lighting designs produced by Körting and Matthieson, wallpapers by Rasch Brothers & Co., and textiles by M. van Delden & Co. Furthermore, many designers associated with the Bauhaus became involved with design for industry in their own right, consistently exploring a vocabulary in which ornament was distinctly subordinate to form.

By the late 1920s the stability of the Bauhaus was being undermined by the departure of a number of leading figures: Walter Gropius, László Moholy-Nagy, Herbert Bayer and Marcel Breuer. Furthermore, the economic and political crises of the late 1920s and early 1930s put increasing pressures on its financial viability. The institution was finally laid to rest when the staff chose to liquidate the school rather than co-operate with the Nazi regime.

The Deutscher Werkbund in the 1920s

The Werkbund, which before the First World War had seen such bitter argument concerning the merits of standardized industrial production versus individual creative expression, re-emerged as a significant force in 1920s design debates. This coincided with the stabilization of the German economy, to which the United States greatly contributed. It was felt not only through investment in Germany, made under the Dawes Plan of 1924, but also through techniques of scientific management in industry, epitomized by the automobile production of Henry Ford; in the United States Herbert Hoover and the US Department of Commerce had been promoting standardization vigorously as a means of facilitating cheaper mass-production on a very large scale.

In the more fertile industrial climate of mid-1920s Germany standardization began to re-emerge as a desirable goal. This gave rise to notions of a *Neue Zeit* (New Spirit) which was promoted by the Werkbund in a series of exhibitions, among the most historically significant being that devoted to "Form ohne Ornament" ("Form without Ornament"). With its promotion of formal simplicity and exploration of abstract possibilities, the exhibition opened up a number of important debates about the role and purpose of ornament and marked the beginnings of a shift away from the Werkbund's belief in crafts as a major source of stylistic inspiration. As at the Bauhaus in its Dessau period, the Werkbund's new creed, supported by Le Corbusier, Mart Stam, J. J. P. Oud and Josef Frank from outside Germany, as well as by Mies van der Rohe, Walter Gropius, Bruno Taut and Peter Behrens from within, asserted the primary importance of architecture and planning. The written word was also influential in

ABOVE **Eau de Cologne** for *Au Bon Marché*, Paris.

ABOVE RIGHT **Huntley & Palmer** biscuit tin, *c*. 1930.

ABOVE FAR RIGHT **Paul Brandt**, abstract motifs on a cigarette case in silver and lacquer, *c*. 1930. The strong geometric design and simple but striking diagonal pattern show how far Art Deco traits permeated the design of all kinds of products.

promoting this new functionalist approach, particularly via the Werkbund's magazine *Die Form*. Despite its comparatively limited circulation it was widely read by *aficionados* of the Modern Movement and provided a literary and visual propagandist counterpart to the publications of forward-looking municipalities.

The Move towards Municipal Patronage

Astronomically high levels of inflation in the early 1920s in Germany led to a marked shift away from private to municipal patronage. This afforded many designers an opportunity to implement the Modernist machine aesthetic: ornament was generally restrained, geometrically based and abstract, and seen as symbolically compatible with modern materials and progressive production technology. It also related closely to avant-garde developments in the fine arts. A move to embrace the new-found faith in Modernism, by promoting the spirit of *Neue Gestaltung* (New Design) and *Neue Bauen* (New Archi-

tecture) as appropriate accompaniments to what was termed the *Neues Wohnen* (New Lifestyle), resulted in the publication of magazines such as *Das Neue Frankfurt*, published between 1926 and 1933, and *Das Neue Berlin*, which commenced publication in 1929. Both sought to demonstrate the social worth of modern architecture and design in civic terms and with municipal support. Support was forthcoming especially from Frankfurt, where the City Architect Ernst May instituted several modern architectural programmes, and where another magazine, the *Frankfurt Register*, was, in effect, both a catalogue and a model of modern, functional design.

This new faith in a design approach more in tune with new materials and modern modes of production, associated with the term *Neue Sachlichkeit* (New Objectivity), was paralleled in the more detached and impersonal characteristics found in contemporary progressive literary, fine art, photographic, cinematic and even advertising output. As with progressive architectural trends, the new outlook embraced a reaction against the highly subjective, often anecdotal, aura of Expressionism, replacing it with a stress on qualities of objectivity, reportage and the documentation of reality.

The Blunting of the Modernist Cause in Germany

The political upheaval and uneasy economic climate of Germany in the late 1920s saw a decline in industrial production and foreign investment. In this period of destabilization and uncertainty the impact of the Wall

Street Crash of 1929 was an important contributory factor to the emergence of Adolf Hitler and the National Socialist Party. At such times of crisis, traditional, vernacular forms of ornament and decoration often found a ready audience in large sectors of the population who were reassured by the visual forms of the familiar and intelligible. This was to be seen in much of the style and imagery associated with National Socialist propaganda and values. After simmering away throughout the 1920s, there was an increasingly powerful lobby which attacked the tenets of the Modernist functional aesthetic, characterizing it as foreign and alien to indigenous tradition. The progressive, anti-ornamental outlook of modern architecture (particularly flat roofs) and design embodied in the Weissenhof housing exhibition at Stuttgart in 1927 was seen by nationalistic critics to be antithetical to German culture. Furthermore, progressive tendencies in architecture and design were internationalist in outlook, conditioned by their symbolic associations with new materials and technology rather than individual nationalistic features, and were generally associated with the political left. They were to have limited currency during the Third Reich, which was inaugurated in 1933.

Russian Constructivism

Reference has already been made to Diaghilev's Ballets Russes and the impact of its costume and set design on the fashionable audiences of Western Europe in the years leading up to the First World War. Conversely, in the same years, the activities of the Western European avant garde were also well-known in artistic and art-collecting circles in Russia. The Russians had been exploring a variety of new modes of artistic expression, drawing on their awareness of contemporary developments in France, Germany and Italy as well as on indigenous Russian folk-art traditions. New abstract references evolved, most notably the Suprematist paintings of

Kasimir Malevich and the Picasso-inspired corner constructions of Vladimir Tatlin. The former consisted of coloured geometric shapes set against light grounds and intended to convey the abstract sensations of floating, ascending and falling, configurations which were later applied to many aspects of design including theatre settings and costumes, ceramics, street propaganda and architecture.

The October Revolution of 1917 and the throwing-over of the old order provided the Russian avant garde with an opportunity to play a creative role in the furthering of new social, political and economic horizons, although artistic response to the Revolutionary spirit was by no means one of universal and deep commitment. None the less, many artists became involved in the design of propaganda posters, leaflets and the striking decoration of the agit-trains and ships which travelled round the country carrying the message of the Revolution. Artists were also instrumental in the reorganization of art education, designing for the theatre and the staging of mass political celebrations.

However, by 1920 there emerged strong differences of opinion about the role of the arts in post-Revolutionary Russia. Naum Gabo and Wassily Kandinsky were among leading figures committed to an outlook which laid stress on spirituality and pure creativity as the mainspring of artistic production, independent of considerations of practical implementation. Others, including Vladimir Tatlin, Alexander Rodchenko and his wife Varvara Stepanova, argued that artists should work for the benefit of society as a whole through the exploration of the direct social and utilitarian applications of their endeavour, harnessed to the realities of mass-production technology. Such artists, known as Productivists, won the backing of the Proletcult (Organization of Proletarian Culture) which in turn had links with the trade unions. Protagonists were involved in the design of textiles, banners, posters, furniture, pottery and stamps and other printed ephemera.

LEFT **Agit-prop train**, *c.* 1920. During the civil war many artists created Bolshevik propaganda for trains, steamships, theatres, posters and ceramics.

RIGHT **Sergei Burylin**, *Tractor* cotton print, produced at Ivanovo Vosnesensk, 1930. A dynamic rhythm and geometric abstraction reveals links with the avant garde. The subject matter is overtly concerned with messages about the Soviet economy and relates to other themes portrayed in textile designs, such as collectivization, transport, industry or construction.

Many of the designs for ceramics were also closely allied to avant-garde developments in the fine arts and graphics. For example, in the early 1920s, Malevich, Il'ya Chashnik and Nikolai Suetin applied their geometric Suprematist forms to china, producing many striking dinner services, coffee and tea sets. Following the Revolution, ceramic production also heavily utilized Revolutionary slogans, motifs such as the hammer and sickle, and pictures of Red Guards, sailors and other heroic figures. Ceramic artists drew widely on indigenous sources, whether primitive woodcuts, folk art or fairy tales. Two of the most important figures in this respect were Sergei Chekhonin, responsible for the reorganization of artistic input to the State Porcelain Factory in Petrograd in the immediate post-Revolutionary period, and Alexandra Shchekotikhina-Pototskaya.

Links between art and the spirit of progressive technology were exemplified by the typographic experimentation of El Lissitzky and the rich contemporary vocabulary explored in the magazine, poster and packag-

ing designs of Rodchenko. Similar characteristics pervaded the striking printed-cotton designs of Liubov Popova and Stepanova, both of whom worked for the Tsindel textile factory near Moscow in the early 1920s, at a time when the Soviet textile industry was attempting to re-establish itself after a period of economic crisis. In many of their designs there was a strong geometric feel, allying them symbolically with a modern technological approach. Nevertheless, as has been remarked upon by a number of historians,[5] many of these designs reflected little understanding of mass taste and often bore strong similarities to Western "capitalist" textile designs such as those of contemporary Paris. Increasingly, Soviet design of the period embraced visual references to everyday life, factories, industrial machinery, agriculture, electrification, transportation, sport and other activities, all of which could be seen as reflecting a healthy, pro-

ductive society. Such visual ornament, based on themes of everyday life, did much to further socialist ideas since these designs were sold throughout the Soviet Republic. The trend continued through the 1920s into the 1930s, when the progressive aesthetic language of the avant garde fell out of official favour and was replaced by Socialist Realism, which was felt to be a more effective means of propagandizing social and economic change.

Modernism and the USA

While the more decorative tendencies of European design made a significant impact in the United States in the wake of the Paris Exhibition of 1925, the starker, more purist message of the Modern Movement also found its admirers, particularly at the Museum of Modern Art (MOMA) in New York, which was founded in 1929. As well as promoting modern fine arts and many of their sources, MOMA did much to encourage European Modernist design through its Department of Architecture and Industrial Art, founded in the wake of the contro-

BELOW **Walter Dorwin Teague**, *Design for the Machine* exhibition at Pennsylvania Museum (now Philadelphia Museum of Art), 1932. This was one of a number of contemporary exhibitions which sought to relate art to technology. The abstracted letter forms and sweeping, banded façade typify the period.

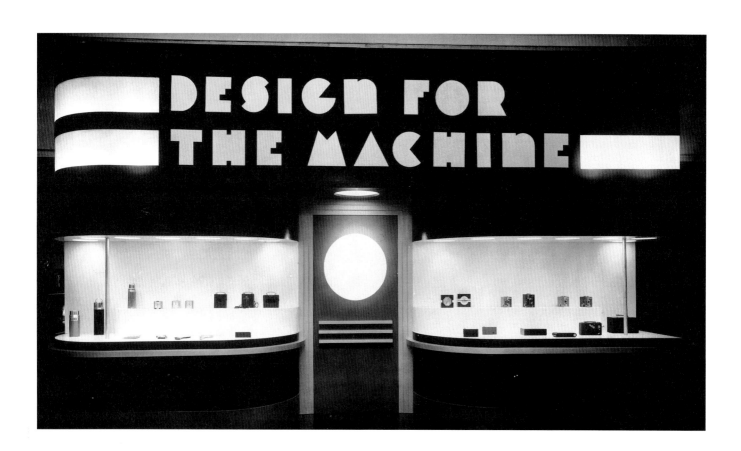

versial Modern Architecture International Exhibition mounted in 1932. This exhibition included work by leading Europeans—Walter Gropius, Mies van der Rohe, J. J. P. Oud and Le Corbusier—as well as American contributions by Raymond Hood, Howe and Lescaze, and others. The Machine Art exhibition, mounted at MOMA in 1934, also furthered the Modernist cause with a strong emphasis on pure forms redolent of the values of modern mass-production technology. However, more potent forces were changing the face of American society: the mass media, technological innovation, transport and communication systems and the rapid development of a fully fledged consumer society. Edward O'Brien, in *The Dance of the Machines: the American Short Story and the Industrial Age* of 1929, saw life in the United States as manipulated by

> the spiritual dictatorship of machinery, warfare, and magazines and newspapers of large circulation. To these shaping influences are now to be added the motion picture, the radio, the gramophone, the automobile, the corporation, queen-bee finance and all forms of national and international advertising and propaganda.[6]

A number of other writers and critics were similarly disturbed by what they felt were the constricting forces of a machine-dominated society—widespread assumptions that machines were above human fallibilities—and by their fears that mechanization restricted the creative spirit. None the less, the far more widespread association of technological progress with higher standards of living dominated the 1930s, even for a while breathing life into the ideals of the Technocratic Party under Howard Scott. In the Depression years such a vision became a more tangible reality than many of the extravagant celluloid fantasies of the contemporary American cinema.

American Values

In its earlier phases, the quest for a modern American style was often concerned with the iconography of everyday American life. For example, Edward Steichen, the American photographer, explored the possibilities of textile design from 1926 using a vocabulary of everyday things. He photographed common objects such as matchsticks, cigarettes and sugar cubes, employing a variety of lighting angles to create striking, almost abstract, patterns. These designs were printed on silk by the Stehli Silk Corporation of New York, a progressive company that promoted modern work by a number of American designers. An example of this trend could be seen in the American Prints series of 1927 which included designs such as "Gentlemen Prefer Blondes" by Ralph Barton, "Manhattan" by Clayton Knight and "Hollywood" by Neyea McMein.

Organizations also played a fruitful role in bringing modern design to public attention. The most important of these was the American Union of Decorative Artists and Craftsmen (AUDAC), founded in 1928. Seeking to promote modern American design, the group mounted an AUDAC exhibition at the Grand Central Palace, Manhattan, in 1930, followed by a more significant showing at the Brooklyn Museum in the following year when it also published *The Annual of American Design*.[7] Although the economic pressures of the early 1930s effectively curtailed its activities, many of the members of the group made a significant impact on the wider design consciousness, particularly in their highly decorative work for Radio City Music Hall in New York.

Technology: Progress and Symbolic Value

Product styling became a growth element in the burgeoning consumer culture of the 1920s, but it was not until the dramatic fall in US manufacturing income in the years following the 1929 Crash that it began to be seen as an important tool in the American economic recovery. The newly established industrial design profession, represented by pioneering individuals such as Raymond Loewy, Walter Dorwin Teague, Henry Dreyfuss and Norman Bel Geddes, sought to promote itself as more than just an agency for superficial styling change, allying itself to an understanding of the principles of engineering and co-operation with production engineers. Despite their impact, however, the heavy emphasis on styling and ornamentation by many leading manufacturers on items such as electric toasters, cocktail-shakers, refrigerators and pencil-sharpeners was simply geared to gaining a temporary market prominence, helped by the increasingly sophisticated business science of "consumer engineering" and advertising strategies.

As the 1930s progressed, what might be seen as a

more fully fledged American style developed in an assured, popular and expressively dynamic manner, embracing the spirit of technological utopianism that began to pervade many aspects of everyday life, albeit still heavily prompted by advertising, styling and other weapons of the corporate armour. This world of technological progress could be seen in the pages of Norman Bel Geddes' manifesto for change, his book *Horizons* of 1932, which emphasized speed, transportation, design and change. Geddes was accused by many fellow-professionals as being too popularist in approach, but nevertheless his evocative visions of streamlined automobiles, buses, trains, ships, aeroplanes, buildings and consumer goods were in tune with the American *Zeitgeist*. Consumers became increasingly eager to purchase goods which carried features of styling and ornamentation symbolizing speed and progress—whether vacuum cleaners, radios or fountain pens.

Several writers[8] have drawn attention to the close parallels which can be drawn with the world of science fiction which flourished in the late 1920s and 1930s, since this too held a Wellsian belief that technological advance would liberate people from mundane and demeaning tasks and create new modes of transportation, new materials and a better way of life. Hugo Gernsback, an important pioneer of popular science who launched the magazine *Amazing Stories* in 1926, aimed to convince his readership that there was a close relationship between science and science fiction. He evolved the maxim "Extravagant Fiction Today—Cold Fact Tomorrow" and, in a 1934 editorial in *Wonder Stories*, wrote:

> When science fiction came into being, it was taken
> seriously by most authors. In practically all
> instances authors laid the basis of their stories upon
> a solid scientific foundation. If an author made a
> statement as to future instrumentalities, he usually
> found it advisable to adhere closely to the
> possibilities of science as it was then known.

Frank R. Paul became Gernsback's leading illustrator, giving a visual dimension to futuristic speculation, and thus encouraging consumers to buy products and ornaments which expressed notions of progressive technology.

LEFT **Edward Steichen**, *Matches and Matchboxes*, printed cotton for the Stehli Silk Corporation, New York, 1928. One of a number of similar themes explored by the photographer Edward Steichen, this was also one of a series of designs commissioned by Stehli Silk which began to explore American subject matter.

Chicago and the Century of Progress Exhibition

In 1933, and again in the following year, an exhibition entitled "Century of Progress" was mounted in Chicago on the general principle of "Advancement through Technology." Originally envisaged before the 1929 Crash, its international scope was limited in the economically straitened climate of the early 1930s. Nevertheless, through the involvement of the National Research Council a coherent exhibition was organized on the theme of technological achievement, past and future. The National Research Council was funded by business and it was therefore unsurprising to find large corporations playing a significant role in the displays: General Motors, Chrysler, Goodyear, Firestone and General Electric were among those participating, in order to awaken the public both to new possibilities and to latent desires.[9] Many of the pavilions, although not radical in their Modernism, adopted the pluralistic values of a capitalist, free-market economy rather than the imposing, monolithic, classical forms favoured by European totalitarian regimes in later 1930s exhibitions.

There was a distinct aura of science fiction about many aspects of the display, particularly the Sky Ride double-decker rocketcars which provided rides of a third of a mile on cables suspended between two 628-foot high towers. Features like George Keck's appropriately named "House of Tomorrow" (complete with aircraft hangar as well as garage), sponsored by General Electric, Libbey-Owens-Ford and others, introduced the public to new materials and appliances. Streamlined modern modes of transport also caught the public imagination.[10] The M10,000 express train (later named *City of Salina*), manufactured by the Pullman Car Company for Union Pacific, epitomized this popular vision of progress and was seen at Chicago in 1934 as part of its nationwide promotional tour. Its sleek, aerodynamic, bullet-like form embodied many of the latest materials and manufacturing techniques and its publicity as "Tomorrow's Train Today" was in harmony with the times, providing the public with an image of modernity which they found reflected in the detailing and ornament of many smaller-scale consumer products. The aerodynamic Burlington *Zephyr* diesel-electric train proved no less popular; it was mobbed by the crowds when it appeared in the finale of the exhibition railway pageant "Wings of a Century," at the end of a dramatic record-breaking run from Denver to Chicago.

The popular impact of the Century of Progress exhibition should not be underestimated as it endorsed and promoted the symbolism of futuristic products. With almost forty-nine million visitors, it was seen by a greater number of people during its double showing than any other exhibition of the inter-war years,[11] and its message was not lost on the public at large. The 1925 Paris Exhibition, about which so much has been written, was seen by less than six million visitors and occupied less than one-eighth of the site acreage.

Streamlining as an Aspect of Everyday Life

Streamlining became an important symbol of the speed-orientated age, epitomized by the highly successful Douglas DC3 passenger aircraft of 1934, itself widely admired as an exemplar of contemporary form. It invaded the styling and ornamentation of all kinds of American consumer products and capital goods, whether capable of movement or not. Domestic appliances and equipment such as radios, lights, toasters, vacuum cleaners and refrigerators were almost as likely to be streamlined as automobiles or railway locomotives. Architecture also took on many features of this vocabulary, whether in the output of highly respected architects such as Frank Lloyd Wright in his Johnson's Wax Administration Building in Racine, Wisconsin, of 1937–9, the more publicly recognized 1936 Texaco service station designs by Walter Dorwin Teague or the widespread proliferation of the roadside diner. This last, a stationary but often streamlined purveyor of good, cheap food, provided a pale reflection of the contemporary luxury interiors of modern trains. Use of up-to-date materials, rounded forms and iconographic detailing associated with speed—such as long horizontal strips of aluminium, chrome or colour applied to surfaces in order to accentuate horizontality and sleekness, as seen on many locomotives, buses and automobiles—meant that customers could continue their associations with speed as they watched the traffic passing by on the highway outside. The extent to which the public saw speed as an all-encompassing metaphor for modernity can be seen in the ways in which diner advertising often juxtaposed the aerodynamic forms of railway locomotives and aeroplanes with diners themselves.

LEFT **American diner**, late 1930s. The use of tiling on the floor and the side of the counter, together with the decorative use of chrome on the stools, stems from the widespread circulation of Art Deco styling from the late 1920s. It is unmistakably American and makes extensive use of the decorative possibilities of Formica on the tabletops, counter and other surfaces.

"Design For Tomorrow:" the New York World's Fair 1939–40

The New York World's Fair (NYWF), which opened on 30 April 1939, made a considerable impact on the public during the two seasons in which it was open. Seen by almost forty-five million visitors, it was a powerful method of convincing them that business, science and technology could provide a better quality of life: production and consumption were the keys to future prosperity. Promotional publicity was unequivocal in its stance:

> To the American people, besieged by propaganda from the right and from the left, industry is giving its account. Here will be told what it has accomplished in the public interest, how it uses its funds, how, as the result of constant study to improve its goods and its services it contributes to the well-being of the nation as a whole, how the machinery of production and distribution is organized and how it seeks to promote prosperity among the men who make its achievements possible—its employees. Industry has found at the Fair a chance to meet the American people face to face and tell them how it is discharging its obligations under the economic scheme the democratic nations believe in.[12]

Industrial design was therefore an important ingredient in this recipe for an affluent free-enterprise culture, lending substance to the central theme of "Building the World of Tomorrow." Walter Dorwin Teague, one of its leading exponents, claimed this was because

> the industrial designers are supposed to understand public taste and be able to speak in the popular tongue, and because as a profession they are bound to disregard traditional forms and solutions and to think in terms of today and tomorrow. . . .[13]

The appetite of a science-fiction-consuming audience (which had reacted with such extraordinary panic to the invasion of the earth as broadcast by Orson Welles in H. G. Wells's *The War of the Worlds* in October 1938) was satisfied by Raymond Loewy's "Rocketport of the Future," a focal point in the Chrysler Building. There, in an ingeniously conceived *son et lumière* display, up to a thousand viewers at a time could see a model rocket-gun shooting a passenger spaceship on an imaginary journey from New York to London. The Chrysler Building also housed a theatre which screened an animated colour 3-D

film about automobile parts, complete with polaroid glasses. No less alluring was the Westinghouse Electrical Corporation's seven-foot tall Elektro Robot which could perform twenty-six movements, responding to commands spoken into a microphone, while its pet robotic dog could beg, bark and wag its tail.

A number of other aspects of the Fair architecture sustained this science-fiction ethos: the Du Pont Chemical Tower, the Westinghouse Singing Tower of Light, the Aqualon Fountains and several of the major pavilions. Many of the comic-strip creations of the era would have seemed entirely suited to such an environment: Buck Rogers appeared in 1929, Flash Gordon in 1934, Superman in 1938 and Batman in 1939.

On a more developed level were exhibits such as Henry Dreyfuss's vast diorama of "Democracity", housed in the 200-foot diameter "Perisphere" which, with the adjacent 700-foot tall "Trylon" (symbolizing flight into the future), provided the striking central motif of the Fair, and gave souvenir manufacturers a tremendous boost. "Democracity" was a vast environmental plan of the future, stretching out over fifteen scale miles with carefully zoned industrial, residential, business and greenbelt sectors, which was viewed by visitors from revolving rings. Such visions of the benefits of a planned environment of the future were typical of the Fair.

By far the most compelling and popular of these futuristic visions was Norman Bel Geddes' "Futurama" exhibit, which took visitors (at a rate of 27,500 per day and five million over the duration of the exhibition) on a series of moving ramps and chairs on a simulated flight over a projected world of 1960, which was divided into separate zones for commercial, residential and industrial purposes.[14] The aim of the exhibit was to examine potential solutions to contemporary traffic problems and project them into the future. But visitors were more likely to be struck by visions of multi-laned highways, with thousands of streamlined cars, buses and lorries travelling at scale-speeds of up to 100 mph, than by any more complex message.

The World's Fair provided manufacturers and industrial designers with a golden opportunity to awaken consumer desires and stimulate the economy. It sustained product styling and ornamentation with a technologically orientated vocabulary, and also provided the opportunity to survey public reactions to future marketing strategies such as those associated with "dream cars," "Motoramas" and "Kitchens of Tomorrow" in the 1950s.

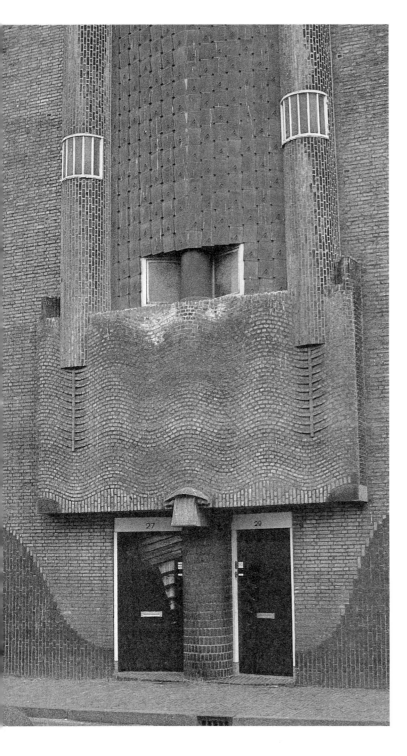

LEFT **Michel de Klerk**, Zaanstraat Flats, Amsterdam, *c.* 1920. De Klerk was the leading figure of the Amsterdam School of architects and designers. He exercised a highly expressive vocabulary, almost a polar opposite from the clarity and precision of the coexistent De Stijl group. This can be seen in the varying rhythms, textures and details which he explored on the façades of his housing schemes, manipulating traditional materials such as brick and tile in an invigorating and exciting fashion.

RIGHT **Michel de Klerk**, interior for t'Woonhuys, 1916, from Wendigen 7, No. 10, 1925–26.

FAR RIGHT **Michel de Klerk**, furniture from the interior of Dr J Polenaar, Amsterdam 1913.

As on the exteriors of de Klerk's buildings, the importance of detail is apparent in his furniture and draws upon a wide range of ornamental sources.

RIGHT **Foyer** of the Tuschinki Cinema, Amsterdam by Jaap Gidding, 1918–21. The ostentatious ornamentation on the exterior of the building by Louis Hyman de Jong was echoed in Gidding's dramatic designs for the interior. His carpet designs and wall paintings explore the decorative possibilities afforded by the peacock, the colour scheme embracing orange, red, green and purple blended by the suffused lighting of the heavily ornate lighting fitments.

FAR LEFT **Robert Mallet-Stevens**, set of the entrance to the engineer's villa from Marcel L'Herbier's film *Inhumanie*, produced in 1923. Mallet-Stevens was in charge of the exterior architecture designs. The strong emphasis on vertical and horizontal lines, together with the rectilinear decoration on the door, indicate a strong familiarity with De Stijl work. The film involved a compendium of decorative designers. These included Lalique, Puiforcat and Luce who were involved with the design of objects, Léger with the engineer's workshop, and Paul Poiret with the costumes.

CENTRE LEFT **Theo van Doesburg**, Cinema Dance Hall, Strasbourg, 1926–8. This was the most important room of the Café Aubette entertainment complex. The striking use of the diagonal shows van Doesburg's move away from the vertical/horizontal basis of earlier De Stijl work towards a more dynamic "Elementarist" vocabulary.

LEFT **Entrance hall light**, designed by W. M. Dudok, from the Town Hall, Hilversum, c. 1928. This fitting reveals links with Frank Lloyd Wright, Berlage and progressive modernist tendencies in Holland. The emphasis on vertical and horizontal divisions shows a stylistic debt to the Neoplasticist theories of De Stijl.

LEFT **Gerrit Rietveld**, Schroeder House, Utrecht, 1924. The interplay of the rectilinear elements and use of red, yellow and blue primaries together with grey, white and black show a close affinity with many aspects of van Doesburg's *Towards a Plastic Architecture*, 1924.

RIGHT **Robert Mallet-Stevens**, table in painted wood, 1920s. This piece, composed of squares and rectangles, exhibits the outward manifestations of the De Stijl aesthetic although the tubular steel stabilizer strikes something of a discordant note.

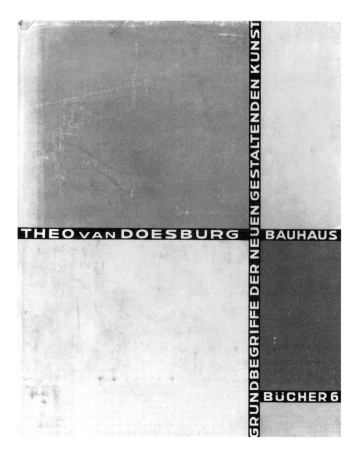

ABOVE LEFT **Theo van Doesburg**, cover design for Bauhaus Book No. 6, *Grundbegriffe der Neuen Gestaltenden Kunst*, designed in 1924, published by the Albert Langen Press, 1925. The rectilinear design, with panels in red, grey, yellow and blue, on the cover of this German publication reflects international interest in De Stijl amongst the avant garde.

ABOVE RIGHT **Walter Gropius**, Director's office at the Bauhaus, Weimar, 1923. The crisp forms of this interior, together with its furnishings and fitments, reveal a growing concern with the activities of De Stijl and Russian Constructivism. There is a move away from the more Expressionist inclinations seen in earlier Bauhaus work. The vertical and horizontal emphases of the light fitting, designed by Gropius himself, have something of the aesthetic outlook of both such groups.

RIGHT **Gunta Stolzl**, design for a hanging tapestry, 1927–8. This colourful abstract design reveals Stolzl's interests in dyeing and textiles which she had developed while a student at the Weimar Bauhaus. After setting up a weaving workshop she returned to the Bauhaus where she was in charge of the weaving workshops from 1927 to 1931.

LEFT **Josef Hartwig**, chess set in lacquered wood, Germany, 1923. Hartwig was a master craftsman in the sculpture workshop at the Weimar Bauhaus from 1921 to 1925. Although the pieces are conceived in relation to their possibilities of movement and echo the move towards a "machine aesthetic" discernible at the Bauhaus after 1922–3, they nonetheless exhibit a distinctive ornamental character.

ABOVE **Fritz Becher and Erich Kutzner**, dining room in a house for the professional classes at the Düsseldorf Exhibition, 1926. The light pendant apart, the use of ornament is restrained and the overall feeling is one of the blending of traditional forms with the modernist spirit.

LEFT **Ernst May**, a room in May's house, Frankfurt, 1925. May was the City Architect in Frankfurt, responsible for the implementation of a great deal of modernist housing. Emphasis was placed on forms and materials which were aesthetically compatible with the spirit of the machine age and modern modes of production. As a result, ornamental interest is largely confined to personal belongings, as in the floor rug.

RIGHT **Theodore Bogler**, earthenware
containers for kitchen supplies seen at the
1923 Bauhaus Exhibition, mass-produced by
the Velten-Vordamm ceramic factory. Such
clean, simplified shapes were compatible
with the machine aesthetic so favoured at the
Bauhaus from this period onwards. Even the
lettering was far removed from the
individualistic, expressive qualities seen in
the 1921 Festival Programme and elsewhere,
but nonetheless lends a machine-oriented
decorative, as well as functional, aesthetic
character.

BELOW **German tableware** of the late 1930s
in a traditional table setting. It shows the
völkisch ornamental traits popular at the time,
which reinforced nationalistic inclinations.

LEFT **Interior view** of the Sommerfeld House by Walter Gropius and Hannes Meyer, 1921. Such decorative tendencies at this time revealed a penchant for the more expressionist, anti-standardization views still prevalent in the early post-War Weimar years of the Bauhaus. However, in those days of material shortages in Germany resulting from the First World War, there was still a delicate balance between the anti-standardization, anti-industrial tendencies of the political left, who viewed such factors as having contributed to the initiation of hostilities, and their concern to develop a more progressive socio-economic aesthetic.

BELOW LEFT **Herbert Bayer and Rudolf Paris**, wall painting at the Bauhaus, Weimar, 1923. This abstract decorative scheme reflects the growing influence of the international avant garde at the Weimar Bauhaus from 1922–3, particularly stimulated in this instance by the arrival of the Russian Constructivist painter Wassily Kandinsky in 1922. One of the concerns of the wall-painters at the Bauhaus was to stress the importance of colour in the architectural environment.

RIGHT **Festival programme** for the Sommerfeld House, 1921. The strong graphic quality of this illustration reveals the importance of the anti-industrial thrust of early Bauhaus thinking. There is a close similarity between this and Feininger's founding manifesto. It ties such tendencies to those anti-capitalist leanings which Gropius, the Bauhaus Director, affected in the early post-War period. The graphic form of the lettering, with its strong calligraphic idiosyncrasies, coincides with such a standpoint.

BELOW **Gerhard Marcks**, portrait of Otto Lindig on an earthenware vase by Theodore Bogler, 1922. There is a strong craft feel in the decoration which is removed from the machine aesthetic, standardization-oriented forms of the later Bauhaus years.

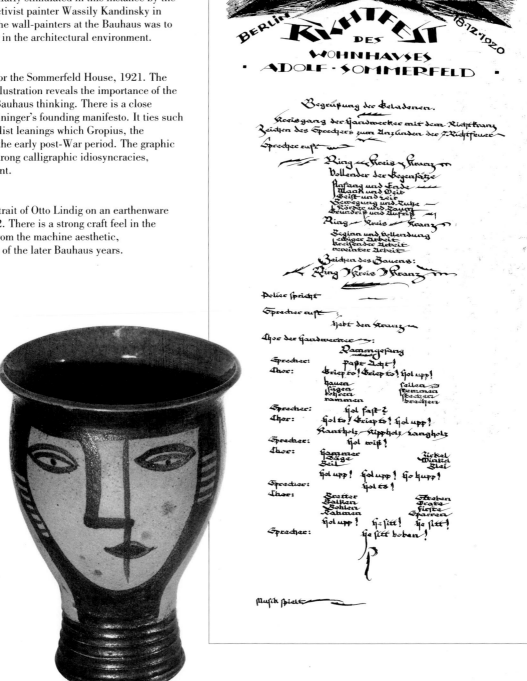

LEFT **Alexander Rodchenko**, box for *Nasha Industria* (Our Industry) caramels, 1924. The strong geometric layout and formal decorative motifs show a concern among the Russian avant garde in the 1920s to orient their designs to economic mass-production.

BELOW **Vladimir Mayakovsky**, "Red Army Star" (Krasnoarmeiskaia Zvozda) caramel wrapper, 1924: *Indianech Came to Red Petrograd—And They Stuck Bayonets in His Side*. Mayakovsky was a key propagandist artist who drew upon easily intelligible forms such as woodcuts and gingerbread moulds to convey the revolutionary cause to a largely illiterate population. Their directness is in clear contrast to the abstract Constructivist tendencies of the avant garde which came under question in the years of the Stalinist oppression.

LEFT **Alexander Rodchenko**, fabric design, 1920s. The spirographic, mechanically realized decorative forms show a concern to move away from individualistic and idiosyncratic tendencies towards a more progressive, technology-based idiom.

RIGHT **Nicolai Suetin**, coffee pot, 1926. The Russian Suprematists began working in ceramics in 1922, although much of their work, which explored the dynamic sensations of abstract forms in space, remained under the umbrella of experimentation. There was a wider European interest expressed in such work as a result of exposure in the 1925 Exposition des Arts Décoratifs et Industriels in Paris.

BELOW **Alexander Rodchenko**, teapot design, gouache on paper, 1922. This striking design explores the decorative possibilities of abstract motifs.

FAR LEFT **Cotton print**, late 1920s. This anonymous pattern shows the easy absorption of Soviet symbolism into traditional decorative forms, with the hammer and sickle set in a star and bordered by wheatsheaves becoming unobtrusive elements in the overall scheme.

LEFT **Plate** in "traditional" style, 1920s.

BELOW **Plate** with witch/devil blowing horn, *c.* 1920.

In the post-Revolutionary years many designs, whether geared to ceramics or textiles, explored the decorative possibilities of traditional Russian culture. Folk traditions, fairly tales and myths were all fields from which ornamental motifs were drawn.

RIGHT **Plate** with hammer and sickle motif, 1918.

FAR RIGHT **Plate** with star motif, *c.* 1920.

Devices with clear agitational subject matter provided
readily identifiable ornament, often blended with traditional
decorative traits.

BELOW ***The Tunnel***, cotton print, *c.* 1930. The design is
clearly intended to support the spirit of industrial progress, a
key aspect of Soviet propaganda. The emphatically
geometric, almost abstract, formal composition relates to
Constructivist textile designs by Stepanova and Poponova.

BELOW RIGHT **P. Leonov**, decorative cotton print, 1927.
Such striking designs reflected the interest in expressing
something of the progressive ambitions of the Soviet
economy: productive factories billowing the smoke of activity
and widespread air transportation.

RIGHT **Paul Browne**, design for a torpedo car, 15 May, 1935. The dramatic teardrop shape, functionally justifiable in an aerodynamic context, provided a rich source of stylistic affectation in countless stationary product designs.

BELOW FAR RIGHT **Walter Dorwin Teague**, Robert J. Harper and A. M. Erikson, tower of the Du Pont Company, New York World's Fair, 1939–40.

BELOW RIGHT **Aqualon fountain** at the New York World's Fair, 1939–40.

The almost science-fiction form of these two landmarks of the NYWF relates to the widespread public faith in technological progress as a route to material utopianism. The Du Pont tower, with its strong molecular connotations, looks forward to the 1950s affectation for such globular forms, while the Aqualon (with its upright glass tube containing goldfish) relates more closely to the fictional exploits of Flash Gordon or Buck Rogers.

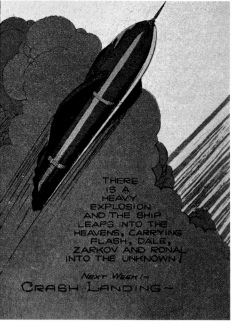

ABOVE **Norman Bel Geddes**, Ocean Liner, 1932. This streamlined liner was illustrated in Geddes' influential book *Horizons* (1932). Geddes did much to promote the adoption of aerodynamic forms in a wide range of everyday products.

LEFT **Flash Gordon**, comic strip, 1930s. This comic strip did much to sustain the ethos of progressive technology. The streamlined rocket forms were widely echoed in many real products of everyday life.

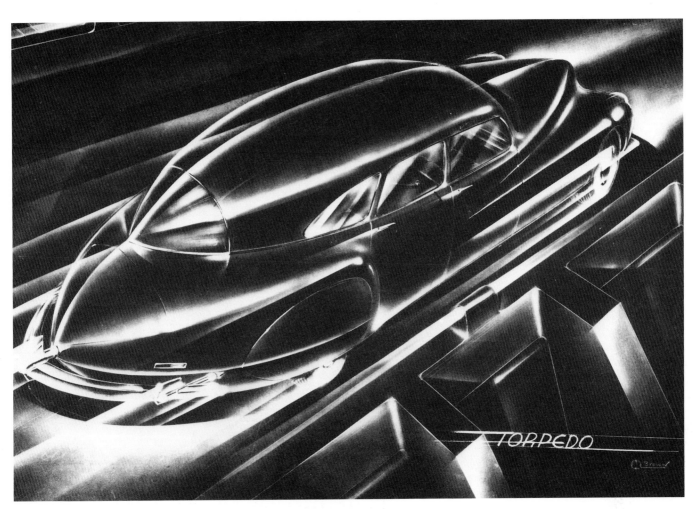

TORPEDO

BELOW **Watergate to the Electric Group**, Century of Progress Exhibition, Chicago 1933–4. Allusions to ancient myth and style indicate the wide range of styles considered appropriate to further the cause of science and industry, a view which had altered significantly by the time of the New York World's Fair at the end of the decade.

ABOVE **Holabird & Root**, Chrysler Building, Century of Progress Exhibition, Chicago 1933–4. The strong vertical lines in the central section are common to the ornamental devices to be found on refrigerators and other appliances. The sunrise motif was a favourite ornamental conceit of the period.

RIGHT **Tabletop** in micarta with anodized
aluminium inlay designed by Winold Reiss
for the Longchamps Restaurant, New York
City, 1933. All the tabletops in the restaurant
bore a different design. The American Indian
motif reflected a wider tendency among
American designers to draw upon indigenous
subject matter. There was also a strong sense
of a formal relationship between the Indian
handicrafts and certain decorative trends in
modern design.

BELOW **High Voltage** Railway Electrification
Panel in micarta for the Westinghouse
Pavilion at the Century of Progress
Exhibition, Chicago, 1933–4.

LEFT **American diner**, 1940s. Like many locomotive exteriors, this low-lying, aluminium, "speed-whiskered" economic purveyor of fast food epitomized something of the technological ethos enjoyed by so many Americans since the late 1920s.

BELOW **Century of Progress** Exhibition, Chicago 1933–4, Olson Rug Company truck and *Burlington Zephyr* locomotive. The exterior of the train, realized through consultants Holabird & Root in conjunction with the Edward G. Budd Manufacturing Company, helped to establish the vogue for streamlining motifs on a wide range of products, from vacuum cleaners to refrigerators. The long, horizontal "speed whiskers", running around the front and along the sides of the train, are echoed on the lower edges of the truck, itself also exhibiting a fashionable teardrop shape.

LEFT **Frank Lloyd Wright**, furniture designed for the Johnson Wax Company, Racine, Wisconsin, 1936–9, manufactured by Steelcase. The chair and desk, in enamelled and brass-plated steel with American walnut work surfaces, show that Wright was not impervious to the streamlined aesthetic. The curved desk drawers swing, rather than pull out.

BELOW LEFT **Robert Mallet-Stevens**, Rue Mallet-Stevens, No. 5, 1927. The development of which this is a part was perhaps Mallet-Stevens' most significant work. The curvilinear edges to the flower beds, together with the sweeping horizontal accents at the lower level, bear some relationship with streamlining concerns across the Atlantic.

BELOW **John Vassos**, Coca-Cola Soda Fountain dispenser, c. 1934. The strong vertical fluted lines which animate the dispenser relate it to the wider world of streamlining and are typical of similar decorative bandings which pervade a wide range of appliances.

ABOVE **Lydia Bush-Brown**, *New York Waterfront*, resist-dyed hanging (silk batik), 1920s. The New York waterfront, a source of inspiration for Fritz Lang's anti-Fordist film *Metropolis* of 1926, also provided many American designers with indigenous subject matter.

LEFT **Paul T. Frankl**, *Skyscraper* bookcase in elm and painted wood with brass handle, late 1920s. Like a number of other examples illustrated in this chapter, the bookcase reflects part of the drive to establish an America-based iconography in the late 1920s. Paul Frankl, in conjunction with the "Art in Trade" exhibition at R. H. Macy & Co. of 1927, lectured on the theme of "The Skyscraper in Decoration".

RIGHT **Ruth Reeves**, *Manhattan*, block-printed cotton for W. & J. Sloane, New York City, 1930. Reeves studied in Brooklyn, New York and in Paris with Fernand Léger. Printed in a variety of colour schemes, this design reflects this background, blending the iconography of New York modernity with Cubist-inspired compositional devices.

LEFT **Shelvador** electric refrigerator, by
Crosley, USA, 1935. The stepped, rounded
forms of the top of the appliance show a
concern to reflect the appearance of
streamlining while the ornamental use of the
trademark badge relates it to automobile
insignia.

FAR LEFT **Radio** by Harold Van Doren and J. G. Rideout, manufactured by Air-King Products Co., Brooklyn, 1930–3. Like many domestic appliances and items of furniture, the stepped form of this radio design reflects the shape of contemporary skyscraper designs. The vertical and horizontal flutings can also be related to the symbolism of streamlining. Available in Plaskon in a variety of colours, the radio also reflects the growing American trend to employ designers to bolster sales.

LEFT **Radio**, designed and manufactured by Philco, 1930. This radio, traditional in its deployment of ornamental motifs, is in complete contrast to the Air-King radio. Its historicizing appearance is a reminder that the legacy of the past was an important aspect of the American (and European) market in the 1920s and 1930s.

BELOW **Abel Faidy**, settee in the "skyscraper" design for the Charles and Ruth Singleton penthouse, 1244 Sloane Street, Chicago, 1927. Despite obvious links with European decorative trends, the use of the skyscraper motif indicates the concern of a growing number of designers to develop an American iconography.

LEFT **Duncan Grant**, butterfly and leaf fabric for Allan Walton, 1930s, one of many artist-designed commissions by Allan Walton in the 1930s.

BELOW **John Adams and Truda Carter**, *Streamline* tea set, manufactured by Carter, Stabler & Adams Ltd, 1936. The contemporary vogue for streamlining can be seen in the smooth, sweeping form of the spout and lid of the teapot. The applied decoration, designed by Truda Carter, is much simpler than the majority of traditional patterns and has an overall feeling of restrained modernity.

RIGHT **A. E. Stenlake**, *Big Tulip* design in pencil and watercolour for roller-printed cotton, 1929. Such traditional forms typified the more widespread and enduring taste for floral motifs in furnishing fabrics.

LEFT **White Tower diner**, Chicago, 1928.

BELOW **White Tower diner**, Syracuse, New York, 1934.

RIGHT **White Tower diner**, New York, 1932.

BELOW FAR RIGHT **White Tower diner**, Camden, New Jersey, 1936.

White Tower was a pioneering hamburger chain, founded in 1926, which sought to devise an eye-catching appearance for its outlets. Initially the style was medieval in flavour, with castellated forms in white glazed bricks, a format seen in the 1932 New York diner. The influence of European decorative motifs could be seen in outlets such as the 1928 Chicago diner, with its geometric moderne stylistic concerns. More popular and enduring in terms of European influence was the 1934 Syracuse diner which was constructed of porcelain-enamelled sheets held in place by stainless steel strips. The Camden diner was not in fact built by White Tower, but taken over by the company in 1941. Its wrap-around windows and aerodynamically softened corners were all part of the streamlined aesthetic.

Tower # 1
144 West Onondaga St.
Syracuse , New York

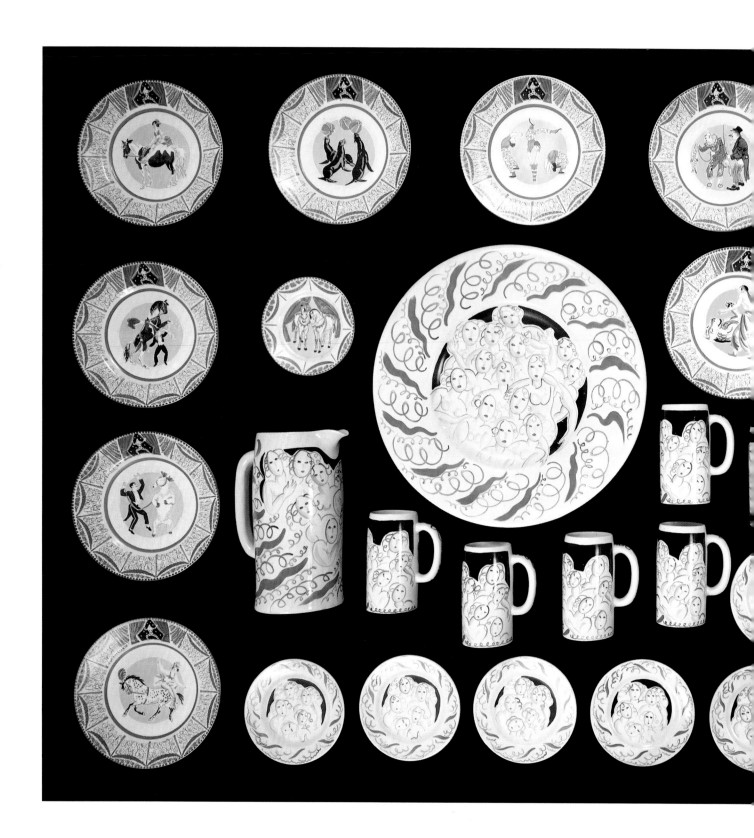

LEFT **Laura Knight**, *Circus* tableware, 1930s. These designs, produced by the Burslem firm of A. J. Wilkinson under the direction of Clarice Cliff, reflect a contemporary trend in Britain to marry art and industry.

BELOW **Berthold Lubetkin** and Tecton, mural for Finsbury Health Centre, Pine Street, London, 1937–8. This piece of propaganda for healthy living, with its stress on fresh air, sunshine and exercise, reflects a balance between certain references to continental modernism and the need to convey a message in an unambiguous manner. Such visual propaganda had a decorative function.

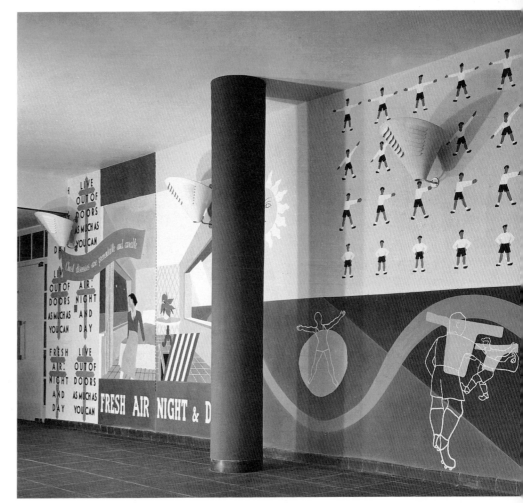

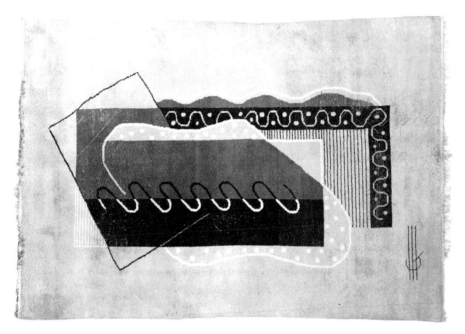

LEFT **Ronald Grierson**, rug design, 1920s. This strikingly bold abstract design owed much to the more decorative elements of continental modernism, with a clear debt to some of the later phases of Synthetic Cubism.

BELOW **Marion Pepler**, carpet, 1929–30. Like those of Dorn and other progressive designers of the period, many of Pepler's pieces sought to provide a fresh, modern impetus to British design.

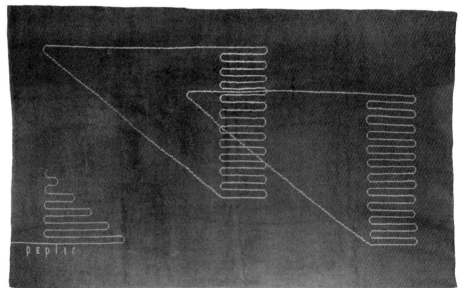

BELOW **Phyllis Barron and Dorothy Larcher**, *Hazlitt*, hand block-printed textile, 1930s. This design shows the softer, British side of the quest for a modern aesthetic, blending personal expression with a desire to explore abstract forms.

BELOW RIGHT **Marion Dorn**, moquette for London Transport, 1939, with small repeats and limited colour range.

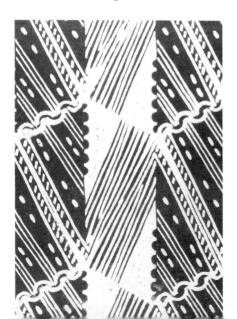

RIGHT **Ashley Havinden**, *Ashley's Abstract*, Edinburgh Weavers, 1937. These forms, blending calligraphic intensity of line with abstract shapes suggestive of Continental artists such as Miró, show the desire of a number of progressive British artists and designers in the 1930s to redress the conservatism and insularity of the majority of British designs at this time.

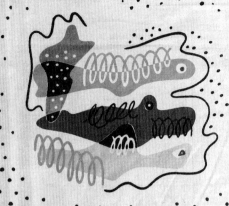

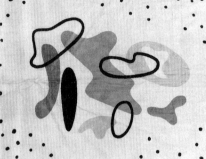

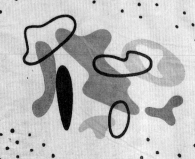

4
Design and Ornament in a Totalitarian Climate 1920 to 1940

Ornament and decoration played an important propagandist role in the totalitarian climate of Italy under Mussolini, Germany under Hitler and the USSR under Stalin. Politics, economics and industrial production were inextricably linked, and design was seen an important means of giving visible form to the overt ideals of the regimes. Fascism in Italy and Germany looked to both traditional and Modernist vocabularies to promote its message, albeit in rather differing ways. Traditional form and ornamentation implied some continuity with the past, while the application of a more modern syntax was able to demonstrate a commitment to progress, particularly of a technological nature. While the scale, grandeur and idealized heroism associated with antiquity provided the basis for many large-scale public visual statements, it is not surprising that the more vernacular ornamental traits associated with the home and its furnishings should have looked towards established models, compatible with the Fascists' stress on family, patriotism and nationhood. In the USSR there was a more straightforward rejection of Modernism during the course of the 1920s, with a marked shift away from the abstract, Constructivist forms associated with avant-garde designers in the immediate aftermath of the 1917 Revolution. Under Stalin the state looked to more readily intelligible forms

of ornament and decoration. These drew on the traditions of folk art, realism, monumentalism and symbols of agricultural and industrial production to convey the power and purpose of the new regime to the population as a whole.

Italian Modernism: the Rationalist Movement

In the immediate aftermath of the First World War, there was a period of political, social and economic turbulence in Italy with five different governments holding office between 1918 and 1922. This was accompanied by a dramatic rise in unemployment, fierce inflationary pressures and a fall in industrial production and overseas trade. The Fascist Party, founded in 1919, came to power in 1922 in this atmosphere of uncertainty and confusion. By the mid-1920s it had suppressed political opposition, independent trade unions and the free press: Mussolini was dictator, with Parliament little more than a rubber stamp.

Despite the progressive, dynamic and distinctly twentieth-century profile of the Italian Futurists, headed by Marinetti in the years before the First World War, Modernism in Italy formally began only in 1926, with the establishment of Gruppo 7, consisting of seven recent graduates from Milan Polytechnic. Initiating what became known as Rationalism, they and their followers

LEFT **L. Raitser**, *The Mechanization of the Red Army*, textile design, 1933. The propagandist, yet decorative, use of technological and militaristic motifs is clear and accords closely to the Stalinist emphasis on social realism.

were aware of avant-garde developments elsewhere in Europe and involved themselves with a number of international centres to which they sent projects, including the Weissenhof housing exhibition at Stuttgart in 1927, Breslau in 1929 and New York in 1931. With a design language allied to the clean, abstract forms of the machine-age buildings and products of their avant-garde counterparts in other countries, they hoped to establish Rationalism as *the* style of Fascism.[1] Nevertheless, there were also attempts to locate Rationalism in a particularly Italian context[2] and its exponents warmed to the emphasis that Fascist propaganda placed on youth and dynamism since it appeared to offer an opportunity for a cultural revolution alongside a political one.

The first Esposizione dell'Architettura Razionale (Rationalist Architectural Exhibition) was mounted in 1928 with approval and sponsorship from the Union of Fascist Architects. The newly formed Movimento Italiano per l'Architettura Razionale (MIAR) was an attempt to establish the Fascist credentials of a Modernist style. Exhibition organizers Gaetano Minucci and Adalberto Libera proclaimed in the catalogue:

> We feel that this is *our* architecture, because we are inheritors of Roman building power. Profoundly

rational, utilitarian, and industrial were the characteristics of Roman architecture . . . we turn to our youth, and in true Fascist spirit, ask them to follow us, because it is they who will be able to refine the new Italian architecture and make it great.[3]

The recognition sought by the Rationalists and MIAR proved hard to come by, particularly since the exhibition was highly critical of major civic commissions by leading Roman academics. In the ensuing furore, MIAR collapsed, which rather dented the aspirations of those who had sought to marry Rationalist ideas firmly and enduringly to the Fascist cause.

Rationalism can broadly be seen to oppose ornament for its own sake, and to embrace notions of standardization and an aesthetic which is spiritually, if not actually, compatible with modern life, materials and production technology. In the design field this tended to find favour

BELOW **Giuseppe Terragni**, Casa del Fascio (House of Fascism) at Como, Italy, 1936. These Party buildings were found in many towns in the 1920s and 1930s. Uncompromisingly modern in style with a minimum of ornament, it is in complete contrast to the overladen ornamental symbolism of the Tuscan House of Fascism (see page 176).

among industries with new products such as radios, office equipment, automobiles and other forms of transport. Unlike the more traditional historicizing values which people liked to see in the furnishings, ornament and decoration of their homes, new products were not steeped in past associations nor necessarily clothed in the ornamental styles of the past, and could more readily be seen as symbols of progress than more long-standing domestic artefacts.

However, it was not merely in terms of style that the Modernist cause was pursued. Important too, as in Germany, was the impact of American business methods and efficient factory organization.

The influence of the American industrial outlook was seen at Fiat in the years immediately after the First World War in, for instance, the highly systematized production lines of the Lingotto factory with its roof-top test-track, designed by Giacomo Matté-Trucco and described as "the most nearly Futurist building ever built."[4] The impression left by Fordist mass production could be seen in the Fiat 500 of 1936, but American automobile modelling also proved alluring in the Fiat 1500 of 1935 which made clear reference to the streamlined Chrysler Airflow of 1933. Pininfarina, the automobile stylist, had seen the Ford plant in Detroit and was also clearly influenced by contemporary American product streamlining in his designs for the Lancia Aprilia of 1935.

American business methods also left their mark on the Olivetti office equipment company, whose image was soon informed by a clean Modernism, whether in typewriters such as the MP1 of 1932 and the Studio 42 of 1935, the new factory buildings at Ivrea of the late 1930s, or a variety of poster designs of the period. Among their highly talented architects and designers were included Figini, Pollini, Schawinsky, Pintori and Nizzoli.

An unambiguously modern style was also used for the Italian State Railways, often considered to be one of the great achievements of the Fascist era. In 1933 Michelucci and others won the prestigious competition for the Santa Maria Novella railway station in Florence, with a clearly Modernist approach integrating architecture and design of lighting, digital clocks, signage and seating. Modern streamlined forms could be seen in the prestigious long-distance electric trains of the 1930s, such as the ETR 200 of 1936, or the Fiat *littorine* with their bulbous, egg-shaped radiators bearing, as did all Fascist trains, the *fasci littori*.

Muted Modernism: Novecento

The Novecento movement, which inclined towards a modernized form of classicism, was also a contender for recognition as the style of Fascism. Emerging during the same years as Rationalism, its exponents, including Giò Ponti and Emilio Lancia, leaned more towards the decorative arts of France or Austria than the far more stark, machine-based idiom of the German avant garde. Where the Rationalists found their ideals epitomized by the new industries manufacturing new products, so the adherents of Novecento looked to the more traditional industries such as those producing applied arts and interior furnishings as an outlet for their creativity. Many fruitful relationships were forged with craft-based industries such as ceramics, glass, lighting, metalware and furniture, and the growing market for such decorative work among the affluent middle classes encouraged manufacturers to move away from historicizing styles towards a more modern, though often still decorative, aesthetic, as in the familiar Art Deco look found in neighbouring France. The influence of Art Deco could be found in objects as diverse as dancing figurines and the Isotta Fraschina *Flying Star* automobile of 1931.

Modern Design at the Triennali

Exhibitions were important disseminators of the ideology of design and architecture and the most significant of these were the Triennali (originally Biennali) exhibitions of decorative and industrial arts, which were first held in Monza from 1923 and moved to Milan ten years later. Monza was originally selected as the location since it was in a region of rapid industrialization with a newly established institute for the decorative arts. As a result, particularly in the early years, the exhibitions were largely successful in promoting the more traditional aspects of Italian design and ornamentation. It was only in the 1930s, and particularly after the move to Milan for the Fifth Triennale in 1933, that a stronger industrial flavour asserted itself. Although at this, and subsequent, Triennali Rationalist products were shown, manufacturers did little to further this progressive cause as there was limited enthusiasm for initiating large-scale production runs. However, with Mussolini's advocation of an autarchic policy in the mid-1930s, there was a renewed interest in standardization of planning and furnishing, although this was short-lived and generally more speculative than widespread.

Traditional Imagery and Ornamentation

It is interesting that in Italy the promoters of emphatically modern products such as the motor car often deployed traditional imagery to encourage their acceptance. Orna-

Fascist hairstyle, Italy, 1930s. The style obviously plays on the symbolism of the *fasci* which have already been seen in a number of other contexts. Although part of a window display it would seem unlikely that such a style would have proved particularly attractive other than in the context of historical pageants.

mental devices with which the public were familiar were the obvious choice, since much of such imagery also drew heavily upon the iconography of Fascism, in its turn looking back to the heady days of the Roman Empire. Typical motifs were the axes and *fasci* which adorned not only the pavilions at Fascist exhibitions, but also posters, publicity and sleeve badges for the uniforms of the Gioventù Italiana del Littorio (the Fascist youth organization), together with the winged eagles of the legions which became familiar ornamental elements under Mussolini. These related both to militaristic and industrial contexts. For example, Giuseppe Romano, for a 1928 Fiat poster, portrayed contemporary automobiles passing through a monumental Triumphal Arch in the form of the Fiat logo, topped by equestrian statuary. Likewise Plinio Codognato, who worked on Fiat graphics for twenty years, drew on the image of an armed Roman soldier on a rearing horse for his 1928 advertisement for the Fiat 521, and on a griffin-like mythological creature for the 525S of 1930. Mario Sironi, who began working for Fiat during the 1930s, was even more direct: his 1936 advertisement for the Fiat 500 drew on the image of a stone statue of the she-wolf suckling Romulus and Remus, a symbol of ancient Rome, and for his 1941 portrayal of "Legione Romana et autocolonna militare in marcia sull'Amba" (A Roman legion and motor column on the move in the Roman Amba), he alluded to the equestrian statue of Marcus Aurelius on the Capitol.

Stylistic Ambiguity

Something of the ambivalence towards Modernism and tradition in the 1920s and '30s has been seen in the gulf between propaganda and product in the Fiat motor company. Similar ambivalence is found in a number of important commissions in the first dozen years or so of the Fascist era. Propagandists for the regime could show examples of both the progressive dynamism and the traditional heritage of Fascism by citing, on the one

RIGHT **Tom Purvis**, poster for British Industries Fair, 1932. This strident image of Britannia shows the importance of traditional imagery in the increasingly sensitive political and economic climate of the early 1930s. There were many who believed that the British Empire offered a route to future prosperity: the use of strident, nationalistic imagery to bolster such a cause paralleled that found in Germany and Russia in the same period.

TOM PURVIS

Nearest Station
**WEST KENSINGTON
BARONS COURT OR
ADDISON ROAD**

Nearest Station
**SHEPHERDS BUSH
OR
WOOD LANE**

205/8000/3-2-32

WATERLOW & SONS LTD, LONDON, DUNSTABLE & WATFORD.

hand, buildings and designs with a distinctly modern flavour and, on the other, links with the Roman imperial past through reference to other examples which drew heavily on classical prototypes. In this context, comparisons have been made between Enrico del Debbio's heavily classical Stadio Mussolini in Rome of 1928, replete with nude statues of athletes, and the engineering aesthetic of Pier Luigi Nervi's emphatically modern soccer stadium in Florence (originally named after a local Fascist hero); or between Paolo and Vittorio Mezzanotte's classically derived Casa del Fascio in Milan of 1927 and the clearly Rationalist Casa del Fascio at Como, built between 1932 and 1936 by Giuseppe Terragni.

In the realm of exhibitions, stylistic uncertainty prevailed again. At the Tenth Anniversary Exhibition of the Fascist Revolution in Rome in 1932, a dramatic modern façade for the Palazzo dell'Esposizione by Libera and de Renzi bore almost abstract 25-metre-high *fasci littori*, thus updating and modernizing traditional imagery which was generally more conventionally delineated by academic monumentalists. Inside, in the Sala del '22, Terragni created a powerful piece of Modernist propaganda, using three-dimensional graphics, photomontage and an almost abstract rhythm of massed hands raised in the Fascist salute (itself deriving from Roman tradition).

However, later in the 1930s, Mussolini came down firmly in favour of the more strongly neo-Classical repertoire of architectural and decorative form seen in many of the major commissions of the late 1930s, especially at the great international exhibitions. At New York in 1939 the main feature of the Italian Pavilion was a huge tower surmounted by a statue of Roma, with water cascading down marble steps by way of a backdrop, and in the Hall of Nations the Italians had a statue of Il Duce, with large-scale maps in black marble showing the Italian Empire outlined in copper.

Such were the dominant public visualizations of the régime, linking modern Italy and her prospective role as the seat of a latter-day Mediterranean government with the Roman Imperial past. But the rather architectonic forms of classicism could also be closely linked with the somewhat diluted form of Modernism which found visual embodiment in many aspects of domestic equipment and decoration seen at the Triennali, although ornamentation was relatively subdued after the early 1930s. However, a fresh breath of ornamental expression was to be found in the decorative arts. Deco-inspired furniture and furnishings were widely available during the Fascist era, as well as the enduringly popular traditional vernacular forms which were conventionally associated with ideas of home and comfort and which continued to have a dominant role in the market-place.

Germany: the Assault on the Avant Garde

The social and economic upheaval in Germany during the late 1920s and early 1930s witnessed an increasing polarization of the political parties together with a sharp rise in unemployment. During this period, the liberal climate enjoyed by culture and the arts in the relative stability of the mid-1920s was severely jeopardized by the closure of theatres, opera houses and a number of art schools. At the same time the critics of Modernism and other avant-garde tendencies began to gain strength, voicing similar concerns to those raised by opponents of the Weissenhof housing exhibition at Stuttgart in 1927: the involvement of a large number of foreign architects and designers and the disregard of German tradition. Conservative furniture manufacturers tried hard to get themselves represented and campaigned to prevent chairs by Marcel Breuer and other experimental designers from being shown. Avant-garde designers and architects were increasingly portrayed as displaying harmful moral and political characteristics, particularly after the founding in 1929 by Alfred Rosenberg of the Kampfbund für Deutsche Kultur (Fighting League for German Culture), which attacked progressive cultural ideals, often portraying them as having Negro, Jewish or Bolshevik (and thus undesirable) roots.

Just as Modernism was threatened by the changed political tenor of the times, so was the outlook of the Deutscher Werkbund which had sought to promote standards of good and efficient design in German industry since its foundation in 1907. After the difficult post-war years it had re-established itself with the German recovery in the mid-1920s and supported an ideal that was compatible with notions of standardization and rationalization in industry. However, as an organization dependent on the health of industry to provide financial support, its position became increasingly difficult to chart on the choppy economic waters of the post-Crash era. The rather austere appearance of many Modernist products in which ornamentation played a relatively minor role was incompatible with the National Socialist outlook. The decoration of these products, relating to the abstract forms associated with avant-garde art movements as well as having symbolic links with machine-age technology, new materials and internationalism, was increasingly seen as inimical and foreign to the traditions of indigenous German culture. After Hitler's accession to power in January 1933, the Werkbund soon found itself under the control of the National Socialists, and in 1934 was affiliated with Joseph Goebbels' New Reichskulturkammer (Reich Chamber of Culture) before being absorbed into the Reichskammer der bildenden Künste (Reich Chamber of the Visual Arts).

Völkisch Culture and the Acceptable Face of Modernism

German design of the 1930s is commonly associated with *völkisch* ("folk") characteristics. Indeed, craftsworkers had placed a great deal of faith in the anticipated economic role that they felt would arise with the opportunities of the "Blood and Soil" ethos of the Third Reich, especially as they had been a major source of political support in the run-up to the 1933 elections. There was an outlet for German traditional design in the furnishings and fittings of many of the Party buildings and in 1934 the Amt Schönheit der Arbeit (Office of Beauty in Work) was established under Robert Ley. It aimed to "awaken joy in work and kindle in the worker the will to organize his working world in a beautiful and dignified manner."[5] However, although the Office produced work which often took on simple vernacular styles, drawing on an essentially craft-based idiom and using traditional materials, the organization was also responsible for developing prototypes compatible with industrial mass production and included a wide range of products from office furnishings and lighting to works canteen tableware.

The Third Reich has often been portrayed as an era when all aspects of Modernism were repressed,[6] but in reality the position was far more ambiguous. As in 1930s Italy, a policy for Germany's re-armament and militarization emerged as a major objective with a consequent impact on economic planning. Clearly industry was a key element and the concerns of standardization and rationalization, the symbolic standard-bearers of the mid-1920s machine culture, assumed a high profile. There

was still scope for designers working in industry to produce modern work, just as there was a need for up-to-date, efficient industrial buildings. Guidelines were produced for neat, functional design in housing, domestic furnishings and equipment, alongside requirements for good design and construction. Many designers who had been successful before the Nazis came to power in 1933 continued to have modern design mass-produced during the years of the Third Reich. Among these were Hermann Gretsch (porcelain, glass and furniture), Margret Hildebrand (textiles), Trudi Petri (tableware), Wilhelm Wagenfeld (tableware, glass and lighting) and Heinrich Löffelharrdt (tableware). The extent to which the Modernist spirit was tolerated can be seen from the 1939 *Deutsche Warenkunde*, essentially a National Socialist catalogue of officially approved designs in current production which could both promote better design standards in Germany and earn invaluable foreign currency.

Propaganda and Ornament

In his inaugural speech for the Great Exhibition of German Art at Munich in 1937 Adolf Hitler proclaimed:

> Until the moment when National Socialism took power, there existed in Germany a so-called "modern art," that is, to be sure, almost every year another one, as the very meaning of this word indicates. National-Socialist Germany, however, wants a "German Art," and this art shall and will be of eternal value, as are all truly creative values of a people. Should this art, however, again lack this eternal value for our people, then indeed it will mean that it also has no higher value today.[7]

The iconography of such "eternal" values embraced key symbols of the Third Reich such as the swastika, the eagle and the flag, all of which were given great prominence throughout the design and propaganda media. The fine arts often utilized the idealized heroic forms of classical antiquity and explored "universal" themes such as work, family duty, motherhood and patriotism, while film and photography were instrumental in the promotion of Third Reich ideology, whether in recording and thus disseminating to an even wider audience the dramatic power and scale of the mass rallies of the Nazi Party or in the advancement of approved subjects and racially ideal

stereotypes. The operation of a well-oiled propaganda machine under Josef Goebbels, the Reichsminister für Volksaufklarung und Propaganda (Minister for Popular Education and Propaganda) did much to ensure the co-ordination and proliferation of such material.

Architecture was also seen as an important propagandist tool, with the planning of ambitious public building programmes intended to surpass those of ancient Rome.[8] Many of the National Socialist buildings, like those of 1920s Modernists, had comparatively little ornamentation. Their decoration was generally conceived in terms of ennobling sculptural reliefs, or the presence of masses of people without whom the intended effect would have been rather incomplete. The most widely known Nazi architect was probably Albert Speer, who organized the large-scale spectacles of the Nuremberg Rallies, having been put in charge of "Artistic Design of Demonstrations" (a department located within the Reichsministry of Propaganda), in 1933.

The power of German monumental architecture could be seen in Speer's massive Reichsparteitag Grounds at Nuremberg of 1934–5 or, in a more obviously internationally propagandist context, his German Pavilion at the Paris International Exhibition of 1937. The 54-metre-high tower for the latter was topped by an eagle and a swastika and the scale of the building, like many of its National Socialist counterparts, dwarfed the individual. Speer saw the new Berlin as the embodiment of a German cultural renaissance on a magnificent scale, with huge buildings planned both as international showpieces and as massive stages for political assemblies. Although most of his ambitions were effectively curtailed by the Second World War, several vast German buildings were constructed, to be distinguished by their monumentality and the sustained propaganda which promoted them as representatives of the enduring values of modern German culture. Their overall form, as well as their design and ornamentation, were by no means homogeneous and a variety of styles were drawn upon in different contexts, whether functional glass-and-steel modern buildings for industry, vernacular forms and detailing for housing, furnishing and fitments, or monumental classicism and decoration in the public arena.

LEFT **Albert Speer**, German Pavilion at the International Exhibition in Paris, 1937. This propagandist building was intended to dwarf the individual with its 54-metre tall tower, topped by an eagle and swastika. The decorative panels between the pilasters play on the swastika motif for their effect.

The Soviet Union in the late 1920s and 1930s: Moves towards Socialist Realism

The period from the late 1920s to the early 1930s saw many changes in the political, economic and cultural outlook in Soviet Russia, much of it shrouded in a certain amount of historical confusion. It was a time during which Stalin gained control of the Party, emerging as an increasingly dominant political figure after assuming the General Secretaryship in 1922. With the ambitious First Five Year Plan of 1928 there were concrete moves to strengthen "the economic hegemony of large-scale socialist industry over the entire economy of the country" as a means of competing successfully with advanced industrial nations of the West. During this time Party membership increased dramatically, much of it drawn from the new industrial workforce, with a consequent rise in support for the Stalinist ideology. There was a distinct change in the cultural climate, with growing pressures on the avant garde in architecture, design, the fine arts and literature, and powerful attacks on foreign artistic influence and intellectuality. Although there was a certain lack of clarity concerning contemporary cultural policy there was, none the less, a clear move to strengthen the proletarian position in architecture, film and the fine arts, thus preparing the way for Socialist Realism. A whole series of proletarian cultural associations were initiated, including VOPRA (The All Union Association of Proletarian Architects) which was established in 1929 under Karo Alabyan. The Association represented a distinct move away from a functionalist aesthetic, perhaps seen at its most exciting in buildings such as Melnikov's Russian Pavilion at the Paris Exhibition in 1925, towards a more archaicizing monumental style, evident in the competition for the Palace of the Soviets in the early 1930s. Experimentalism of all kinds was attacked while intelligibility and the communicative value of State propaganda overrode what became increasingly considered as the obscurantism of avant-garde, formalist or constructivist art and design.

By 1932, the year of the adoption of the Second Five Year Plan,[9] there was a bewildering number and variety of related associations. Accordingly, the Party Central Committee decided to reform the various groupings, creating single unions for each discipline which were in

turn subordinate to the ideological objectives of the Party. Socialist Realism, formulated by Andrei Zhdanov and Maxim Gorky, was presented at the first Soviet Writers' Congress of 1934, and became the new aesthetic creed affecting all the arts: literature, theatre, sculpture, painting, film, even music. Visual propaganda was an important means of education, and posters, textiles and ceramics all carried clear messages in support of the regime, celebrating industrial and agricultural progress, electrification and building—very different visual considerations from the pluralist, decorative ethos enjoyed by the majority of consumers in the West.

The new spirit of architectural monumentalism was seen in competition entries, both for the Commissariat of Heavy Industry by Melnikov in 1934, based on the Roman numeral V (after the Five Year Plan) and complete with heroic sculptures, and for the design for the Palace of the Soviets by Boris Iofan, of 1933. After revisions the latter was intended to be topped by a 245-foot-high statue of Lenin and, had it been built, would have been taller than the Empire State Building. Both were part of Stalin's replanning of Moscow but due to their enormous scale were never built.

Nevertheless, the Soviet presence was very marked in the international exhibitions of the late 1930s. At the Paris Exhibition of 1937 the Soviet Pavilion was designed by Iofan and was, with the German Pavilion facing it, among the most striking on the site. Clearly signifying the economic emphasis on industry and agriculture so much a part of the Five Year Plans, the building was topped by a gigantic sculpture by Vera Mukhina of a Worker (holding a hammer) and a Collective Farm Girl (holding a sickle) with arms raised and joined together. The emphasis on Socialist Realism was also apparent in the displays of architecture, design, popular theatre and the fine arts. The formula at the New York World's Fair of 1939 was organized along similar lines, with an equally imposing and monumental Pavilion designed by Iofan and Alabyan. Its tower was the tallest structure on the site apart from the Trylon centrepiece, and was surmounted by a 79-foot-high stainless-steel statue of a heroic worker (apparently dubbed "Big Joe") holding a Red Star in his raised right hand.

LEFT **Boris Iofan**, USSR Pavilion at the International Exhibition, Paris 1937, topped by the Worker and Collective Farm Girl sculpture by Vera Mukhina. The propagandist tenets of Social Realism can be seen at their most imposing in this contribution to the Paris Exhibition, which faced the equally dominant German pavilion.

LEFT **Fortunato Depero**, poster for Società
Nazionale Gazometri, 1934.

BELOW **Fortunato Depero**, Depero tapestry
workshop, Via 2 Novembre No. 14, Rovereto,
1920–30. Like Balla, Depero had a
background in the fine arts and moved into a
wide range of design disciplines. He also
designed a number of Futurist environments,
the most renowned being for Giuseppe
Sprovieri in 1921.

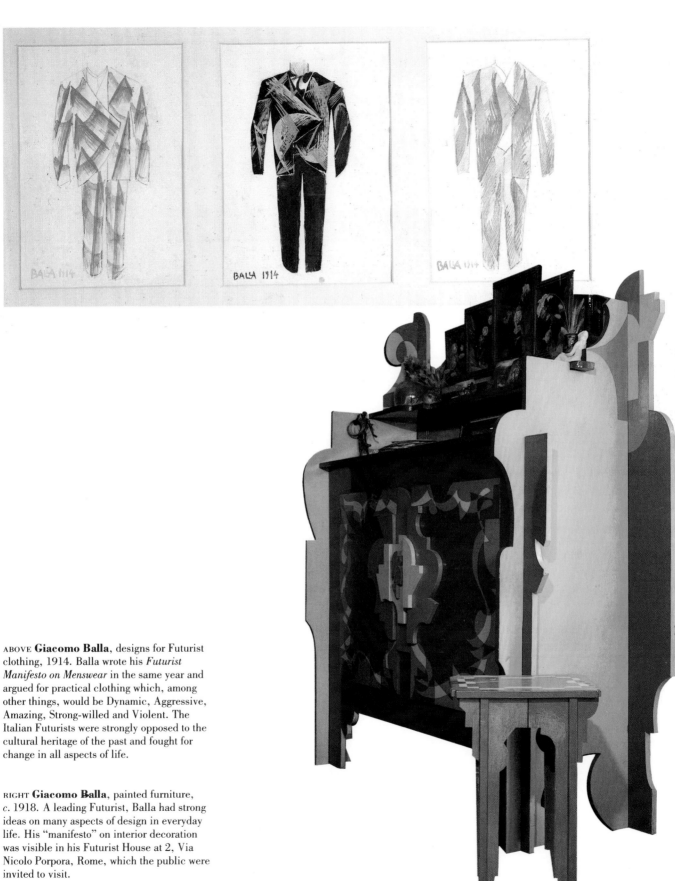

ABOVE **Giacomo Balla**, designs for Futurist clothing, 1914. Balla wrote his *Futurist Manifesto on Menswear* in the same year and argued for practical clothing which, among other things, would be Dynamic, Aggressive, Amazing, Strong-willed and Violent. The Italian Futurists were strongly opposed to the cultural heritage of the past and fought for change in all aspects of life.

RIGHT **Giacomo Balla**, painted furniture, *c.* 1918. A leading Futurist, Balla had strong ideas on many aspects of design in everyday life. His "manifesto" on interior decoration was visible in his Futurist House at 2, Via Nicolo Porpora, Rome, which the public were invited to visit.

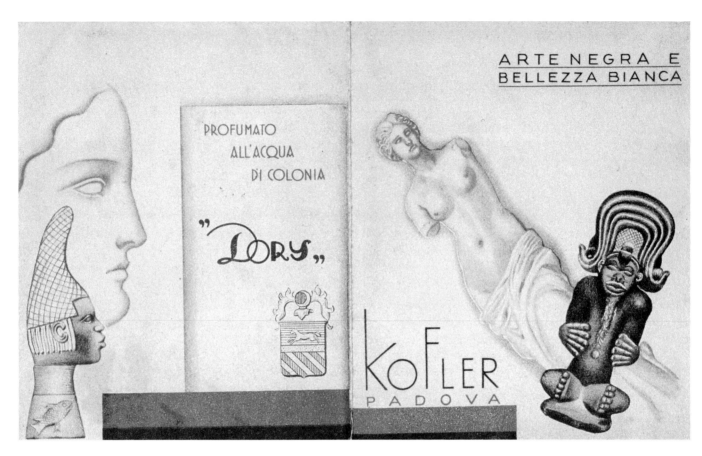

ABOVE *Arte Negra e Bellezza Bianca*, booklet pull-out for exhibition, 1936.

RIGHT *Fasci e Bandieri* pattern, brocaded silk, produced by the Ferrari Company, 1930. The *fasci* were bundles of rods which were carried ceremonially before high-ranking magistrates in Ancient Rome. Such ornamental motifs were incorporated as symbols of Fascism and were to be found in many designs.

RIGHT *Alla Finestra* pattern, brocaded silk, designed by Giò Ponti and produced by the Ferrari Company, 1930s. His decoration relies on small accents of designs against a neutral ground.

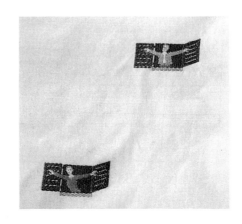

FAR RIGHT **Swimming pool** at the Foro Mussolini, Rome, in 1937. The use of traditional, classicizing imagery reflects Fascist aspirations to make Italy the centre of a second Roman Empire.

LA VETTURETTA DEL LAVORO E DEL RISPARMIO

LEFT **Mario Sironi**, poster "Fiat 500, La Vetturetta del Lavoro", 1936. This advertisement draws heavily on classical allusion and myth, with the stone statue of the She-Wolf suckling Romulus and Remus set alongside an achievement of modern production techniques.

BELOW **A historical pageant** marking the opening of a House of Fascism in Tuscany. The importance of Roman traditions are absolutely explicit in this illustration, which shows participants in togas as well as contemporary fascist uniform. The ornamental references to the commemorative columns, ceremonial *fasci* and axes all contribute to the ethos of building a "Roma Secunda".

RIGHT **Milan Railway Station**, detail showing *fasci*. The ubiquitous *fasci* were found in many contexts on the railway, particularly on the front of locomotives.

LEFT **Luciano Baldessari**, *Luminator* light, 1929. Designed for the Barnocchi stand at the Barcelona Exhibition of 1929, this chromium-plated steel design has a distinct flavour of Art Deco.

ABOVE **Giò Ponti**, white porcelain vase for Richard-Ginori, late 1920s. This amphora-like vessel has a strong historical feel, despite being designed by one of the leading figures of modern Italian design.

LEFT **Piero Fornasetti**, prototypes of glasses in the shape of musical instruments, Venini-Murano, 1939.

ABOVE **Ottavio Cabiati**, dining room, Milan, *c*. 1933. This room reflects a somewhat awkward attempt to marry modern and traditional forms. The imposing, yet obviously modern, light-fitting has undertones of old-fashioned candelabra.

RIGHT **Scatolificio** S. D. Modiano-Trieste, 1931. This range of package designs shows the wide variety of decorative styles current in the output of one packaging manufacturer.

LEFT **Ludwig Holwein**, Deutsche Lufthansa poster, 1936. This design draws heavily on classical imagery, much in keeping with the heroic forms favoured by the Nazi regime.

BELOW **Locomotive No. 2000**, manufactured by Krupp, Essen, 1939. This was the fastest steam locomotive in Europe and the aerodynamic, streamlined form is reminiscent of similar designs in the United States, particularly in the sweeping, horizontal decorative stripes. Advanced technology and its symbolism were emphatically modern counterparts to the völkisch and classicizing tendencies favoured in other fields of design.

LEFT **Josef Becvar and Viktor Rucza**, entrance hall to the RDV Bureau, Vienna, 1938. There is a flavour of muted modernism in this design as seen in the clock and the unobtrusive use of the swastika in the decorative grills on either side of the double doors.

BELOW **Trophy** presented to Hermann Goering, 1938, made by H. J. Wilm, Berlin. This heavily decorated trophy was a present from the Province of Pomerania to Goering on his 45th birthday. The swastika motif on the band immediately beneath the lid is, interestingly, the most restrained element of the decoration.

LEFT **Leonhard Gall and Gerdy Troost**, living room in the Führerhaus, Munich, late 1930s. The triptych of *The Four Elements* by Adolf Ziegler epitomizes official taste in the fine arts.

BELOW LEFT **Trinkstube**, 1939. This drinking room is emphatically German in its decoration, with its checked table cloths and carved wood.

RIGHT **Albert Speer**, Hitler's study in the New Reich Chancellery, Berlin, late 1930s. The grandeur of scale was important in terms of propaganda since the interior of the building was frequently publicized in National Socialist film and photography. Hitler had declared at Nuremberg in 1937 that "the buildings of today should not be destined for the year 1940 or 2000, but should be towering, like the cathedrals of the past, in the milleniums of the future. These monumental works will be, at the same time, the rehabilitation of the political strength of the German nation."

RIGHT **Luftwaffe sitting room**, late 1930s. The fireplace is made of sandstone, the ceiling beams of sanded pine and the floor of granite slabs. There is an emphatically traditional emphasis in the decoration, from the floral motifs on the chair coverings to the wrought-iron fire basket. Many buildings relating to state organizations provided opportunities for the use of German traditional design in their furnishings and fitments.

BELOW **Houses** under construction at Oeschelbronne in the German vernacular style, 1930s. The style was improved by the National Socialists through their emphasis on tradition. Photographs of such work were important as political propaganda and this illustration was accompanied by the following caption: "Where thirteen months ago blazing flames and thick wafts of smoke lay over the ruins of Oeschelbronne, through a remarkable effort and the sacrifice of the whole nation a new village has come into being within the space of a year: bigger, healthier, than the old . . . Fortune came out of Misfortune since from Oeschelbronne's ashes grew a prototype for rustic living."

RIGHT **Memorial Chapel** for Hans Mallon on the Island of Rugen, 1930s. The memorial has a strongly *völkisch*, almost primitive, character, the hip-thatched roof reflecting local building traditions. Each of the heavy doors is decorated with two heavily embossed, almost Wagnerian, shields accompanied by two swastikas which add to their rich ornamental effect.

LEFT **Tea Service** commemorating the opening of the Moscow Underground, produced by the Lomonosov Porcelain Factory, Leningrad, with designs by L. V. Protopova, 1935.

FAR LEFT **Mural** on the Moscow underground, 1930s.

BELOW **Booking Hall** of the Kosomolskaia Square Underground Station, Moscow.

The building of the Moscow Underground was a highly propagandized event and was celebrated in posters and other visual media. The architecture was imposing, with a monumental classical character. In keeping with the Social Realist climate of Stalinist Russia, decorative mural schemes provided unambiguous propagandist messages. The commemorative tea service shows the ways in which icons of achievement were used to serve decorative ends.

LEFT **Mityaev**, *The Five Year Plan in Four Years*, textile design, *c.* 1930. The almost abstract decorative motifs relate to industrial activity and include a heavy hammer and elements of gearing. However, as a result of the adoption of a progressive visual vocabulary the precise propagandist message may well have eluded many. Such designs fell out of favour as the 1930s unfolded.

BELOW **Decorative cotton print**, Russia, 1930s. This design has a heavily propagandist flavour and its easily intelligible forms are in keeping with the move away from progressive art forms in the late 1920s. Nonetheless, use is made of a number of interesting abstract devices to blend the various scenes together. Almost a microcosm of State endeavour, the blend of agricultural and industrial workers, marching youths, schoolroom, factories and railway locomotive provide a striking pattern.

5
From Austerity to Affluence
1940 to 1960

The impact of the Second World War on design production and consumption was widespread. Restrictions on the non-military applications of a wide variety of materials, and the generally prevailing climate of austerity, led to a correspondingly restrained aesthetic in which ornamental excess and exuberant decoration played no part. However, in the years following the war, with the gradual easing of restrictions and rationing and the move towards greater economic stability on both sides of the Atlantic, a considerable range of ornamental motifs began to be deployed. These featured in the everyday decoration, furnishings and equipment of the rapidly growing number of new homes, as well as in the public environment of shops, restaurants, and hotels.

Many consumers hankered after the historicizing and traditional ornamentation which they associated with the warmth and familiarity of the domestic environment of the pre-war years. But public awareness of war-time scientific and technological advances together with developments in new materials, also proved to be significant in the way in which ornament made itself felt in everyday life. In the United States, in particular, ornamental imagery associated with the developing science of rocketry began to invade many spheres of life, whether in the styling and detailing of automobile radiator grilles, dashboards and tail-light clusters, the proliferation of all kinds of kitchen equipment, or the jukeboxes which were to become such potent symbols of 1950s American culture. The international impact of the American consu-

LEFT **Volkswagen Commercial** Type 2, first produced in 1950. The variety of painted decorations provides an interesting social history of ornament over many years: the vans have been used for a wide range of tasks, from commercial delivery vehicles to travelling homes.

merist way of life ensured that such decoration appeared (in a rather more inhibited fashion) on many European products, especially those concerned with domestic technology.

Other scientifically oriented ornamental symbols appeared to catch something of the "spirit of the age." Molecular forms and images were widely applied in ornamental design of all kinds; crystallographic structures provided the basis for surface decoration especially in Britain, while the rather wiry, linear motifs combined with geometric and organic elements had a much wider international currency, appearing in the applied surface patterns of Formica, in furnishing fabrics and in the output of an increasingly buoyant wallpaper market. Organic, amoeba-like shapes were another decorative characteristic of the early 1950s which featured widely in many design media.

Design, Austerity and the War in Britain

Following the outbreak of war in 1939, many of the middle-class lobbyists who had argued for "better" standards of design in British industry in the 1930s were presented with an opportunity to demonstrate the efficacy of some of their egalitarian ideals and forthright propositions with the introduction of the Utility Schemes by the Government's Board of Trade in 1942. These soon covered a wide range of media, including furniture, fabrics and household textiles, clothing, shoes and bedding. During the war years Utility production had to conform to established specifications in respect of materials and construction, thus providing a means of maximizing those materials and labour that were available. In 1943 a Design Panel to review the role of design was set up under Gordon Russell, who had in effect drawn up for the Utility Advisory Committee a job description that fitted his own particular talents. Wartime Utility designs were characterized by a simplicity of construction and a minimum of applied ornament. The pottery industry, although not covered by the Utility schemes as such, was in many senses extremely close to it in spirit, as "decorative" and "inessential" ware was prohibited and output was largely restricted to glazed, undecorated natural clay colours: brown, cream and white. Furnishing fabrics and textile designs were austere and restrained: small repeats were used to avoid wastage and, until 1946 when yellow was added to the palette, the designs were confined to rusts, blues, greens and creams.[1] However, the *Architectural Review*, a tireless propagandist for the Modernist cause ever since the late 1920s, was quite acute in its forecast for the long-term future of Utility-style products. In its own rather condescending manner it commented on Utility furniture (although the criticism was equally applicable to other areas of Utility design):

> The taste of the public is a highly controversial topic. Nobody really knows it or can know it. But one thing appears certain: the nostalgia of those in drab jobs and with little variety in their leisure hours for something jolly or glamorous. The cinema, the sham half-timbered house with the jazzy fittings and the jazzy wallpapers, and the Modernistic furniture paid for at three times its value on the hire-purchase system, have to supply this need . . . But honesty of design is not an argument that will on its own cut much ice. It is not a quality inherent in all good art, although Ruskin thought so. The public at large has never accepted this tenet, and so long as furniture looks as austere and institutional as the Board of Trade's, the majority of the forced purchasers will, at their very first opportunity, return to the wildly grained H.P. walnut suite with stuck-on moulded ornaments.[2]

Indeed, such predictions were largely fulfilled in the post-war period as the public yearned for a variety of styles and ornamental decoration far removed from the Government-imposed rather puritanical aesthetic which was available to them in the straitened circumstances of the war years. During the late 1940s the Utility specifications were gradually relaxed and manufacturers were

able to gain stylistic latitude through downgrading quality. A considerable amount of anxiety was expressed in official circles since, in many peoples' eyes, Utility goods had at least represented value for money due to strict quality controls on materials and production. As a result, a number of Government Committees were set up[3] but in any case the move away from austerity to affluence during the course of the 1950s brought with it a new climate of ornamental indulgence, both traditional and "contemporary."

Affluence and Aspiration in the 1950s

The 1950s saw considerable expansion of the housing market in the mass-produced, suburban developments of the United States, Britain and elsewhere. In the United States the most remarkable developments in suburban construction were associated with the company Levitt and Sons, whose factory was producing one four-roomed house every sixteen minutes by the early 1950s. Stylistically, such housing drew on many of the traditional features associated with home-making but combined them with the layout and equipment which the new home-owners wanted in their "dream houses." The Levittowns, as they were called, typified 1950s American suburbia, and became the subject of sociological scrutiny.

With growing levels of affluence and higher disposable incomes, interest in home-centred leisure activities increased: watching television, listening to hi-fi, working on Do-It-Yourself improvements or gardening were all popular pursuits. Likewise extra attention was paid to the embellishment of the domestic environment, which now became a priority. The widely encouraged use of ornament and decoration was characteristic of the late 1940s and 1950s; and all manner of contemporary motifs were employed, often combined with the latest technology to indulge the whims of a public eager to display its material affluence. Plastic laminated surfaces, the high-tech imagery of cooker control panels and the science-fiction inspirations of pendant lights or electric heaters in the

RIGHT **The Villa de Mon Oncle** from the film *Mon Oncle* by Jacques Tati, 1958. This humorous film satirized High Tech gadgetry and automated lifestyles: the architectural setting has an almost Post-Modern sense of pastiche.

form of flying saucers were all as typical as the organic and crystallography-derived motifs of furnishing textiles or the transfer decorations applied to the sides of drinking glasses, to name but a few of the outlets for ornament. It should be remembered that the plundering of historic styles for furniture and furnishings continued much as it had in the years preceding the Second World War, but with the rapid increase in the number of new homes on the market there was a clear demand for modern as well as traditional styles. Well aware of the potential growth in the consumer industry, particularly in relation to science and technology, the government had, as early as 1944, set up the Council of Industrial Design (COID) to promote better standards of design in industry and consumer products. In its early days the Council exhibited a strong sense of social idealism married to a belief that it was genuinely possible to bring about improved design in the competitive post-war climate. Most members of the COID were drawn from the familiar names of the good design campaigns of the recent past and so a predictable aesthetic code was given rein over the next decade, particularly in the pages of the Council's magazine, *Design*, which was launched in 1949 and soon became an important mouthpiece for post-war Modernism.

Organic Motifs

A dominant ornamental and decorative motif of the post-war years was the organic amoeba-like blob. One writer on British design of the 1940s and '50s has, a little fancifully, suggested that the widespread preoccupation with such motifs stemmed from the fact that many artists had been involved in camouflage painting during the Second World War.[4] However, its roots can be seen both in design and the fine arts of the pre-war years, whether in the paintings of Joan Miró, the mobiles of Alexander Calder or the glassware of Alvar Aalto. Both in Europe and the United States, amoeba-like abstract forms provided the basis for the shape and decoration of countless products which furnished the home, ranging from

RIGHT **Kingsley Fire** advertisement, Britain, *c.* 1960. These interiors reflect popular ideas of luxurious living and, with the emphasis on patterned carpets and hand-crafted wrought iron gates, are far removed from the more austere modernist "Good Design" favoured by the Council of Industrial Design.

DESIGN No. CWRM. 92

No. SS. 1

DESIGN No. HCC. 96.

DESIGN No. CM. 93

DESIGN No. WM. 94

DESIGN No. CS. 97

dinner-services, fruit-bowls and ash-trays to the tops of occasional tables and patterns on printed textiles and laminates, as well as decorative elements featuring in neon signs, advertisements, menus, labels and a wide range of other graphic ephemera. Generally such organic motifs seemed to reflect something of a spirit of contemporaneity and modernity and were therefore of interest to the average taste-conscious consumer. In the growing affluence of the 1950s more and more money was spent on enlivening domestic environments with a wide range of products and furnishings that embraced such ideals. Other organic forms contributing to the design vocabulary of the period included the kidney shape which, with its amoeba-like counterpart, featured across the design spectrum from side-plates to door-handles.

In the United States the exploration of such forms had been stimulated by an "Organic Design in Home Furnishings" competition in 1940, under the auspices of that proponent of American élitist taste, the Museum of Modern Art in New York. The competition was won by Charles Eames and Eero Saarinen, who produced sculptural designs for seating and other living-room furniture in moulded plywood for mass production. Eames was a graduate of, and Saarinen a teacher at, the Cranbrook

RIGHT **Eero Saarinen**, *Tulip* chair, manufactured by Knoll, early 1950s. One of a number of Saarinen chairs produced by Knoll in the 1950s, this design became a classic.

Academy, which had been founded in 1926 and went on to produce a number of graduates who became distinguished in the fields of furniture and the applied arts in the 1940s and 1950s. The strongly sculptural aspect of their work continued during this period, culminating in Saarinen's famous pedestal chair which was manufactured by Knoll Associates in 1956, and Charles Eames' renowned chair and ottoman in rosewood leather and steel for the Herman Miller company in the same year. However, while organic motifs soon proliferated in a wide range of mass-produced consumer goods which were to be found in all facets of American life, the Museum of Modern Art tended to approve of the organic only as the underlying basis of form rather than as indiscriminately applied surface decoration.

Organic Tendencies versus Minimal Styling: Germany's Dilemma

Organic shapes and forms, though at the root of much European design of the period, were not exclusively popular. In Germany, for example, there were two dominant tendencies in the post-war years, both seeking, in their own ways, to re-establish the design profession on a sound footing. The more dominant reflected a growing belief in scientific management and rationalism in science and industry, stimulated by American industrial practice and the management techniques espoused by the Harvard Business School. This outlook was associated with the educational philosophy of the Hochschule für Gestaltung at Ulm, which had opened in 1955, and found expression in the rather austere, clean forms of Braun electrical products of the 1950s and '60s, where ornamental embellishment and decorative detail were kept to a bare minimum—a far remove from the *volkisch* design vocabulary of the Nazi regime as well as any resonances of the old industrial order which had played such an important role in the 1930s. However, the other major tendency in 1950s Germany looked to the organic as a basis for furniture and textile design, sharing common characteristics with much design production elsewhere in Europe and reflecting a belief in the importance of individual artistic creativity and expression as well as in forging links with arts and crafts. The fine arts

were an important formative influence, particularly the technique of action painting which seemed to explore large-scale, vigorous, expressive forms appropriate to a new dynamic age. Not surprisingly, given the widespread American influence in Germany in the post-war period, streamlining too found its way into the styling and ornamental vocabulary of domestic appliances, as well as graphics, textiles and other forms of surface decoration.

Italy's Design Diversity

In Italy, as in Germany, there were a number of conflicting design ideologies in the late 1940s and '50s. In the anti-Fascist left-wing political climate of the immediate post-war period, there was a belief in intellectual circles that Italian society could be reconstructed along genuinely democratic lines. This outlook was echoed in contemporary design debates which looked to the progressive Modernist principles of the pre-war Italian Rationalist architects and designers as a means of providing new forms appropriate for post-war living. However, this inherited machine-based attitude placed comparatively meagre emphasis on ornament, stressing instead the importance of economy, practicality and good taste in design, as seen at the RIMA (Riunione Italiana per le Mostre di Arredamento) exhibition of popular furnishings, mounted in Milan in 1946. Attendant publicity and criticism pointed to the advantages of flexibility, lack of affectation, space-saving and practicality in well-designed goods geared to the pockets of the majority.

But over the next decade there was a move towards centrist politics that was accompanied by an economic boom, with a parallel shift in the design world away from the democratic idealism of the Rationalists towards a more middle-class, style-conscious aesthetic. Giò Ponti, one of the stalwarts of twentieth-century Italian design, resumed editorship of the highly influential design magazine *Domus* in 1948 (twenty years after he had originally founded it) and did much to promote a new language of visual expression.

One of its more outspoken characteristics was an emphasis on organic, sculptural form that could be detected in such diverse products as Corradino D'Ascanio's Vespa motor scooter for Piaggio of 1946, with its bulbous, almost streamlined, engine housing;

RIGHT ***Tapetti*** **plate**, the shape designed by Olga Osol with decoration by Birger Kaipainen, manufactured by Arabia 1953–64. This Finnish design, with its stylized blue flowers, is typical of the period and marks the re-emergence of Scandinavian design in the international markets of the 1950s.

Marcello Nizzoli's Lexicon 80 typewriter for Olivetti of 1948 with its rounded casing; Giò Ponti's 1949 coffee machine for La Pavoni, with its associations with automobile styling; and the elegant, curvilinear forms of Carlo Mollino's furniture of the late 1940s and '50s. Such work shared a stylistic vocabulary with contemporary sculpture, such as that by Hans Arp, Max Bill, Bruno Munari and Alexander Calder. The mobiles of the latter, carefully balanced constructions of rods and wire from which hung series of organic shapes, often painted in bright, primary colours, particularly caught the mood of the period and could be seen as the three-dimensional forerunners of the strongly linear motifs overlying flat geometric coloured shapes that were so popular in contemporary textiles in Europe and the United States.

Arts and crafts took on a similar new lease of life in Italy, particularly Venetian glass, which underwent a revival with the arrival of Paolo Venini from Milan. A marked emphasis on bright colours, abstract forms and motifs, often with a strong asymmetrical feel, underlined the relationship with contemporary fine art. Craft traditions in other fields were also an important factor in the growing international recognition of Italian design in the 1950s, enabling designers to develop a consciousness of the expressive potential of form in furniture, furnishings, ceramics, glass and metalwork, all of which were important aspects of the export drive.

Form and Function in Scandinavia

A powerful organic, sculptural element characterized much Scandinavian design work of the period, ranging from the silverware designs of Henning Koppel for Georg Jensen in the late 1940s and '50s and Tapio Wirkkala's glass for the Finnish Iittala factory, to the output of the leading Swedish glass companies of Orrefors and Kosta-Boda. Scandinavian design, which in the inter-war years had been seen to represent the more human face of the Modern Movement through its respect for natural materials, once more emerged as a significant force in the post-war period. Its basis lay in the successful reconciliation of its arts and crafts origins with the more starkly functionalist outlook of the avant garde in Germany and France. The approach was maintained in the 1950s despite increased industrialization and the population shift into the towns. The new urban market stimulated the manufacture of domestic goods, and Scandinavian Modern, as the style became known in the 1950s, also made a major impact in the domestic furnishings and equipment markets of Europe and the United States.

A significant impact had already been made in the USA at the New York World's Fair of 1939 through the design of the Swedish and Finnish exhibits, and was further stimulated by a number of exhibitions mounted during the mid-1950s, as well as the successful operation of exporting agencies such as Artek and Portex. Also instrumental in establishing an international vogue for Scandinavian goods were the strong Scandinavian contributions to the Milan Triennali and the mounting of the Hälsingborg (H55) Exhibition in Sweden in 1955. Held in commemoration of the twenty-fifth anniversary of the 1930 Stockholm Exhibition, it was devoted to housing, domestic furnishings and design in industry; it attracted over one million visitors and much favourable press coverage, both at home and abroad.

Scandinavian design, with its strong links between industry and the crafts and a penchant for natural materials, presented an attractive, yet still progressive, alternative to mainstream European and North American developments. Although many of the forms of furniture, glassware, silver and ceramics often relied on clean, abstract forms for their effect, pattern and decoration also played a key role in design of the period. While acknowledging the crafts-based peasant traditions out of which they had evolved, there was none the less a freshness and spirit of contemporaneity which appealed to many middle-class consumers of the 1950s. In woven textiles and rugs, designers drew on motifs from nature and folk art and utilized traditional techniques. In the field of printed textiles Josef Frank, once associated with the austere Modernism of the 1920s, had moved in the direction of far more decorative patterns, often drawing on floral and naturalistic motifs, and greatly influencing the tenor of interior decoration of the period. Connections with contemporary art practice were also developed: not only did many manufacturers use leading craftsmen and women, but Swedish textile companies employed abstract painters, as in a wide range of designs for the Stobo Company in Stockholm in the mid-1950s.

Ornament and Images of Technology in Post-War USA

The romance of technology and science, so much part of the product-streamlining fashion of the 1930s, increasingly found material form and expression in the styling and ornamentation of the American automobile of the 1950s. General Motors had concluded that at the end of the war the purchasers of automobiles would rank styling first, automatic transmission second, and high compression engines third.[5] After an initial determination simply to satisfy public demand with vehicle output in the immediate aftermath of the war, the three big manufacturers—General Motors, Ford and Chrysler—soon

LEFT **Benton Dales, Ted Koeber and Dave Chapman**, the *Decorator* refrigerator with abstract decoration, produced by International Harvester Co., 1954. Abstract art was not always widely admired in the art galleries, but provided an acceptable face of modernism in the vinyl-coated fabric applied to the surface of appliances. The decorative finish was able to be varied at the discretion of the consumer who could change it to fit in with any colour scheme.

placed a major emphasis on styling as a means of gaining a competitive edge in the marketplace. One of the most striking innovations was the appearance of the "tail-fin," inspired by the vertical stabilizers of the Lockheed P-38 fighter plane. It first appeared in a rather modest form on the Harley Earl-designed Cadillac of 1948, but soon became a major feature in the 1950s "Battle of the Tail-fins." During these early post-war years General Motors also built a series of experimental ("dream") cars, exhibiting them to the public in order to test their reactions to certain styling features before implementing them in a toned-down fashion on their production models. Amongst the early "dream cars" of the period were the XP-300 and the Le Sabre of 1951, both of which caught the public imagination, no doubt influencing General Motors in their decision to launch the first of their "Motoramas" in 1953 at the Waldorf-Astoria Hotel in New York. These were lavish and spectacular stage shows with all the razzmatazz of a Hollywood musical, showing the futuristic "dream cars," extravagantly styled with a heavy emphasis on the iconography of rocketry and science fiction, alongside the latest production models.

The Frigidaire Division of General Motors also used publicity shows to capture public imagination, commencing in 1953 with the first "Kitchen of Tomorrow" event at the Waldorf-Astoria. In 1954, this feature was included alongside the more elaborate "Motoramas," making a not incongruous bed-mate through the concentration on futuristic gadgetry and lifestyle. For example, the 1956 Motorama Kitchen of Tomorrow boasted an Electro-Recipe File on IBM cards which activated an automatic dry-ingredients dispenser; an Ultrasonic dishwasher; a Thermopane domed oven heated by quartz lamps; a Planning/Communication Center, and a number of other appliances of the future. Ideas like this were in tune with contemporary advertising for gadgets already in production. A contemporary critic commented on the correlation between the advertising and promotion of kitchen apparatus and the language of aero-auto styling:

> Individual appliances have had a face lift in the direction of moulded "car"-colour plastic wraps on the works—chrome spears, speed lines and similar fragments of iconography are in character, but the best giveaway is in the language and techniques of presentation which sell them. References to "aquamatic action", "jet-spray", "centrifugal clutch-drive", in the washing-machine, figure well with General Electric's new cooking range names—

the Stratoliner and the Liberator. A quote like "New Extra Hi-Speed Giant 2,600 Calrod Unit is 20 per cent faster than by gas—by actual test", is straight out of 56 auto ad-speak, and with push-button control, "a flick of the finger selects your cooking heat" as well as your gear-change. Automatic "cut-offs", "oven-timers", "circuit-breakers", "washer and timer swirl-out" signalled the general preoccupation with robotics, and the "WondR dial automatically pre-selects" everything from defrosting to the year's breakfasts.[6]

Automobile-derived styling and ornament was typical of many products during the 1950s: cooker instrument panels reflected car dashboards; the chrome-plated character of other domestic appliances looked to car door handles and makers' marques and badges; even radios shared similar technologically orientated ornament and styling. Built-in product obsolescence through annual (or more frequent) styling changes was a means of maintaining a buoyant consumer market and, as a result, most products with pretensions of remaining abreast with the latest technological advances shared this dominant philosophy of the automobile industry.

The Jukebox: Symbol of an Era

Popular music was a powerful social force in the post-war years and the jukebox became almost an icon of the 1940s and '50s, reflecting in its appearance many of the preoccupations of other competitive markets. As with its automobile counterpart, the jukebox industry had its own dominant manufacturing companies which had emerged in the inter-war years. These were AMI (Automatic Musical Instrument Co.), Rock-Ola, Seeburg and Wurlitzer. By the mid-1950s jukebox decoration had moved away from streamlining and Deco as major ingredients and instead drew on the more potent, and particularly American, source of automobile styling as a means of gaining a competitive edge. The "wraparound" windscreen which General Motors had introduced commercially into the car market of 1954 was echoed in Wurlitzer's Centennial jukebox of 1956 which boasted a "one-piece panoramic Super-Vu window." This metalanguage of technology advertising was shared by both industries: General Motors' Hydra-Matic transmission system was countered by Seeburg's Select-o-matic record choice system and

Ship's Westwood logo, Los Angeles, 1958. This striking and easily recognizable motif for a restaurant chain reflects widespread public interest in imagery relating to flight.

Wurlitzer's "shape of tomorrow today" was the echo of countless contemporary promotional automobile brochures.[7] However, one of the most striking examples of car-inspired imagery was incorporated into the Seeburg Model K jukebox of 1957 which sported three large tail-fins across the loudspeaker, complete with red lights, referring, perhaps somewhat incongruously, to the same sources as seen in the Baroque technological ornamentation on the rear of contemporary cars: the tail-burn of jet engines. There were other examples, perhaps culminating in the Rock-Ola Tempo I of 1959 with its wraparound viewing window, the chrome "automobile" marque emblazoned on the speaker, and fins rising off the button-selector bank.

Las Vegas, The Strip and Roadside Vernacular Ornamentation

The automobile made an impact not only in terms of its own applied ornamentation but also through its increasing influence on the ornament and signage of the urban environment, whether relating to shops, shopping centres, car-washes, motels, restaurants, drive-in cinemas, drive-in churches or casinos. Perhaps the most publicized location for such phenomena was Las Vegas, which expanded dramatically in the post-Second World War era. Although Reyner Banham saw Las Vegas as being "as much a marginal gloss on Los Angeles as was Brighton Pavilion on Regency London"[8] its effect has been considerable in terms of cultural criticism and theory, whether via Tom Wolfe in *The Kandy-Colored*

Tangerine Flake Streamline Baby of 1965 or through Robert Venturi's *Learning From Las Vegas* of 1972 in which architectural semiotics became the prime consideration.

"Californian Coffee Shop Modern" did much during the 1950s to develop this car-orientated ornamentation, with adventurous roof elevations and raised, sculpted or neon-lit signs geared to attract the attention of the automobile traveller. It was in this period that the distinctive architecture and signage of McDonald's evolved as a result of the McDonald brothers' aim to develop a striking corporate image which would enhance the prospects of franchising their operations. The original motif of two yellow parabolic arches was integrated with the buildings of the original hamburger bars, and echoed in the roadside signs. However, as the image changed in the 1960s a new look was introduced, although the two arches became incorporated into the logo.

It should be remembered, however, that at the opposite end of the design spectrum from the imagery of high technology in everyday ornament, traditionally based decorative forms and motifs continued to be a major force in North American decoration and furnishings, just as they had been in the first half of the century. While the symbolism of progressive technology was highly prized in the kitchen or as an element in cleaning equipment, the reassuring historicizing motifs of traditional home-making were widely adopted in the living and sleeping areas, from the designs applied to bedroom furniture, tableware and curtain material to the highly ornate woodwork of many television cabinets.

While the Modernist aesthetic did play a role in the domestic environment of the "taste-conscious," well-to-do consumer of the 1950s, its most conspicuous expression was to be found in the corporate sector. Its associations with progressive forms and modern technology provided the ideal metaphors for conveying the spirit of a forward-looking, businesslike enterprise.

The Impact of Science and Technology on Attitudes in Britain

After the end of the Second World War there was a considerable fascination with scientific and technological development, innovation and application. Until the late 1950s and '60s these concerns were generally seen as benevolent and progressive forces, potentially ushering in a better quality of life through labour-saving and automation. At the large-scale "Britain Can Make It" Exhibition, organized by the newly formed Council of Industrial Design (COID) and mounted at the Victoria and Albert Museum, London, in the last months of 1946, this outlook was reinforced in several sections, particularly those devoted to "From War to Peace," "What the Goods are Made of" and "Designers Look Ahead." The latter was rather a fanciful display, including an "Atomic Cooker" designed by William Vaughan and Milner Gray, an "Air-Conditioned Bed" by F. C. Ashford, a "Super Streamlined Cycle" by Ben Bowden and a "Space Ship" by Warnell Kennedy which, according to the *Catalogue Supplement*, acknowledged the "possibility of travel through inter-planetary space [which] must now be considered seriously. The control of atomic energy brings it within the compass of reality." Similar futuristic ideas were followed through in the Ideal Home Exhibition held at Olympia, London, in the following year, where there was a section entitled "Science Comes Home" which was concerned with applying scientific wartime research to domestic ends.

Other media also did much to portray sympathetic visions of the future. For example, the *Eagle* comic, launched in April 1950, featured the exploits of Dan Dare, Pilot of the Future; films such as George Pal's *Destination Moon* of 1950 sought to give space exploration a dimension of conviction through considerable attention to detail; and science fiction began to be seen as a far more serious literary genre in the 1950s than its more frivolous pulp-fiction antecedents. Many of the more persuasive portrayals of the future were of a utopian outlook, as in the writings of Isaac Asimov, one of the new breed of authors in this vein. He had written a series of stories about robots in the 1940s, representing them as non-aggressive, rational beings, able to understand moral and social principles. Although it must be acknowledged that there were other contemporary classics which looked to the future with far greater trepidation—George Orwell's chilling vision of *1984* published in 1949 and John Wyndham's *Day of the Triffids* of 1950, for instance—they merely added to the futuristic inclinations of the post-war years.

Science and the 1951 Festival of Britain

The fascination with science found a significant outlet in the Festival of Britain of 1951, which was devoted entirely to a celebration of Britain: the land, the people and achievements in arts, sciences and technology. There was a strong whiff of science fiction in the massive aluminium-covered, flying-saucer-like Dome of Discovery by Ralph Tubbs which not only dominated the South Bank site but inspired the forms of a number of domestic appliances such as electric heaters and vacuum cleaners. The dominant motif of the towering 300-foot-tall Skylon by Powell and Moya also had a strong futuristic flavour to it, spawning many souvenirs such as Biro pens in stands. Several exhibition sites, in London in particular, incorporated the iconography of science in their displays. Notable among these were the molecular features of Edward Mills' large screen on the South Bank which was the major national Festival venue, and the large screen at the entrance to the Science Museum by Brian Peake which was based on the structure of the carbon atom. Indeed, the COID, which effectively controlled design policy for the Festival, saw this as an opportunity to use science literally as a basis for ornamentation in design.

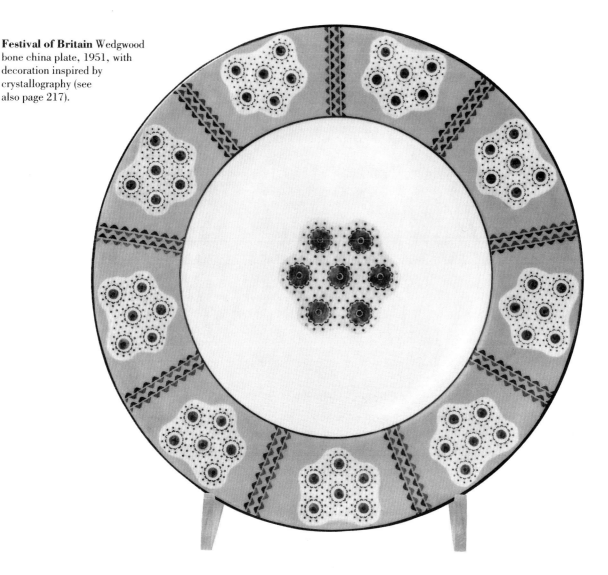

Festival of Britain Wedgwood bone china plate, 1951, with decoration inspired by crystallography (see also page 217).

Crystallography, a field in which Britain was a world leader in the late 1940s, provided the basis of designs for textiles and other applied surface decoration on glass, packaging, pottery and furniture. Boric acid, insulin, aluminium hydroxide and haemoglobin were among the substances whose crystallographic structures inspired the designs of the so-called Festival Pattern Group: 26 manufacturers contributed to this scheme, among them Wedgwood, Goodearl Brothers, Chance Brothers, London Typographical Designers, Warerite and Spicers. The eight and a half million visitors to the South Bank were able to view a wide range of atomic, crystallographic and molecular structures throughout the site, walking past the atomic patterns and "snowflakes" which were used as decorative elements in the Dome of Discovery, eating off Festival Pattern Group plates in the restaurant, and sitting on the sinuous Antelope chairs designed by Ernest Race, which had "molecular" feet.

The Wider Ornamental Impact of Molecular Science

"Molecules" became a widespread ornamental trait in the early 1950s: in the feet of the increasingly ubiquitous plant pot holders or domestic appliances, in the decorative elements of balustrading and space dividers in public buildings and stores, or in other environmental features of everyday life. This trend was not restricted to Britain, and a similar approach was evident throughout the late 1940s and '50s in both the United States and Europe, as at the 1958 Brussels International Exhibition, whose main theme was devoted to International Science, and which was dominated by a 360-foot-high Atomium, designed by André Polack with André Waterkeyn. Its form was derived from a magnification by 165 million times of an iron molecule and, with its steel and polished aluminium structure, it made a significant impact on the forty-one million visitors to the exhibition, many of whom ate in the restaurant at the top or drank in the bar on a lower level. Other successive exhibitions did much to sustain the theme of science and progress; in the United States, Seattle's "Century 21" Exhibition had as its central attraction a 600-foot-high Space Needle (with "flying saucer" restaurant) and a special monorail system which carried visitors from the centre of town to the exhibition site.

Aftermath of the Festival of Britain

Reyner Banham regarded much that was said about design at the Festival of Britain in subsequent years as a considerable distortion of the truth, one which had been framed by those who had ushered in and supported the "Festival Style" with such enthusiasm, including the

people associated with the COID, the *Architectural Review* and other middle-class arbiters of taste who sought to impose their vision of "good design" on the general public. He wrote:

> Reduced to its two basic propositions, and baldly put, the myth proposes that: the Festival of Britain created a style that was new and valuably English; and that this style was influential, especially on popular taste. The first proposition is so easily falsifiable, and was known to be so even in 1950 before the Festival existed, that one must now wonder about the second. But both have been so tenaciously held that their value as "official legends" is almost as interesting historically as the romantic fallacies they enshrined.[9]

BELOW **Mahogany sideboard** with recessed rosewood door fronts, designed by Booth and Ledeboer and manufactured by Gordon Russell Furniture. The thin, wiry decorative motifs on the front of this piece are typical of the period.

It is clear that certain aspects of the style derive from American, Scandinavian and, most obviously, Italian precedents. It is also evident that the crystallographic sources for the efforts of the Festival Pattern Group were short-lived. But it seems fair to comment that, at least among middle-class consumers, the Festival helped to stimulate an interest in modern, or "Contemporary Style," design in Britain, which in modified form found a Festival afterlife in the coffee-bar culture which became such a hallmark of the decade. Nevertheless, although plenty of media coverage was devoted to modern design during the decade, the majority of people were still relatively unmoved by the values promoted by the COID, progressive furniture firms such as Hille and Ernest Race or high-class retailers like Heals and Liberty, preferring instead to surround themselves with the reassuring familiarity of more traditional styles, motifs and ornament. The plethora of historical references and ornamental motifs still played an important role in the economic survival of many manufacturers, whose skills were used effectively to decorate the legs of a dining-room table or to put a floral pattern on a tea-service. After all, as Michael Frayn wrote in his witty Festival essay: "Festival Britain was the Britain of the radical middle classes— the do-gooders; the readers of the *News Chronicle*, the *Guardian*, and the *Observer*; the signers of petitions; the backbone of the BBC."[10]

Opposition to Ornamentation in the United States

In the inter war years the Museum of Modern Art in New York had sought to promote the Modernist tendency in architecture and design through a series of exhibitions such as "Modern Architecture" in 1932, "Machine Art" in 1934 and "Bauhaus 1919–28" in 1938–9. This policy continued during the 1940s under the guidance of Eliot Noyes, appointed as director of the Department of Industrial Design on the recommendation of Walter Gropius, former Bauhaus Director and current Professor of Architecture at Harvard. Noyes' links with European Modernism were consolidated further through his work in the architectural practice of Gropius and Breuer in Cambridge, Massachusetts.

In 1950 the first of a series of "Good Design" Exhibitions was mounted at MOMA under the control of Edgar Kaufmann Jnr, who had succeeded Noyes as Director after Suzanne Wasson-Tucker's brief interregnum. These exhibitions, running in parallel to the design conference initiatives of Egbert Jacobsen (Director of Design at the Container Corporation of America) at Aspen, were formally linked with the Merchandise Mart of Chicago which hoped to attract manufacturers of modern furniture and design to display their wares there. The further intention was to introduce good modern design to a wider audience of consumers and manufacturers. The Selection Committee for these shows, which lasted until 1955 when Kaufmann resigned his post at MOMA, comprised Kaufmann and a representative from both the design and the retailing professions. This tastemaking triumvirate over the years included such figures as Alexander Girard, who became Director of Design of the Textiles Division of Herman Miller in 1952, and Serge Chermayeff, who had played an important role in bringing the Modernist aesthetic into Britain in the late 1920s and 1930s prior to emigration to the United States in 1939. Kaufmann was wholeheartedly opposed to any design language that transgressed the Modernist creed. Streamlining, in particular, was an anathema which he saw as a

> widespread and superficial kind of design . . . used to style nearly any object from automobiles to toasters. Its theme is the magic of speed expressed in teardrop shapes, fairings and a curious ornament of parallel lines—sometimes called speed whiskers. The continued misuse of these devices has spoiled them for most designers . . .[11]

Expounded at a time when there were an increasing number of sociological and cultural analyses of the repercussions of mass culture on American society, Kaufmann's views were seen by a number of contemporaries as élitist, equating good design with status, and out of touch with the wider social, economic and psychological realities of materialism. MOMA conformed to Russell Lynes' notion of *The Tastemakers* in his book of 1954, by endorsing design which was opposed to notions of obsolescence, the mainspring of the post-war American economy, and which exhibited a minimum of ornamentation and thus, for many, a minimum of meaning. Such an outlook continued in succeeding decades, leading one critic to observe:

> [The] Museum does not want anything to look *bakockt* with ornamentation, although preferences here were for so long dogmatic as to discourage the

development of any flexible ornamental sense in design. Normally an object has entered the collection only if it looks inorganic and not substantially affected—certainly not affected in a formal way –by the workmen who made it.[12]

America, Consumer-Culture and the British

Such attitudes were not confined to the United States during the late 1940s, but found expression in Europe too. Edgar Kaufmann Jnr warned the British about the dangers of unfettered styling in the pages of the *Architectural Review* in an article entitled "Borax, or the Chromium-plated Calf."[13] Borax was seen as "a trade term for flashy, bulbous modernistic design" and streamlining as "the Jazz of the drawing board." Kaufmann had the ears of the COID, whose members reflected the same concern over standards of quality. Many British writers and critics shared the fear that the United States and its consumer-culture values would sweep aside the established British way of life and order of things.[14] Concerns about "Americanization" were heightened in the heated debates surrounding the introduction of commercial television, which commenced broadcasting in September 1955 in London. Television, however, was not the only culprit; the whole ethos of the American "good life" came under fire. Just as Kaufmann and MOMA in New York had done, the COID in Britain attacked what it saw as the meretricious styling and ornament of many American goods. John E. Blake, writing in *Design* in 1954, deplored the imagery of American consumerism which drew heavily on science fiction, rocketry and space exploration. He commented that

It is not enough, apparently, that the instruments of a motor car dashboard should register the behaviour of the various parts clearly and simply. Indeed the dashboards of many new, particularly American, cars look, and are obviously intended to look, as though they would control nothing less than a spaceship. Likewise the most commonplace of mechanical devices in the home—clocks, radios or cookers—are beginning to vie with each other in the extent to which they satisfy a popular taste for the "romance of science."[15]

Other Promoters of the "Good Design" Cause

There were organizations in Continental Europe and elsewhere which sought to encourage modern design in industry. In Germany, these included the Stuttgart Design Centre, established in 1949, and the Advisory Board for Design in Darmstadt, founded in 1951; in France, the Institute d'Esthétique Industrielle was founded in 1950, and in Italy, the La Rinascente stores fulfilled the same function. Many people concerned with such organizations, just as with Britain's COID, had been advocates of the Modernist aesthetic in the inter-war years. They campaigned for similar ideals through the mounting of exhibitions, the awarding of labels which could be appended to goods adjudged to epitomize "good design" (commencing with the MOMA awards made in conjunction with the Chicago Merchandise Mart in 1951), the publication of magazines, and the organization of conferences of retailers, industrialists and buyers. None the less, such idealism began to founder on the realities of increased affluence and consumer aspiration in the more stable economic climate of the later 1950s. Consumers wanted to express their new-found status through choice rather than the adoption of an "approved" and seemingly restrictive aesthetic.

LEFT **Utility furniture** in room setting, 1940s.

BELOW LEFT **Enid Marx**, *Chevron* utility printed fabric.

RIGHT **Utility ginghams** from the Spring/Summer 1945 Empire Stores (Bradford) catalogue.

The Utility Scheme was established in Britain in 1942 by the Board of Trade in order to contend with shortages of materials. It originally involved furniture, but soon applied to several areas of design, including clothing, shoes, fabrics and textiles. Designs were made under licence to precise specifications. A number of campaigners for design reform were involved, including Gordon Russell, and the resulting products were characterized by emphasis on proportions, practicality and economic production. There was little ornamentation; where it was used in textile designs it was characterized by a limited colour range with small repeat patterns to minimize waste. The rather austere aesthetic soon gave way to ornamental extravagance once wartime restrictions were eased.

For the Home and the Family

D 3765

D 3566

D 3765 (Top)
An exceptionally smart Pram Rug in double texture **Woollen Material.** Has various attractive designs in appliqué work and is soft and warm. In **Blue.**
Size approx. 26 x 34 ins. **32/1**

D 3766 UTILITY
This Rug is suitable for either pram or cot, is made from soft **Woollen Material** and is light yet very warm. Neatly bound round the edges.
In **Rose, Sky** or **Beige.** **7/8**

EACH OF THE ABOVE PRICES INCLUDES 3D. DELIVERY CHARGE.

D 3767 Shown also on the front cover of this catalogue. Curtain Material in **Folk-weave effect.** Hangs beautifully and always looks attractive at any type of window. In the latest shades of **Brown/Green, Green/Brown, Rose/Blue, Blue/Rose.** Width 47 ins. Per yard **18/4**

THE ABOVE PRICE INCLUDES 1D. DELIVERY CHARGE.

Curtain lengths and Gingham are not sent on approval. When we have cut the material we cannot accept its return.

D 3768 UTILITY
Brightly coloured Gingham, suitable for children's frocks, curtains, overalls, etc. In large or small checks and in **Green, Mauve, Blue** or **Red.** Width approx. 36 ins.
Per yard **1/9**

THE ABOVE PRICE INCLUDES 1D. DELIVERY CHARGE.

NEWEST DESIGNS

LEFT **Ernest Race**, *Antelope* chair, produced by Race Furniture, 1950. This design was seen widely at the South Bank, London, site of the Festival of Britain in 1951. Originally the legs of the chair were given "molecular" feet. These, together with the sinuous linearity of the backrest, gave it a contemporary idiom.

BELOW LEFT **Earthenware** cooking pot and cover with cheese dish, part of the *Picknick* range designed by Marianne Westman, produced by Rostrand, Sweden, from 1956 to 1969. This graphic style with blocked areas of colour was typical of the period.

BELOW **Raymond Loewy** tableware, with wiry calligraphic decoration.

RIGHT **Fabric** designed by Marion Mahler, 1950s. The use of strongly graphic linear forms on abstract shapes was typical. There are also some hints of molecular forms in one foot of the "bird" and "bowls".

FAR LEFT **Frederick T. Day**, dustjacket for *Passe Partout for School and Home*, 1950s. This book was typical of the many home decoration volumes published in the 1950s and shows the kinds of ornamental devices produced in many British homes of the period.

LEFT **Readicut** rug-making advertisement from the *Ideal Home Year Book*, 1949–50. This rug design is close in appearance to those produced by modernist designers of the 1930s such as Marion Dorn. The striking abstract design is none the less aimed to capture the more traditional British market as seen by the wrought iron magazine holder, armchair and fire screen.

ABOVE **"A Complete Home in One Room"**, English interior by the Times Furnishing Co., 1950s. The desire for a plethora of patterns is evident in the carpet, wallpaper and furnishing fabrics. Although a display room, the tasselled decoration on the standard light, the mantelpiece ornaments and lightshade on the sideboard are all typical of the period.

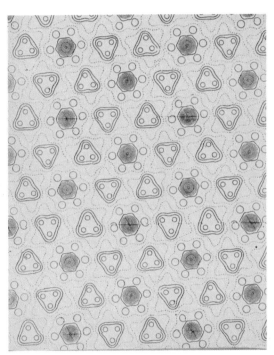

FAR LEFT **Frits Wichard**, *Quercus* curtain material, produced by De Ploeg, 1949. Although based on the oak leaf, the design has a strongly organic, yet linear, character.

FAR LEFT BELOW **Marianne Straub**, *Surrey* textile, Warner & Sons Ltd, 1951, one of a large number of designs based on crystal structures which were launched at the Festival of Britain in 1951. In 1949 the Festival Pattern Group was set up to develop designs on this theme, stimulated by the work on crystallography carried out by Dr Helen Megaw of Girton College, Cambridge. Twenty-six manufacturers in a variety of fields contributed to the scheme. Straub's *Surrey* design was seen in the Regatta Restaurant on the South Bank, London, site of the Festival (see also page 204).

LEFT **Die-lines** based on insulin, late 1940s. Die-lines were issued to manufacturers participating in the Festival Pattern Group to help them develop their own designs.

BELOW **Raymond Loewy**, hand-printed wallpaper design from the Centenary Hand Print Collection, Sanderson, 1960. This design, with its almost snowflake-like motifs set on flat blocks of colour, superficially resembles designs by the Festival Pattern Group.

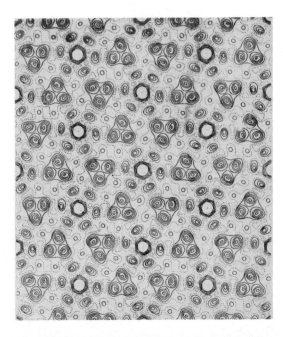

ABOVE FAR LEFT **The Atomium** by André Polack and André Waterkeyn at the Brussels International Exhibition of 1958, seen in the background on the cover of *La Vie Parisienne*, June 1958. This design, which was widely known in the late 1950s, was derived from a magnification by 165 million times of an iron molecule.

FAR LEFT **Edward Mills**, *Abacus* screen on the South Bank, London, site of the Festival of Britain, 1951. Science was an important aspect of a number of the displays at the Festival and Mills' use of molecular elements in red, yellow, blue and white is aesthetically in tune with many other designs of this period.

LEFT **Coatstand**, French, 1950s, with molecular forms in red, yellow and blue, blended with wiry curvilinear rods.

ABOVE **George Nelson**, Clock for Howard Miller, 1949. This clock, with molecules representing the hours, makes an interesting wall decoration.

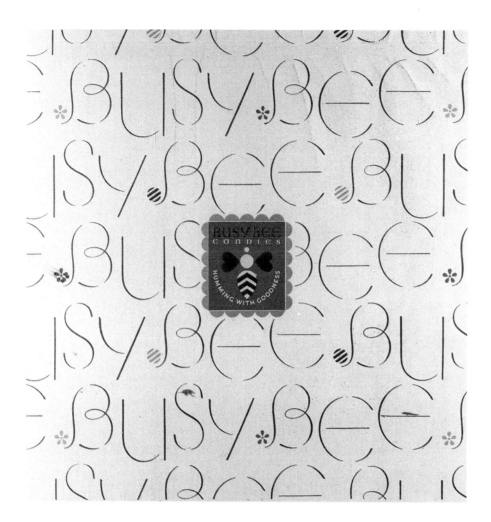

ABOVE **Busy Bee Candies**, 1950s. The linearity of this decorative
lettering gives the packaging a distinctly 1950s look.

RIGHT **Abstract textile**, Laverne originals, 1953, with reliance on line
and Miró-like abstract forms.

ABOVE **London County Council Restaurant**, Drayton Park, 1949.
The rather exotic decorative mural scheme is in marked contrast to the
utilitarian canteen furniture.

RIGHT **Public Bar of _The Happy Prospect_**, Coronation Square,
Southcote Estate, Reading, 1958, designed by R. E. Southall ARIBA
and H. & G. Simonds Ltd. This interior is typical of British public
houses of the period, especially in the decorative vignettes above the
bar.

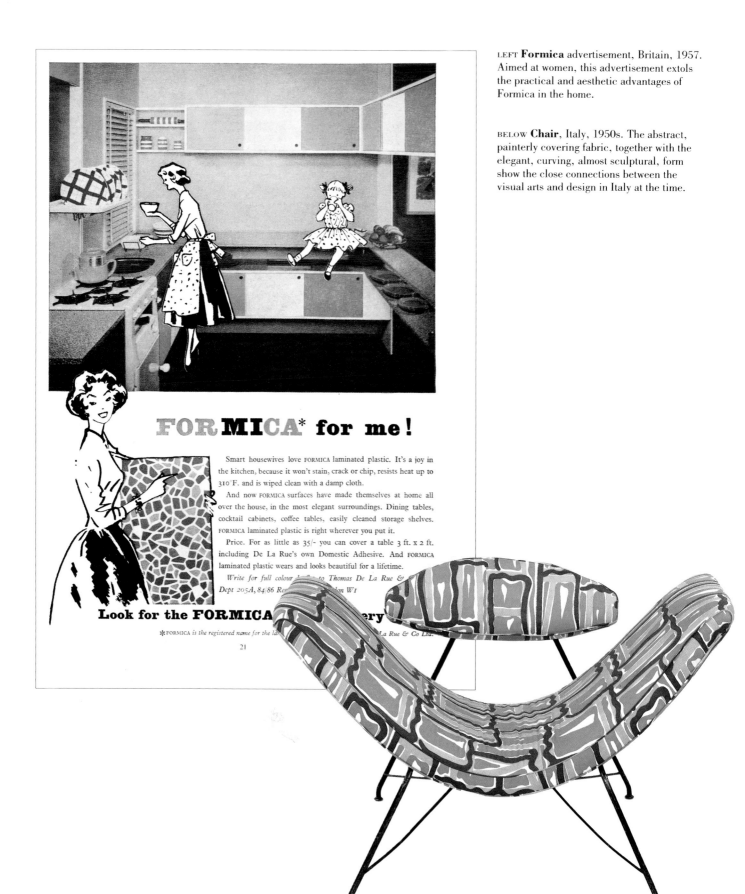

LEFT **Formica** advertisement, Britain, 1957. Aimed at women, this advertisement extols the practical and aesthetic advantages of Formica in the home.

BELOW **Chair**, Italy, 1950s. The abstract, painterly covering fabric, together with the elegant, curving, almost sculptural, form show the close connections between the visual arts and design in Italy at the time.

LEFT **Public Bar of *The Favourite***, Luton, 1960. The British predilection for a variety of contrasting ornamental patterns is evident in this interior. The use of decorative plastic laminates for tabletops was especially popular.

BELOW FAR LEFT **Formica** Coral Syylark 81–1–30, American range, late 1950s. The use of curvilinear graphic forms relates this pattern to many wider international ornamental trends. The organic kidney shape, picked out in coral pink, echoes the form of many coffee tabletops and side-salad dishes of the period.

BELOW LEFT **Formica** Sky Blue Nassau 17–NA–38, American range, late 1950s. The use of overlapping blocks of colour can be found in many surface pattern designs in the 1950s. Formica laminated plastic was used increasingly during the 1950s, whether for work surfaces in the kitchen, coffee tables or shelving.

BELOW **Cees Braakman**, SM 01 Chair, produced by U. M. S. Pastoe, 1954. This design exhibits the fashionable, spindly quality found in much European furniture of the period. The pattern on the synthetic covering on the seat and backrest owes a superficial debt to the work of De Stijl artists in the 1910s and 1920s.

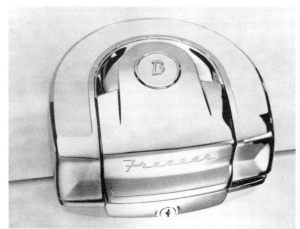

TOP **Harold van Doren**, Philco cooker instrumentation, USA, 1954. In the 1950s there was a vogue for cooker controls to draw on automobile dashboard design in order to give them the feeling of being in tune with the latest technology. Such ornamental devices were to be found on both sides of the Atlantic.

ABOVE **1950s launderette**. The metal door ornament recalls automobile design.

ABOVE RIGHT **Bendix** freezer latch handle, designed by J. M. Little and Associates, 1954. The use of chromium plate, with the manufacturer's marque inset, together with raised lettering, clearly draws on an ornamental vocabulary based on the automobile industry.

RIGHT **Lincoln *Futura***, USA, 1959. This "Dream Car" was never intended to be put into mass-production as it was one of the futuristic designs promoted by large-scale automobile manufacturers in order to help stimulate sales. The influence of space-oriented imagery is obvious, especially in the moulded transparent canopy, which has much in common with contemporary science fiction illustration or aircraft cockpits. The dramatic, sculptural fins and the tail-light clusters set in chrome also reflect such highly popular concerns with the iconography of space.

RIGHT **Josef Frank**, furniture designed for Svenskt Tenn, produced from the 1930s onwards, an example of "Swedish Modern" in which there was much interest in Europe and the USA in the 1950s. Ornament, where used, is restrained and elegant.

BELOW **Josef Frank**, *Vegetable Tree* printed fabric, designed in 1944 and produced by Svenkst Tenn in 1981. Frank's designs, which often rely on bright and unusual colour combinations, have been highly influential in Scandinavian design over many decades.

RIGHT **Giò Ponti**, *La Pavone* espresso machine, Milan, late 1940s. The design draws on a wide range of sources of inspiration, from the American automobile industry to the organic abstract forms of contemporary sculpture.

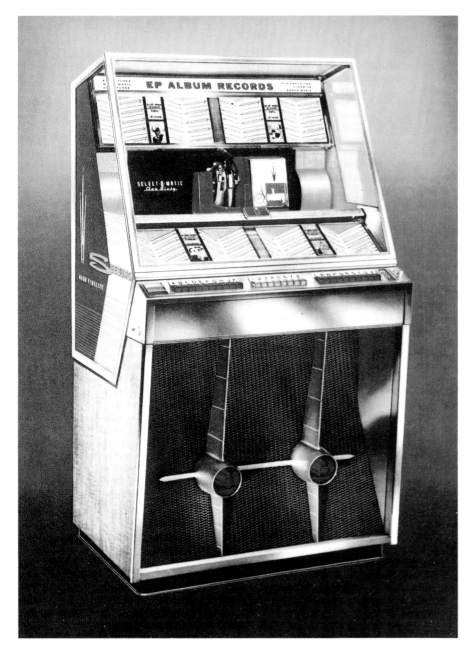

LEFT **Seeburg Jukebox**, Model 161, 1958. Based on the Model K of the previous year, this design shows the allure of space imagery for all kinds of products. The rocket motifs, with small red lights to simulate tail-burn, were one of a number of automobile-oriented details employed by jukebox manufacturers. These included the application of chromium manufacturers' badges and wraparound viewing windows.

RIGHT **Brooks Stevens**, cycle design proposal for the Cleveland Welding Company, USA, 1948. This design makes an interesting comparison with Ben Bowden's bicycle (below), seen at the "Britain Can Make It" exhibition in London two years earlier.

BELOW RIGHT **Ben Bowden**, *Super Streamlined Cycle*, shown at the "Britain Can Make It" exhibition at the Victoria & Albert Museum, London, in 1946. The illustration shows the original full-scale prototype, made of wood and plaster. It was intended for mass production with a frame made of light alloy pressings and shows the extent to which 1930s streamlined forms were still considered appropriate in the years following the Second World War.

FAR RIGHT **Vespa 50** scooter, designed by Corradino d'Ascanio, produced by Piaggio, Italy, from 1946. The tapered rear end echoes the streamlined forms of the 1930s, especially the teardrop engine casing. There is a combination of the functional and the aesthetic, as in the foot-rests which are reminiscent of the "speed whiskers" of the previous decade.

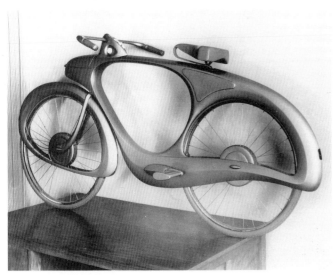

LEFT **Printed textile**, designed by Renato Birolli, 1950s. The painterly, abstract pattern owes a debt to developments in the contemporary fine arts which provided a fresh vocabulary for textile design.

BELOW **Decorated ceramic** vases by Fantoni, Italy, 1950s. Many designers in Italy at this time were forging links between the fine and decorative arts.

ABOVE LEFT **Ties Honcoop**, *Rayure Vibrante* wallpaper design, produced by Rath & Doodeheefver, Holland, 1958. This exclusive hand-printed paper shows a debt to contemporary developments in painting. The cock motif could be applied by the wallpaper hanger wherever desired, as an extra screen for printing was supplied for this purpose.

LEFT **Printed textile**, British, 1950s. Abstract coloured shapes set on a network of thin lines were typical of the period. Similar decorative patterns were to be found on a wide range of products, whether plastic laminates or teacups.

COLOR GUIDE

color of object					
white	turquoise	gray	purple	black	white
gray	white	yellow	henna	black	gold

LEFT **Page** from *Designs and How to Use Them* by Joan B. Priolo, New York, 1956.

BELOW **Frou Frou** chocolate packaging, New York, 1950s.

The growth of foreign travel encouraged the decorative use of vignettes drawn from popular symbols of countries like France and Italy. France was a particularly potent source for such designs, encouraged by the popularity of films like *An American in Paris* and *Gigi*. Motifs could be applied to a wide range of surfaces, from wallpaper to tea-trays.

6

Pop and Post-Pop
1960 to 1975

The Pop era of the 1960s has often been heralded as challenging accepted values across many aspects of life as well as aesthetics. Concepts of expendability, disposability and flexibility made an assault on traditional attitudes, which had been far more concerned with notions of permanence and durability. However, as the writer of one recent study on Pop has observed, the consumer values that Pop furthered were not seen as a serious threat to the social status quo until the end of 1966, when hallucinogenic drugs, free love and an interest in Eastern religions became associated with Pop culture and began to undermine social structures and middle-class values[1]. It can also be argued that Pop was the ultimate stimulus behind the inevitable recognition by manufacturers, market analysts and the advertising profession of the new, untapped energies and desires of the affluent youth of the late 1950s and 1960s. This emergent market sector was young enough to be unwilling to conform to the patterns of outlook and tastes of an older generation which had been conditioned by notions of durability and "value for money." It was also affluent enough to express itself in new and exciting ways.

Youth Culture

The new-found voice of youth found expression in the United States in the mid-1950s, where for a while it was portrayed as socially unsettling in films such as *The Wild One* of 1954 starring Marlon Brando, *Rebel Without a Cause*, starring James Dean, and *The Blackboard Jungle*, both of 1955. Music also reflected a distinct shift in attitude with the emergence of Rock 'n' Roll. Bill Haley

and the Comets exported the new vogue to Europe, both on the cinema screen in *Rock Around the Clock* of 1956, which was banned in many British cinemas for fear of violence, and in person in 1958, at a concert in Essen, West Germany, where several thousand fans rioted. Chuck Berry, Little Richard and Elvis Presley soon became the standard-bearers of this modern, vibrant culture, which found another route to Europe via the jukebox, itself a potent symbol of the American consumerist ethos.

Pop in Britain

London rapidly became, by international consensus, the major hub of the new Pop movement, which had extended, by the mid 1960s, to the fine arts, furniture, fashion, textiles, all aspects of graphic design, photography, music, magazines and even store design. The new "boutique" culture, which became such a feature of urban-centred life in the later '60s, with the proliferation of elaborately decorated fascias, had its roots in London of ten years earlier. Outlets such as *Bazaar*, which first opened in 1955 in the Kings Road with clothes designed or bought by Mary Quant, and John Stephen's boutique in Carnaby Street, which commenced business in 1957, were the harbingers of the later, more effervescent, decorative and mass-orientated boutiques.

LEFT **The Fool**, mural for the Apple Building, Baker Street, London W1, 1967, by Simon Posthuma, Marijke Koger, Josje Leeger and Barrie Finch. This mural with its vibrant, colourful patterns reflected the widespread craze for psychedelic imagery, which could be found on record sleeves, clothing, posters, interiors and boutique façades.

Bright colours and strong geometric motifs such as targets and the Union Jack flag were applied to all kinds of surfaces, from jackets and carrier bags to record sleeves, coffee mugs, trays and painted furniture, all of which could be purchased from shops such as Gear in Carnaby Street. Traditional notions of stability and status in furniture design were challenged by concepts of expendability and flexibility, as had been the case in the realm of fashion. Many young designers emerged, and enterprising firms such as Hull Traders began to market furniture made from cardboard and chipboard, finished in strong colours—three-dimensional counterparts to the bold geometric patterns of contemporary textile designs.

The comic strip, so symptomatic of mass culture and ephemerality, was popular among both artists and designers. On the one hand, it was used by the celebrated American Pop artist Roy Lichtenstein as the basis for many of his paintings, and on the other, it became a potent source of inspiration for Pop ornamentation such as shop window display, murals or contemporary advertising. The barrier between fine art as a preserve of aesthetic élitism and the concept of ephemerality appeared to have dissolved with the advent of consumerist icons; thus the hamburger or the Coca-Cola bottle were absorbed into contemporary artworks by Claes Oldenburg, Andy Warhol and others. Similar consumer-orientation lay behind the furniture which could be bought at Mr Freedom, the fashion and furniture boutique opened by Tommy Roberts in the Kings Road, London, in 1969.

Technology and the Consumerist Status Quo

The Pop era saw continued faith in technology as an agent of change. Just as it had been in the 1950s, scientific and technological progress was still seen as allied to the quest for material affluence, an outlook that was boosted by man's landing on the moon in July of 1969. Science fiction also maintained a sustaining role: while Britain concentrated on the adventures through space and time of *Dr Who*, a television series launched by the BBC in 1963, the Americans were entertained by the neo-imperialist explorations of the space-carrier *SS Enterprise*, complete with interplanetarily and racially integrated personnel, which commenced in 1966 with the NBC television company. Stanley Kubrick's film of 1968, *2001: A Space Odyssey*, based on a short story by Arthur C. Clarke, made a striking impression.

Into this milieu stepped the British avant-garde architectural group, Archigram, which organized itself around a magazine of the same title launched in 1961. Members of the group were architecture graduates who readily endorsed notions of expendability, progressive obsolescence and change, which they saw as the manifestation of a healthy, rather than a morally questionable, society. They looked to science fiction as a source of inspiration for the future and to the latest technological advances, such as the space capsule or the bathyscope, as a means of realizing it. Many of their ideas were

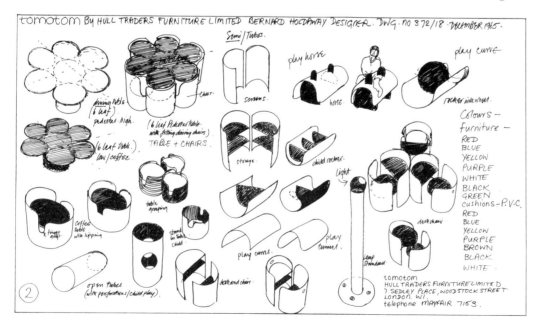

LEFT **Tomotom Furniture** by Bernard Holdaway in conjunction with Peter Neubart of Hull Traders Ltd, Lancashire, designed in 1966. Featured at the Daily Mail Ideal Home Exhibition, this cheap, expendable furniture retailed in a range of bright colours (red, purple, yellow, blue and green) which, in addition to its simple shapes, gave it a strong Pop character (see page 247).

RIGHT **Japanese radios**, Matsushita, late 1960s. These brightly coloured novelty bracelet radios sought to capture the youth market.

presented in their magazine in comic-strip form from 1964. A wide range of propositions was put forward, including Walking Cities, Underwater Cities and Instant Cities. The last of these was to involve the group travelling around the country, revitalizing the community with exhibitions, sound/light presentations and the latest in educational technology, information communication and entertainment.

Japanese Design: the American Influence

In the 1920s and '30s Japanese design had been seen as something of a threat to Western markets, often producing for export products which were considered potentially competitive in their heavy dependence on the appearance of Western consumer goods. This outlook was still apparent in the 1950s, although many Western producers remained complacently convinced that the quality of their goods would see them through. In the post-Second-World-War years American influence on Japan was particularly significant and made itself felt in a number of ways: social, economic, technological, political and cultural. Much of the initial impact stemmed directly from reforms initiated while Japan was still under American occupation in the late 1940s and early 1950s. As had been the case in Germany in the early years of peace, there was also a strong reaction in Japan against its own old-established industrial order, which many associated with the war effort. The United States was seen as a healthy breeding ground for new design management techniques and industrial organization, and many leading Japanese industrialists and young designers visited America to experience such ideas at first hand. Such influence extended to the nascent Japanese design profession: Raymond Loewy, one of the most successful American industrial designers, visited Japan along with others in his profession to promote the role of the designer in a consumer society.

On a more everyday level, the impact of the lifestyle of the American forces in Japan was significant. Many Japanese, particularly the young, were fascinated by American packaging and consumer products and associated them with notions of democracy and the idea that the majority of Americans enjoyed a high standard of living. The American "flavour" exerted a significant impact on urban consumer culture, several major cities becoming increasingly laden with large-scale, American-influenced advertising signs and hoardings. Japanese attempts to evolve ornamental motifs which reflected a Western lifestyle were often rather stilted and clumsy, but as the design profession developed greater confidence within a more affluent consumer climate many more original designs began to emerge.

The Olympic Games of 1964 and the Osaka World Exposition of 1970 did much to bring the qualities of original Japanese design and traditions to international attention while at the same time causing Japanese designers to re-evaluate such traditions in the context of a technologically orientated consumer society. The tech-

RIGHT **Car** at the Isle of Wight Pop Festival, Britain, 1969. The painting of all kinds of surfaces was a feature of everyday life in the late 1960s, whether murals, boutique frontages or cars. Pop festivals were a feature of the late 1960s, with Woodstock in the United States attracting an estimated 500,000, Hyde Park in London about 250,000 and the Isle of Wight 150,000. They did much to render an "alternative" lifestyle orthodox, with a rapid growth in the commercialization of the hippy ethos.

nological drive of the 1960s and '70s was accompanied by the integration of Pop culture with consumer goods, graphic design, architecture and fashion, where the emphasis on youth, dynamism, and bright colours was readily absorbed. Not surprisingly, much ornament and decoration drew heavily on the iconography of Western consumer products. But as Japan's position as a leading economic power became more established and Western eyes turned increasingly eastwards, Japanese designers began to grow in confidence, blending traditional Japanese forms and outlook with the imagery of a technologically oriented culture. More recently, Japan has contributed imaginatively to international fashion, and the world-wide appearance of the minimalist interiors of expensive retail outlets reflects the growing impact that Japanese ideas have exerted on the West. Japanese designers have also contributed to the output of the Memphis group, participating fully in the Post-Modernist debate.

"Alternatives"

The 1950s and 1960s saw the emergence of a number of behavioural "alternatives" within mass-consumer society. The "beat" subculture which sprang up in the United States in the late 1950s was the antithesis of the material values and all-American imagery promulgated by the agencies in New York's Madison Avenue, the mecca of the advertising world: "beat" clothing, language and lifestyle were totally opposed to bourgeois cultural norms. The "hippie" movement of the 1960s shared a number of these values, embracing to a large extent the concept of free love and the new drug culture of LSD. Just as the popular habit of wearing beards had undermined the clean-shaven, upright American look, so the hippies' long hair symbolized reaction to the tyranny of social conformity. Emphasis was placed on individuality, resourcefulness and creativity, allied to a distaste for the values of conspicuous consumption, an attitude that pervaded all aspects of hippy philosophy and that was apparent in many of their "underground" magazines, which were often mildly pornographic and scatological. Among the artists who emerged from this genre were Robert Crumb, creator of *Fritz the Cat* and *Mr Natural*, and Gilbert Shelton, who drew *Fat Freddy's Cat* and *The Fabulous Furry Freak Brothers*. Similar values were embodied in the British underground magazines *International Times* (later renamed *IT*) and *Oz*, launched in 1966 and 1967 respectively.

There were attempts to legitimize some of the positive aspects of the hippy outlook, as in the American publica-

tion *The Whole Earth Catalog* of 1968, an encyclopaedia of the means of self-determined living. Altogether glossier in outlook and presentation was Charles Jencks' and Nathan Silver's book of 1972, *Ad Hocism*. In it they argued that the "ad hocist" makes do with the materials to hand, cutting through the usual delays caused by bureaucracy, hierarchical organizations and specialization. They felt that the spirit of ad hocism could bypass conventional modes of thought, resorting instead, for instance, to using a knife as a screwdriver or flushing a toilet as an effective means of washing grapes. In reality the spirit of ad hocism was found in many aspects of everyday life: the growing interest in customized cars, motorcycles and other products was commercially validated by the introduction of customizing kits. What began as an exciting form of individual ornamental and decorative expression became increasingly available "off the shelf."

Psychedelia as a Source of Ornament and Decoration

The imagery and colours associated with the experience of taking LSD were in some quarters a rich source for all types of applied surface decoration, including jewellery,

furniture, clothing and posters. The West Coast, especially San Francisco, was particularly associated with such developments, but they were soon to be found in many other urban centres such as Chicago and New York, while the graphic work of artists such as Wes Wilson, Rick Griffin and Victor Moscoso became widely known throughout the United States.

Psychedelic art also made an impact in Britain through posters, album covers, murals, and other outlets. Among the most widely known artists were Martin Sharp (an Australian who had been heavily involved in the early editions of *Oz*), Michael English and Nigel Weymouth (creator of "Hapsash and the Coloured Coat"). Hallucinatory motifs and colours were blended with a wide variety of sources, ranging from the *fin-de-siècle* forms of Aubrey Beardsley, whose work was seen in an exhibition at the Victoria and Albert Museum in 1966, through to the more fantasy-laden imagery of science fiction, Tolkien or Hieronymus Bosch. Posters were readily affordable and widely available and soon became very much part of the trappings of the "weekend" or "plastic" hippies, who affected the outward appearance associated with the subculture but brought with them few of the underlying premises on which the movement had originally been based. Such was the widespread fashion for applied decoration in this vein, that even the COID's magazine *Design*, which had at first been very slow to accept the inevitability of the ephemeral, fashionable nature of Pop, asked "Are We Suffering from Psychedelic Fatigue?"[2]

Italy: the Impact of Pop

The Pop phenomenon made an impact on Italian design in the early 1960s. Many Italian designers had visited the United States and seen the work of the Abstract Expressionists and Pop artists; American Pop Art was exhibited at the Venice Biennale of 1964, and the Milan Triennale of the same year was dubbed "the Triennale of Pop." However, although Pop imagery and iconography provided a colourful and diverse inventory of forms and motifs that were immersed in consumerism, the ends to which these were directed by the design avant garde were in fact critiques of conventional expectations of "good taste" and elegance: references to popular styling, kitsch and nostalgia, particularly in the decoration of everyday artefacts, were among the means of undermining such élitist concepts. There had been increasing criticism of the ways in which the freedom of designers and consumers had been constrained by manufacturers' overriding concerns to raise levels of production and consumption through the creation of artificial needs. Designers envisaged a future utopian world of leisure in which material needs were addressed by self-sustaining technology while the individual could rediscover her or his own creative potential, freed from the cultural élitism associated with a society that placed a premium on conspicuous consumption.

Archizoom Associati and Superstudio were two avant-garde groups that began to explore such concepts in 1966, providing the roots of the Anti-Design movement of the late 1960s and 1970s in their manifestos, exhibitions and environments. It was this tradition of experimentation, away from the dictates of manufacturers and conventional notions of taste and aesthetic sensibilities, which gave rise to the wide range of ornamental motifs, references and decorative effects of the highly influential Milanese avant-garde design groups of the late 1970s and early 1980s, most particularly Memphis, which was to become an international byword for fashionable decorative design of all kinds.

Wider Critiques and the Imagery of Nostalgia

Faith in technological utopianism was widespread at the beginning of the 1960s, whether in President Kennedy's vision of an age in which he felt that "science can fulfil its creative promise and help to bring into existence the happiest society the world has ever known" or Harold Wilson's pledge that "the white heat of technological innovation" would be a key aspect of the British Labour Party's planning after winning the General Election of 1964. But the quest for material affluence and the acquisition of status through consumption, trends which had gathered such pace in the late 1950s and '60s in industrialized countries, were not without critics. Vance Packard, in writings such as *The Hidden Persuaders* of 1957, and later publications exploring parallel themes (including *The Waste Makers* and *The Status Seekers*) attacked notions of consumer manipulation, built-in obsolescence and design as a tool for corporate profiteering rather than catering for genuine need. Ralph Nader and others reproved the American automobile industry, with its emphasis on styling rather than safety and social responsibility, in books such as *Unsafe at Any Speed: the Designed-In Dangers of the American Automobile* (1965), while J. K. Galbraith denounced the economic, political and social power of the large-scale corporations in *The New Industrial State* (1967).

By the late 1960s and early 1970s many penetrating questions were also being asked about the detrimental ecological, environmental and social consequences of technological advance. Concern was voiced on the question of non-renewable sources of energy, particularly as a result of the oil crisis stemming from the war in the Middle East in 1973. But adverse criticism was also raised in terms of the impact of complex technologies on ordinary people. Tony Benn, former Minister of Technology under Harold Wilson, articulated this clearly in a speech made in Germany in 1975:

> For a generation we have all been talking about the technological revolution. We have thought of it in terms of brilliant scientific discoveries and miracles

RIGHT *Oz* **cover**, *c.* 1970. Much of the imagery of this British underground magazine related to psychedelia and hallucinogenic drugs, connecting closely with the hippy milieu out of which it was born in 1967.

of engineering skill. We have studied the implications of nuclear weapons and space travel and the cybernetic revolution. Hordes of academics have written their doctoral dissertations on the multi-national corporations. The mass-media has pinpointed a new class of top scientist and corporate planner and focused on the difficult decision-making confronting presidents, prime ministers and chancellors.

As compared with this, we have devoted far less attention to what the technological revolution has done to, and for, ordinary people.'[3]

In such a climate, which had been in the process of formation in the later 1960s, the crafts underwent something of a revival and many designers began to draw increasingly on the imagery of ruralism, wholesome unpolluted living and small-scale cottage industries, virtually untapped sources of decoration for use right across the design spectrum, ranging from packaging and advertising to domestic product design. Such values were typical of the goods marketed by Laura Ashley who, having started with fabric prints in the 1950s, had become increasingly concerned with the marketing of complete interiors, co-ordinating fabrics, wallpapers, paints and sundry other items. In the wake of a certain backlash against the unacceptable face of technological progress and the destruction of flora and fauna by environmental pollution, Laura Ashley's and similar products achieved considerable success in the portrayal of a "country look" and a sense of nostalgia for "better days." The quasi-institutionalized cottage and chintz style in wallpapers, fabrics and frills could be purchased by mail order through the Laura Ashley catalogue, which was

BELOW **Wedgwood**, *Wild Strawberry* fine bone china, 1965. This traditional design is still popular today.

launched in 1981 and further consolidated through the *Laura Ashley Book of Interior Decoration*. The firm was also highly successful in the international market-place having, by 1979, more than forty stores worldwide, including outlets in the United States, Japan and Australia as well as a vast network of "shops within shops."

Punk and the Assault on Traditional Values

The mid-1970s saw the emergence of Punk, in its origins an affirmation of the working-class urban reality which emerged from "nameless housing estates, anonymous dole queues, slums-in-the-abstract."[4] More recently, its roots have been presented in a more glamorous light,[5] no doubt as a result of its appropriation by mainstream commercial interests, which anaesthetized it much as they had the underground and hippy subcultures of the later 1960s. Nevertheless, Punk in its early days was a phenomenon which gained a considerable amount of media attention, attracting outrage and indignation, particularly in response to its anarchic invasion of the popular music scene.

It also made an unmistakable contribution to many aspects of design and ornamentation. Punks saw themselves as alienated from the orthodoxy of the mores of everyday life in a society which was conditioned by the glamour of consumerism and affluent lifestyles. Their dress was "the sartorial equivalent of swear words,"[6] opposed to fashion convention: clothing was ripped, zipped, and "dirty," often made up from "eccentric" materials such as plastic bin-liners or fake leopardskin; hairstyles were dramatic and unnatural, hair was blatantly dyed and make-up worn by both sexes; and personal ornamentation ranged from safety pins through noses and cheeks to dangling chains, themselves often associated with other forms of "deviancy" and contributing to the general air of menace.

In the field of graphic design many ideas stemming from the Punk subculture were to provide the impetus for change in certain aspects of surface ornament. Abdication of law and order was the powerful core of the Punk outlook whether through dress, music or the making of posters and publishing of magazines—in other words a means of presentation which avoided the large-scale controlling interests in such media. What characterized the output was a sense of crudeness, immediacy and vitality that was lacking in more orthodox spheres. Something of this could be seen in the wide range of fanzines, such as *Ripped and Torn* or *Sniffin Glue*, which began publication in 1976. They were produced on a small scale by individuals or groups, stapled together, and circulated complete with typographic errors, deletions and handwritten insertions. Graffiti, an integral part of the 1970s urban environment, provided a certain stimulus and the incorporation of letters randomly torn or cut out from other sources became another characteristic. Album covers and other promotional material such as T-shirts soon absorbed something of these qualities in their artwork.

Among the most celebrated examples which initiated the trend was Jamie Reid's poster, advertisement and record sleeve designs for the Punk band The Sex Pistols, which caused considerable controversy, particularly his work for the single *God Save The Queen*. This image, which caused widespread offence in Queen Elizabeth II's Silver Jubilee Year of 1977, comprised a picture of the Queen's head, defaced with collaged lettering placed across her eyes and lips.

The immediate impact of Punk's outcry against the establishment was relatively short-lived, however, and the features that at first gave such offence were rapidly admired and emulated instead. Punk-derived clothing, packaging and other design media were soon mass-marketed in the fashionable boutiques in most major British urban shopping centres. Nonetheless, despite such emasculation, Punk did much to revitalize Britain as a centre for new and original design ideas.

LEFT **Living room** with girl in a mini-skirt hoovering, Britain, 1960s. This illustration reveals the more widespread picture of ornament in Britain in the Pop years. Although the woman is wearing a fashionable dress and shoes, much of the decoration and furniture is traditional, for example the heavily patterned carpet and the heavy armchair. The wallpaper has a 1950s flavour to it, showing that in many homes there was not the stylistic homogeneity that many period histories convey.

RIGHT **Tableware**, 1960s. These designs were typical of the period, particularly the cast-iron candlesticks of 1962 by Robert Welch. The "Buy British" mugs employing the Union Jack were designed by Paul Clark and made in Stoke on Trent in 1966–7. They were marketed by Perspective Designs, Fulham Road, London. The British flag was a favourite ornamental device in the Pop era and featured on all kinds of products. The image was considerably bolstered by the World Cup football matches, which were held in England in 1966; also by a series of "Buy British" campaigns.

LEFT "**London After Dark**", London Transport poster, 1960s.

BELOW **"Luxury Lounge"** with target wallpaper, Britain, 1960s. The target motif, with its bright, bold coloured stripes, became a favourite Pop motif and could be found on mugs, magazine covers and other surfaces.

RIGHT **Gunnar Cyren**, Pop glasses, manufactured by Orrefors, Sweden, 1966. The use of distinct bands of bright colours shows the widespread international response to the Pop aesthetic.

BELOW FAR RIGHT **Tomotom Furniture** by Bernard Holdaway in conjunction with Peter Neubart of Hull Traders Ltd, Lancashire, designed in 1966.

LEFT *Daisy Chain* textile designed by Pat Albeck for Cavendish Textiles (John Lewis), Britain, *c.* 1964. This pattern, which is still in production, shows the enduring British taste for floral motifs, a commercial undercurrent which predates and has outlasted the more extravagant floral design of the "Flower Power" years.

BELOW *Moonflower* containers and tablemats, made in lightweight metal to a Swiss design in vivid pink, red, blue, green and white, sold at Boots' chemists in July 1969. These products show the mass-market for floral designs and the way in which "alternative" forms of decoration were readily assimilated into everyday retailing.

RIGHT **Pop rug** designed by Peter Blake, Britain, 1960s. Blake was one of the first generation of British Pop painters and did much to spread strong, brightly coloured imagery into graphic and other fields of design. The striking simplicity of the design parallels the use of other geometric devices such as the target or Union Jack.

BELOW **Hippy Wedding** in Paris, 20 August 1975. Hippy styles lived on during the 1970s. The ornamental motifs on clothing were derived from a wide range of sources, drawing on the symbolism of Eastern religions, non-Western cultures, floral and other nature-oriented decorations as well as more mainstream styles such as Art Nouveau. Such ornamental devices were also incorporated into body painting on faces and arms. Jewellery was generally hand-made and was often produced by the hippies themselves as a means of economic survival.

OVERLEAF **Posters**, late 1960s. This range of posters shows the rich diversity of psychedelic imagery of the time and contains the work of a number of leading artists. During the latter part of the 1960s the poster became one of the cheapest and easiest means of establishing "individual" taste or lifestyle projection in room decoration for the young.

LEFT **Peter Blake and Jan Howarth**, printed insert card for the *Sergeant Pepper's Lonely Hearts Club Band* LP, 1967. The page of cut-outs indicated an interest in stylistic revivals in the 1960s, whether hinting at aspects of Victoriana, as here (albeit with a Pop dimension), or adopting the forms of Art Deco or Art Nouveau.

BELOW LEFT ***Granny Takes a Trip*** boutique, King's Road, London, 1967. This striking image, by Nigel Weymouth and Michael English (a partnership known as "Hapsash and the Coloured Coat"), was one of a number of Pop designs with which the boutique was painted. Something of the stark contrast with more mundane stores can be seen by comparison with the adjacent Sunlight Laundry.

RIGHT **Mike Rogers**, Rocket jacket in satin for Mr Freedom boutique, London, *c.* 1970. Mr Freedom, a highly fashionable store, was run by the designer and entrepreneur Tommy Roberts, first in the King's Road and then in Kensington Church Street.

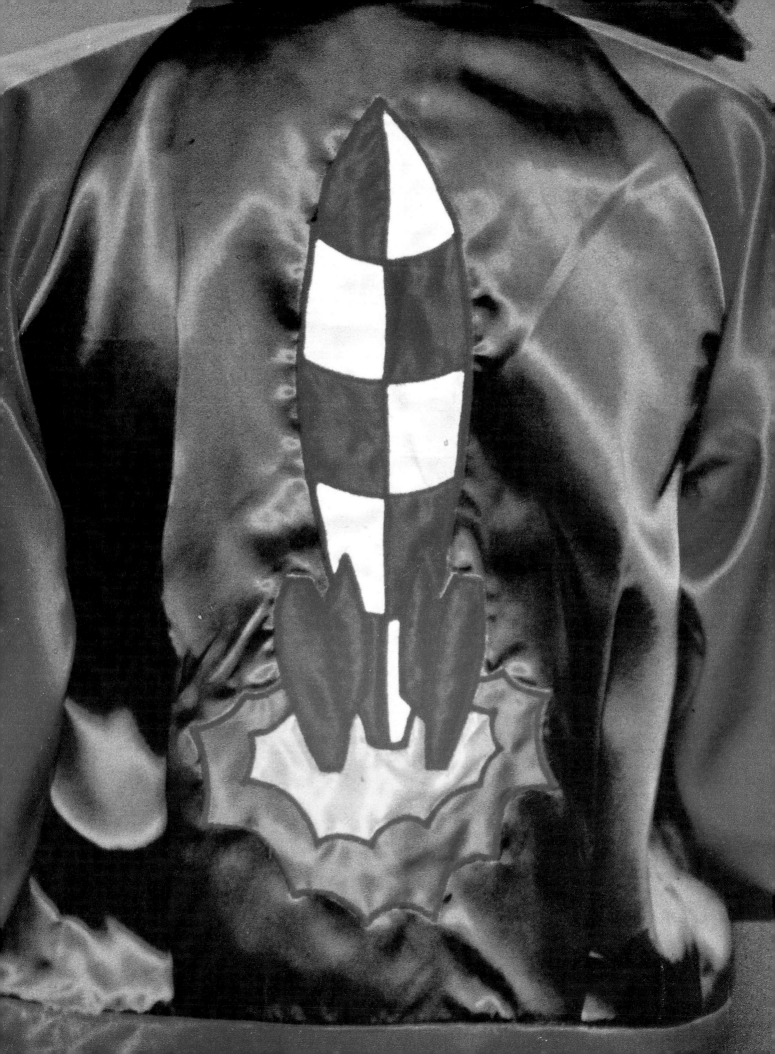

RIGHT **Interior** of Biba's, Kensington High Street, London, late 1960s. This phase of Biba moved away from a rather brash and expendable Pop clothing store to one which exuded glamour, Deco and, above all, a spirit of commercialized nostalgia. Potted plants, mirrors, ostrich feathers and interior decoration reflected a glamorized notion of 1920s design, with geometrically based decorative motifs playing a dominant role in the store furnishings.

BELOW **John McConnell**, design for Biba Catalogue, 1965. Art Nouveau provided an important influence for much graphic design of the 1960s, drawing on a renewed interest in the work of Mucha and Beardsley. There is also a strong element of Celtic revival in this piece.

RIGHT **Milton Glaser**, Bob Dylan poster, USA, 1967. This poster, with its stylized yet psychedelically inspired rendering of Dylan's hair, has become something of an icon of the period.

BELOW **Shirley Craven**, *Simple Solar* textile design, Britain, 1967. From 1960 to 1972 Shirley Craven both designed and commissioned textile designs for Hull Traders, establishing a sound reputation. The curvilinear forms of this particular design reflect something of contemporary interest in the flowing arabesques of Art Nouveau, while the more organic colour fields relate to the more commercial elements of psychedelic art.

RIGHT **Susan Collier and Sarah Campbell**, *Bauhaus* furnishing
fabric, Liberty & Co., London, 1972. This textile design is a
reinterpretation of Bauhaus designs of the 1920s, but exhibits a much
more strident colour range. It is typical of the spirit of revivalism of the
times, following along the lines of Terence Conran's Habitat stores,
which drew on the striking 1920s textile design of Sonia Delaunay in
the 1960s.

BELOW **Hippy** multicoloured Volkswagen van in Haight Ashby, San
Francisco, 1967. This brightly coloured vehicle looks back to avant-
garde styles of the 1920s.

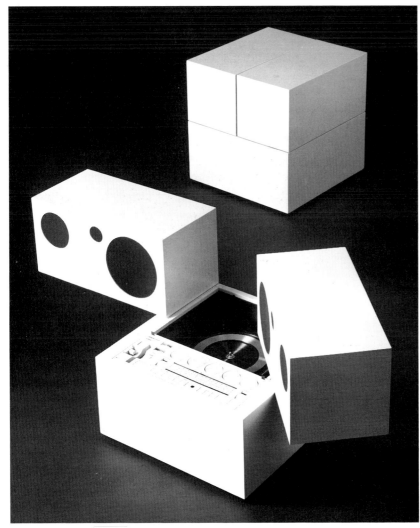

LEFT **Pluvium** umbrella stand designed by Gian-Carlo Pirelli for Anonima Castelli, *c.* 1970.

ABOVE **Gerd Alfred Muller**, Food Mixer KM3, manufactured by Braun, West Germany, 1957.

ABOVE LEFT **Mario and Dario Bellini**, *Totem* hi-fi set with detachable speakers, designed in 1970 and put into production by Brionvega in 1972.

These designs reject unnecessary surface decoration and for effect rely on their formal qualities. The Braun mixer was the product of a highly rational aesthetic which was to become the hallmark of Braun products. Its clean sculptural form, punctuated only by functional elements and the Braun trademark, accorded well with the purist design canons of the Museum of Modern Art in New York and the Council of Industrial Design in Britain. Both Italian designs exhibit the stylistic up-market elegance which accorded international recognition to one dominant strand of Italian design from the 1950s onwards.

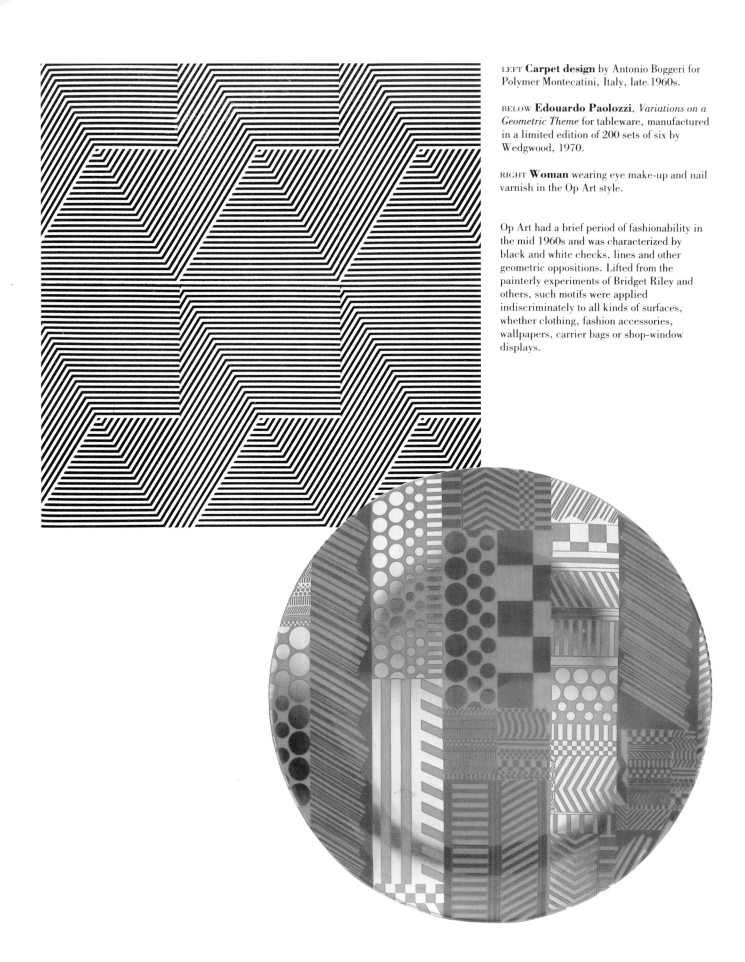

LEFT **Carpet design** by Antonio Boggeri for Polymer Montecatini, Italy, late 1960s.

BELOW **Edouardo Paolozzi**, *Variations on a Geometric Theme* for tableware, manufactured in a limited edition of 200 sets of six by Wedgwood, 1970.

RIGHT **Woman** wearing eye make-up and nail varnish in the Op Art style.

Op Art had a brief period of fashionability in the mid 1960s and was characterized by black and white checks, lines and other geometric oppositions. Lifted from the painterly experiments of Bridget Riley and others, such motifs were applied indiscriminately to all kinds of surfaces, whether clothing, fashion accessories, wallpapers, carrier bags or shop-window displays.

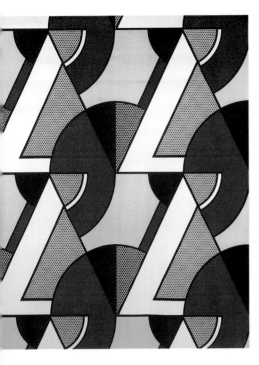

ABOVE **Roy Lichtenstein**, wrapping paper, *c.* 1970. Many of Lichtenstein's Pop Art designs were simply hijacked and recycled in a range of design media. This particular example looks to the Art Deco revivals of the late 1960s.

RIGHT **Eddie Squires**, *Archway* screen-printed cotton, Warner & Sons Ltd, 1968. Another design reflecting interest in past styles, particularly Art Deco, this pattern was inspired by cinema design of the 1930s.

LEFT **Jenny Lowndes**, *Karnak*, screen-printed cotton from the Pharaoh Range for Warner & Sons Ltd, 1967. Based on Egyptian ornament, this striking geometrically based design has much in common with other rivals of the period which looked to decorative aspects of design in the 1920s.

FAR LEFT **Evelyn Redgrave**, *Cascade* fabric for Heal's, London, *c.* 1965. Heal Fabrics were commercially extremely successful in the 1960s, both in Britain and abroad, and many young designers were commissioned by the company. This detail is part of a much larger pattern full of flowing curves, almost a meeting of Pop Art and Art Nouveau which was enjoying such an upsurge of enthusiasm at this time.

RIGHT **Archizoom Associates**, *Presagio di Rose* dream bed, 1967. Radical design groups in Italy reflected a dissatisfaction with the restrictive canons of modernism and subservience to the dictates of marketing strategy. They explored mass culture, being profoundly influenced by Pop and, through the medium of exhibitions, sought to draw upon a diverse range of cultural references, materials and finishes which undermined conventional notions of "taste".

BELOW **Sue Thatcher**, *Space Walk* screen-printed cotton, Warner & Sons Ltd, 1969. Designed to commemorate the moon landing in July 1969, this print shows the continuing fascination for space as a decorative theme.

BOTTOM **Natalie Gibson**, *Vanessa* wallpaper design, 1971. Despite the planetary references, the forms and colours of this painterly design owe a debt to the work of Vanessa Bell and Duncan Grant of the 1920s and 1930s. As such they are yet another aspect of period revivalism.

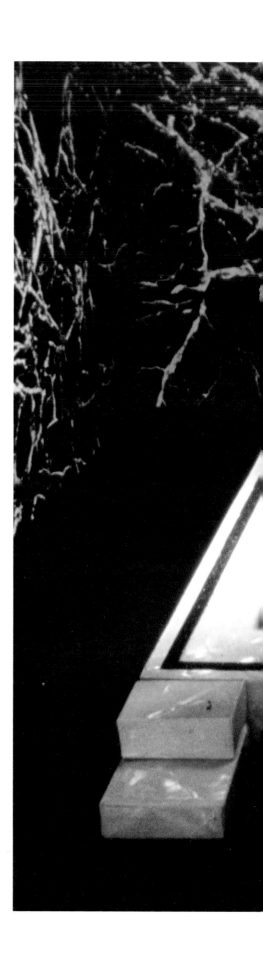

RIGHT AND FAR RIGHT **Punk** emerged in the mid-1970s as the anti-societal expression of disenchanted youth. At its extreme, clothing, body decoration and appearance were akin to an expression of social deviancy, but softer, more decorative applications were also punk-inspired.

BELOW *God Save The Queen* badge. The badge was based on the record sleeve designed by Jamie Reid for the Sex Pistols record of the same title. This image, which defaced the face of the Queen, caused considerable controversy in the British media.

7
Ornament and Post-Modernism
1975 to the 1980s

A legacy of problems

The late 1960s and 1970s saw a change in attitude towards the radical replanning of the urban landscape, with a growth in awareness of the heritage of the past. Just as writers and theorists such as Christian Norberg-Schulz, Robert Venturi or Charles Jencks had articulated the perceptions of the deficiencies of a Modernist aesthetic in a pluralist society, ordinary people were also becoming disillusioned with what they saw as the Modernist legacy or urban planning and high-rise apartment blocks. Many such structures were beset with problems of vandalism, the consequences of untested building systems and widely held opinion that they were psychologically unsuited to the realities of communal living. For Jencks and others, the death of Modernism was symbolized by the dynamiting in 1972 of Minoru Yamasaki's Pruitt-Igoe housing scheme in St Louis in the United States. It had been designed only in 1951 and been given an award by the American Institute of Architects, but later became a victim of the social pressures with which so many similar schemes have been identified.

Heritage and Environment

In many quarters of the industrialized world the distinct feelings of unease inherited from the '60s continued to grow concerning the ecological and environmental consequences of unbridled technological progress, and an increasingly articulate lobby sought to bring notions of

preservation and conservation of the existing fabric, both urban and rural, to the forefront of contemporary planning debates. Such considerations did much to heighten public awareness of the ornamentation of past epochs, which in turn promoted a renewed interest in disappearing craft techniques. Stencilwork, marbling, rag-rolling, stippling and a wide variety of other decorative techniques made a comeback in the 1980s, featuring in popular magazines concerned with homemaking and decorating ideas in manufacturers' paint catalogues. A similarly reinvigorating tonic was given to the crafts by the stylistic and ornamental eclecticism typical of much Post-Modernist architecture and design, with its emphasis on surface texture and decorative motifs in a wide variety of materials and finishes. The marketing, packaging and advertising industries have been quick to appropriate for their own gain the contemporary taste for nostalgia and the fascination for the past, with frequent decorative and pictorial allusions to a mythical bygone age when cottage industry excelled in the making or baking of wholesome jams or breads, untainted by the realities of factory-farming and artificial additives. The vogue for such images has also been fuelled by growing concerns for health, exercise and a "natural" way of life, sustained by an invigorating diet. The countrified imagery of certain fabrics, clothes and furnishings of the early 1980s and their associations with a particular way of life are a formula that have continued to flourish in the

LEFT **Alessandro Mendini and Bruno Gregori**, *Zabro* table/chair, manufactured by Zabro, Italy, 1980s. Studio Alchymia was founded in 1976, and drew upon banal and kitsch subject matter, the fine arts, and continued avant-garde critiques of mainstream industrial production. In this striking design there are resonances of the progressive art forms of the 1920s.

recent past. In a similar vein, the ideals or ruralism represented by sheaves of wheat and further arcadian motifs applied as decoration to electric toasters and other kitchen equipment enhance and complement the newly concocted "traditional" kitchen interiors that they often inhabit.

Tradition at Large

It should also be remembered that throughout the century many manufacturers have continued to produce successful lines of tableware and furnishing textiles which have been in existence for many decades. While rapid changes in style and ornament have played a dominant role in many aspects of domestic living, particularly when associated with products and appliances that consumers associate with "state-of-the-art" technology and a limited lifespan, a large number of patterns and ornamental motifs applied to the more enduring items of the home, ranging from dinner services to major items of furniture, reflect a less emphatically contemporary spirit. For a significant proportion of consumers, the values and associations embodied by such forms and decoration are those which seem to be the most expressive of warmth, security and other traditional characteristics of the home.

However, although nostalgia and retrospection have recurrently and directly affected design, reference has also been made to other historical epochs, cultures and symbols. One of the most powerful trends exploring such ideas is Post-Modernism.

Towards Post-Modernism

In the late 1950s and 1960s a clean, Modernist-inherited aesthetic appeared to provide an appropriate means for expressing the power and progressive face of multinational corporations in their buildings, equipment and furnishings. Olivetti, for instance, continued to set an

example in corporate design by endorsing many aspects of a direct, functional approach (although contemporary publicity by Giovanni Pintori and others was far more varied in its expressive qualities) and set standards which many other companies sought to emulate. In the United States, the architectural designs of Eero Saarinen at General Motors Technical Center near Detroit, the design consultancy of Eliot Noyes at IBM and the furniture and furnishings output of companies such as Herman Miller and Knoll all contributed to this trend. The parallel, and international tendency towards a more scientific and rational system of design, with a greater emphasis on team-work and specialist evaluation and an understandable lack of ornament, was encouraged throughout the late 1950s and 1960s by the Hochschule für Gestaltung at Ulm, and could be seen in designs by Dieter Rams for Braun and Otl Aicher for Lufthansa Airlines' corporate identity scheme.

In the same period an increasing number of critics, theorists and designers became interested in the relationship between visual and linguistic "signs," the correlation between the two being embraced in what has been termed semiology. Writers such as the French sociologist Roland Barthes, the Italian theorist and historian Gillo Dorfles and the American Robert Venturi began to explore the semiotic possibilities of architecture and design. Venturi's book *Complexity and Contradiction in Architecture*, written in 1962 and published in 1966[1] did much to open up debates about the shortcomings of the Modernist aesthetic. In it he spoke of his admiration for

> elements which are hybrid rather than "pure," compromising rather than "clean," distorted rather than "straightforward," ambiguous rather than "articulated," perverse as well as "impersonal," conventional rather than "designed," accommodating rather than excluding, redundant rather than simple, vestigial as well as innovating, inconsistent and equivocal rather than direct and clear.[2]

Such thoughts represented a growing sense of disillusionment with the apparent linguistic and expressive poverty of Modernist architecture and design, with its high premium on form rather than ornament. Inherited from the 1920s and '30s, the ideals of the avant garde of thirty years earlier seemed to many, particularly younger practitioners and theorists, to be extremely limited, particularly in an age where the mass media were able to introduce images and cultures from all over the globe with ever-increasing rapidity. The developments of the previous decade in consumer culture, new youth markets and the related shifts in stylistic outlook which had challenged the dominant professional aesthetic of the post-war years seemed increasingly attractive to individual consumers who wanted to embrace contemporary life and mass culture. Faced with an alluring wealth of styles, symbols and ornamentation, they were provided with a rich visual syntax by which they might express themselves through the purchase of clothes, interior furnishings, furniture and other domestic artefacts.

Designers, architects, manufacturers and retailers were not slow to explore (and exploit) this climate of consumption and rapid change. Advances in electronics technology further defied the status quo, the microchip rendering the old saying "form follows function" rather meaningless. Together with Venturi's reworking of the Modernist adage "less is more" into "less is a bore," such developments gave yet another impetus to designers to explore the expressive and symbolic potential of form and ornament.

Post-Modernist Expression

Post-Modernism, a term which derived from literary criticism but which has subsequently been so widely and indiscriminately applied that it has almost ceased to have any precise meaning, was given widespread currency by the publication in 1977 of Charles Jencks' book *The Language of Post Modern Architecture*. In effect, Post-Modernism has drawn on a wide range of decorative styles, bringing together an extensive range of visual, cultural, historical and aesthetic reference: eclecticism, ornamentation, and decoration are all facets of such an outlook.

The Austrian architect-designer Hans Hollein has produced much stimulating design in a Post-Modernist vein, ranging from a striking series of stores in Vienna to furniture for Memphis and Poltranova and metalware for Alessi. One of his most imaginative and evocative schemes was the interior of the Austrian Travel Bureau in Vienna, dating from 1976 to 1978 but destroyed in 1987, which was full of allusions to travel in the various motifs and images deployed within. Metal palm trees, part of a classical column blended with a stainless-steel shaft, a golden-roofed baldachino, eagles soaring against a pale blue sky, an Austrian flag apparently fluttering in the breeze and a lifebuoy hanging from a railing all conveyed something of the memories of travel to faraway and exotic places. Michael Graves, a leading American architect-designer, also worked in a wide range of media, including furniture for Memphis and Sunar and metalware for Alessi. His Public Service Building in Portland, Oregon, is perhaps one of his most dramatic essays in Post-Modernism. Drawing on the ideas, ornament and forms of 1930s Art Deco, the building's façade also makes clear references to New York skyscraper architecture of the same period.

In the hands of a number of Post-Modernist designers and architects, ornamental references often have

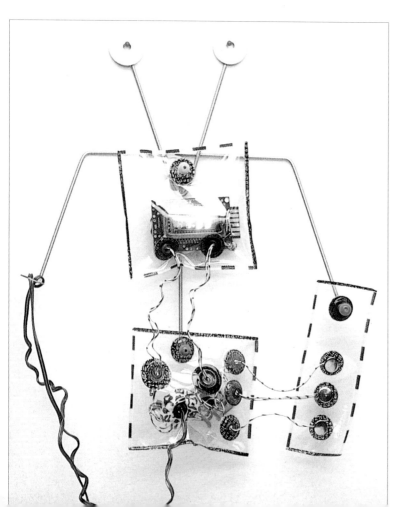

LEFT **Daniel Weil**, bag radio, manufactured by Quartett, West Germany, 1982. With developments in electronics technology and new materials the designer has been freed from the tyranny of form following function. In this design Weil has produced a poetic Post-Modernist essay from the component parts.

RIGHT **The Public Service Building**, Portland, Oregon, designed by Michael Graves, 1980s, and often hailed as an icon of Post-Modernism.

particular meanings which are intended to enhance the particular building or product to which they are applied. However, by the late 1980s the Post-Modernist "look" was visible in an ever-widening range of consumer goods (as well as retail outlet design, advertising, packaging, magazines and television graphics) which were far more concerned with surface than content. Just as the Victorians increasingly ransacked histories and cultures to enhance their ornamental repertoire, often without interest in or understanding of their original meaning, so many designers in the 1980s have treated the full extent of earlier twentieth-century styles as a set of stylistic sources for ornamental and decorative effect, without any attempt at conveying particular nuances of meaning or reference.

Italian Developments: Studio Alchymia and Memphis

Experimentation had been taking place over a number of years among the Italian avant garde, beginning with the debates which had centred on the Milan Triennali in the later 1950s and 1960s. Increasingly, designers and critics were concerned about the growing emphasis placed on style and status as the foremost characteristics of Italian design, feeling that individual and creative energies were being over-ridden by the dictates of manufacturing industry and its markets. The arguments were widely aired in the design press and often articulated through the medium of exhibitions. One of the most important of these was the show mounted at the Museum of Modern Art, New York—"Italy: the New Domestic Landscape"—which brought to the fore the politics, polemics and mainstream production of Italian design of the preceding decade.

Decoration was an area of research that increasingly interested a number of Italian designers, with particular reference to textiles. In 1975, publication of *Decorattivo* commenced—a yearbook that contained illustrations of all kinds of ornamental and decorative fabrics, drawn from an enormous variety of prime historical sources. Often juxtaposed with contemporary cultural images, these visual references were aimed at providing fresh stimulus and impetus. In the late 1970s several leading Italian designers took up the challenge, including the group Studio Alchymia, founded in Milan in 1976 and

listing among its participants Alessandro Mendini, Michele De Lucchi, Paola Navone and Ettore Sottsass Jnr. Their ideas first captured critical attention and controversy in 1978, followed in succeeding years with two exhibitions entitled Bau Haus I and Bau Haus II. Ranging from individual pieces of furniture and lighting to total environments and performances, their work was characterized by ornament and structures resonant with all kinds of echoes of meaning, drawing on references from kitsch to Kandinsky and exploring the communicative possibilities of design. Emphasis was placed on the crafts and small-scale production runs as a means of stimulating experimentation, providing an antithesis to the sterile "industrially styled" forms often associated with mass production. In the ferment of debate in Milan in the late 1970s and early 1980s, there were differing ideas about how to proceed. Mendini was now a leading voice in theoretical discussions, having edited until 1976 the magazine *Casabella*, an important forum for radical ideas in design and architecture. He was among those who saw exhibitions as providing the principal stimulus for critical discussion while others, centring around Ettore Sottsass, wanted a more positive relationship with manufacturers, forcing them to recognize the importance of imagination, metaphor and language as potentially enriching the experience of the consumer through the environment. The latter group, rejecting much of the spirit of utopian idealism that had dominated the radical avant-garde outlook of the 1970s, finally came together under the title of Memphis in Milan in 1981.[3]

Memphis

Like many of their radical predecessors of the previous decade, Memphis explored a visual language outside the limiting canons of "good taste" which had characterized mainstream Italian design since the 1950s. Barbara Radice, a founder member of the group, wrote that Memphis embraced an attitude that "assimilates, or at least acknowledges, anthropological, sociological and linguistic inquiry, from Lévi-Strauss to Barthes to Baudrillard."[4] Memphis's first show of furniture, lighting, clocks and ceramics was mounted in Milan in September 1981, coinciding with the Milan Furniture Fair and causing a considerable critical stir. The ornamental and decorative features of their designs relied extensively on a large number of sources ranging from the icons of American consumer culture to the symbols and motifs of ancient civilizations. The name Memphis itself could refer both to American popular music and Ancient Egypt, but in the group's work little distinction was made between "high" or popular cultural references: the decorative features of suburban coffee bars, the ornamental motifs associated with the Wiener Werkstätte of the 1920s, and Aztec jewellery were all effortlessly assimilated into the Memphis vocabulary. Colours and patterns were often strikingly juxtaposed in such a way as to upset conventional expectations of "tastefulness." Materials were treated similarly, being drawn on the one hand from the accepted design repertoire of woods, metals and fabrics, and on the other from sources normally associated with the mundane and everyday, including, for example, the printed plastic laminates of coffee-bars and seaside cafés or the many decorative finishes seen on mass-produced "ordinary" consumer goods.

The impact of Memphis has been enormously widespread. Exhibitions of the group's work have been seen in Britain, Canada, France, Israel, Japan, Scandinavia, Switzerland, West Germany and elsewhere and they have been given extensive international media coverage. As a result, many other designers and manufacturers have explored and marketed the wider implications of design drawing on a similarly encyclopaedic cultural, linguistic and symbolic range of references. Memphis itself soon became recognizable for the ornamental and decorative look which was their hallmark, applied to all kinds of products from television sets to ice-cream wrappers.

High Tech

Despite such rich essays in decoration and ornament, a more technologically orientated aesthetic also found favour in the late 1970s and early 1980s. "High Tech," supposedly the fusion of "high style" and "technology," was a term which conjured up an image of contemporaneity throughout Europe and the United States, lending itself to the title of a book by two American journalists in 1979.[5] Drawing on the urban chic of Manhattan loft-dwellers, the style featured in upmarket glossy magazines, newspaper colour supplements and even in the pages of Terence Conran's Habitat *Catalogue* where "Tech" was described as "a new look reflecting the

industrial style on home furnishing"[6] and was characterized by, among other features, perforated steel-sheet furniture components, graph-based wallpapers and fabrics and bulkhead lighting. The idea of appropriating ready-made industrial components and redeploying them to create an individual, contemporary, technological aesthetic was hardly new, having been seen thirty years earlier in Charles Eames's house in California, as well as in other instances. Nevertheless, as a style of the late 1970s and 1980s, High Tech was largely a readily marketable, fashion-conscious trend, moving one British critic to write that

> half the fun of High Tech comes from finding everyday uses for highly specialized industrial products. Sometimes it works: Levi's denims, originally designed for factory workers, have long been in everyone's wardrobe. But sometimes it's simply ridiculous, like riding a jeep in central London—it's hungry on petrol, cold in the winter, wet in the rain and open to fumes.[7]

The technological aesthetic made its mark on an architectural scale in Piano and Rogers' Beaubourg Centre in Paris, Norman Foster's Hong Kong and Shanghai Bank in Hong Kong and the same architect's Lloyds Building in London. On a smaller scale its influence was seen in products such as those on sale in Astrohome and Practical Styling, two stores which opened in London in March 1981, and in the interior design of retailing outlets from London to Tokyo, by designers such as Nigel Coates and Eva Jiricna. Fashionable clubs, restaurants and other public places frequented by the affluent were also subject to a High Tech ornamental vocabulary.

New Wave Design

The late 1970s and 1980s saw a renewed interest in Modernism, with graphic designers in particular drawing on the design avant garde of the inter-war years, ranging from De Stijl and Russian Constructivism to the New Typography. The fine arts also played an important role in enriching the vocabulary of graphic design, and the results could be seen in an exciting range of record covers, book jackets, posters and magazines. Style magazines in particular showed something of this trend, especially the two market leaders in Britain, *i-D* and *The Face*. Launched in 1980 by Terry Jones, *i-D* explored a

wide variety of approaches which were common to other New Wave designers: abandonment of the conventional grid-based layout in order to achieve a more immediate, less studied feel; combining handmade marks with typewriter print; the introduction of a variety of textures, decorative devices and photographic finishes. *The Face* was characterized by the typographic experimentation of Neville Brody, who combined a range of typefaces and all manner of decorative motifs to enliven the page. Brody's work was the theme of an exhibition at London's Victoria and Albert Museum in 1988 and has been highly influen-

tial. Indeed, many of its visual mannerisms have been translated by other designers into everyday packaging, store fascia and interior design and all kinds of other surface ephemera, from company brochures to food labelling.

Similar developments and affectations have been seen in European, American and Japanese design of the same period. Californian New Wave graphic design of the 1970s evolved via reactions to the rigidity and clarity of the dominant Swiss International style of typography and layout. There was a growing emphasis on bright

LEFT **Nigel Coates and NATO** (Narrative Architecture Today), exterior of the *Bongo* cage, Parco department store, Tokyo, 1986. Coates is one of a growing number of Western architects and designers who have been working on major projects in Japan. This dramatic sensationalizing fantasy reflects the importance of achieving a good return on the extremely high land values in Tokyo and many architects have been vying with each other to produce ever more striking architectural effects.

BELOW **Neville Brody**, page from *The Face*, May 1983. Started in May 1980, *The Face* was aimed at a young, style-conscious market. Brody's designs drew on a wide range of avant-garde sources of the 1920s: in this instance the horizontal bars running across columns of typeface together with the decorative rhythms of rectangles and squares are resonant of Constructivism and De Stijl. Such visual concepts subsequently became almost *de rigueur* in many areas of graphic and retail design.

colours, layered images and textures, and the mixing of typefaces on a variety of scales. New Wave has since been a powerful force in American graphic design, and a great deal of lively experimentation has graced the pages of certain small-circulation magazines such as *Fetish*, *Raw* and *Emigré*. The latter, launched by Rudy VanderLans in 1980, used computer-generated typefaces but was laid out by hand, combining striking black and white photographs with bold blocks of colour. In the late 1970s and 1980s Holland also encouraged adventurous graphic design with groups such as Hard Werken and

Dumbar Studios producing striking results. Even the Dutch European driving licence, designed on computer by Hans Kruit and Joost van Roon for the Staatsdrukkerij (State Printing Office) in 1986, combines typography, texture and decorative motifs in an exciting manner.

LEFT **Ribbon Trellis** fabric, designed by Dupont in France in 1971, Warner & Sons Ltd. This fabric is still in production and shows how traditional taste is still a prominent force in the market place.

BELOW **Kutani Crane**, fine bone china tea set in a traditional shape, introduced by Wedgwood in 1971 and still in current production. This design relies on traditional notions about the suitability of particular patterns for everyday domestic objects and bears little relationship to progressive developments. It has outlasted many more overtly fashionable lines.

LEFT **Willow Pattern** earthenware
manufactured by English Ironstone, 1980s.
English ironstone produce approximately
25,000 pieces of *Blue Willow* per week for
mail order and retail outlets in Britain, the
United States, Spain, Australia and
elsewhere. In keeping with current decorative
trends, the design may also be co-ordinated
with *Willow Pattern* textiles, housewares and
sundry other items. Willow Pattern was
originated in Britain by Thomas Turner at
Caughley Pottery Works in Shropshire in
1780.

ABOVE **Townhouse *Canton* range**, British
Home Stores, 1989. These blue and white
vases and plates show the enduring appeal of
such patterns to consumers in one of Britain's
leading store chains.

RIGHT **Today Interiors'** *Selwood* range
reveals a nostalgia for the English country
house. The various patterns are designed to
co-ordinate with one another in an overall
decorative scheme.

LEFT **Vivienne Westwood**, *Savage* collection
of clothing, Britain, 1981. These bright,
striking designs show the impact of ethnic
sources, drawing on Aztec, Mexican and
other patterns.

RIGHT **Graham Smith**, *Africa* pattern, from
the Ethnic Originals Collection, Warner &
Sons Ltd, 1977. Widespread interest in
"alternative" lifestyles and travel of the early
1970s led to the setting up of many stores
which specialized in the marketing of a wide
range of ethnic designs, whether from Africa,
Afghanistan, Morocco, India, South America
or Turkey. The resultant reawakening of
interest in techniques such as batik and tie-
dyeing made a strong impact on do-it-yourself
clothing decoration but was soon absorbed
into mass-production industry as a highly
fashionable style.

RIGHT **Hans Hollein**, interior of the Austrian Travel Centre, Vienna, 1976–8 (destroyed 1987). The architectural symbolism of this striking Post-Modern interior is drawn from a wide range of references relating to travel, whether an Indian pavilion, gilded palm trees, a broken classical column or, as can be seen at the far end of the room, the railings of an ocean liner complete with lifebuoy.

BELOW **Las Vegas**, neon-lit cityscape, 1970s. During the 1960s there was considerable interest in popular culture as an important ingredient in the syntax of architecture and design. Many of these ideas were disseminated through the writings of Robert Venturi in *Complexity and Contradiction in Architecture* of 1966 and *Learning from Las Vegas* of 1972, and did much to further ideas of Post-Modernism.

BELOW **John Outram**, view of courtyard entablature detail from a country house in Sussex, England, 1978–85.

BELOW CENTRE **Charles Vandenove**, column detail from the renovations and additions to Hors-Château, Liège, Belgium, 1978.

BOTTOM LEFT **John Blatteau**, ceiling detail from the Franklin Dining Room, State Department, Washington DC, 1983–85.

BELOW **Erith & Terry**, north elevation of the Howard Building, Downing College, Cambridge, 1983–7.

Classical ideals have been absorbed into the Post-Modernist vocabulary. Outram's use of brick for columns and capitals and the heavy rustication on the east and west ends of Erith & Terry's Howard Building show the playful manipulation of a classical language.

very slightly
e animals closely rela

are furnished with skin coverings appropriate to their

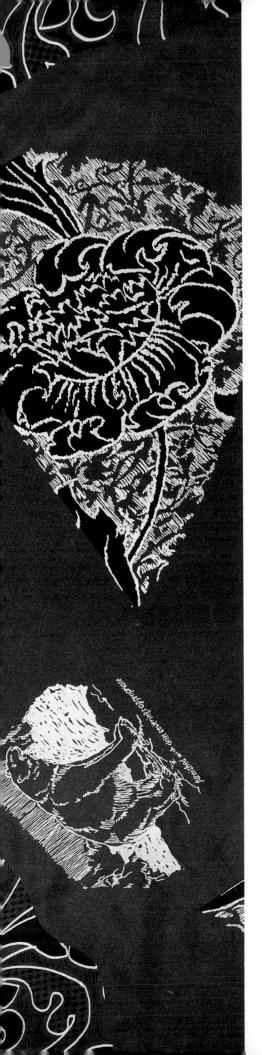

ABOVE **David Tisdale**, picnic flatware in anodized aluminium, USA, 1980s. These pieces rely on material, colour and finish for effect, although the three retaining studs on the handles provide "high-tech" ornamental relief.

LEFT **Helen Littman**, *Arctic* textile for English Eccentrics, 1980s. This culling of a wide range of visual references is typical of the eclectic spirit of the 1980s. English Eccentrics was set up in 1984 by sisters Helen and Judy Littman, and Clare Angel. They designed prints, knitwear and clothes respectively.

BELOW **Jason Pollen**, *Freesia* fabric design for the Larsen Design Studio, New York, 1980s. This striking design is essentially an updating of a traditional theme.

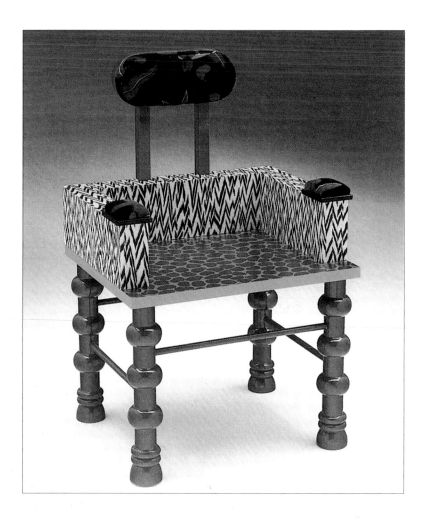

LEFT **Nathalie Du Pasquier**, *Esmerelda* chair in wood and plastic laminate, with arms and back in printed fabric, 1980s. The fresh combination of different materials and stylistic resonances, whether drawn from "high" or popular culture, has much in common with the work of the Memphis Group.

BELOW **Ettore Sottsass, Jr.**, *Ivory* table in reconstituted veneer and plastic laminate and glass top, 1980s, Memphis, Italy. Since the 1960s Sottsass has been a leading figure in Italian avant-garde design. Memphis emerged as one of the major Milanese design groups of the 1980s and sought to extend the vocabulary of furniture, lighting and interior design by combining materials, surfaces, patterns, symbols and decorative devices in new and unexpected ways.

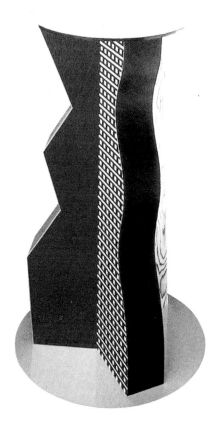

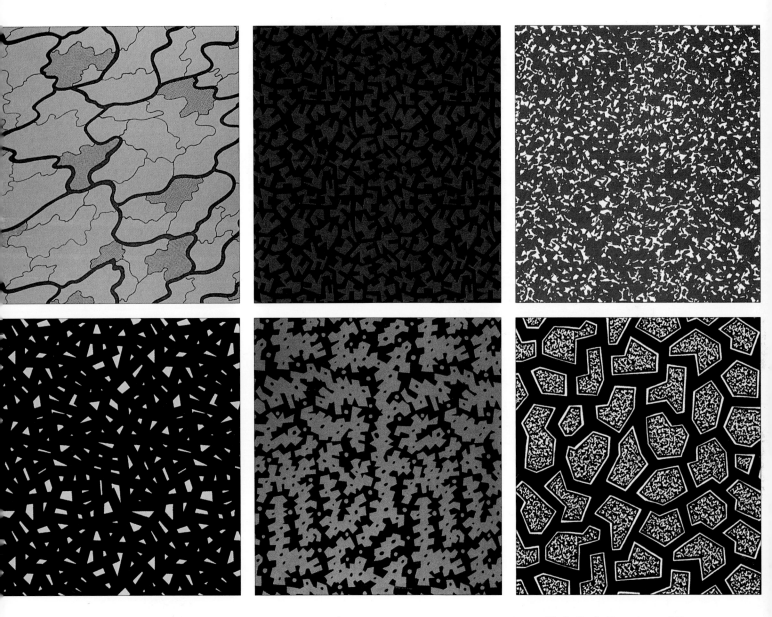

ABOVE **Nathalie du Pasquier and George Sowden**, decorative surfaces from *Progetto Decorazione*, a collection of silk-screen printed papers, 1980s. These patterns by two leading participants of the Milanese Memphis Group reflect the wide range of decorative experiments which were explored in this project. Surface decoration had preoccupied a number of Italian-based designers from the mid 1970s onwards and was an area of research which both these designers incorporated into their output.

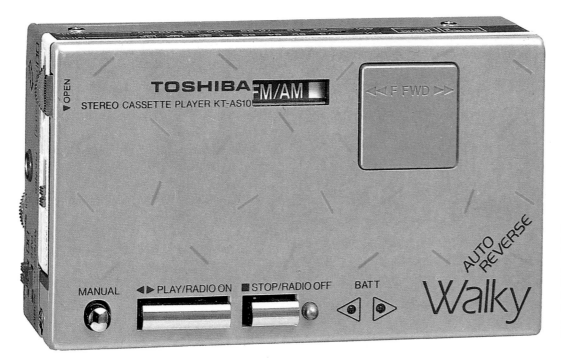

LEFT *Walky* slimline stereo cassette player and radio, Toshiba, Japan, 1980s. Available in a variety of finishes and colours, the use of colour and pattern as applied to both surface and controls has given the product high fashion status.

LEFT **Architectural decoration** by Andrea Branzi and Alessandro Mendini at Giulianova, Italy, 1978. This surface decoration by two leading figures of the Milanese avant garde reveals the extent to which the environmental uses of ornament and decoration were being explored in progressive circles. Branzi was involved in the publication of *Decorattivo* in 1975 as well as three volumes on colour projects for industry, including one on "Environmental Colours" in 1977.

BELOW *Festival* porcelain dinnerware by Hans Hollein manufactured by Swid-Powell Design, USA, 1980s. These surface decorations relate closely in appearance to the work of many other Post-Modernist designers in the 1980s.

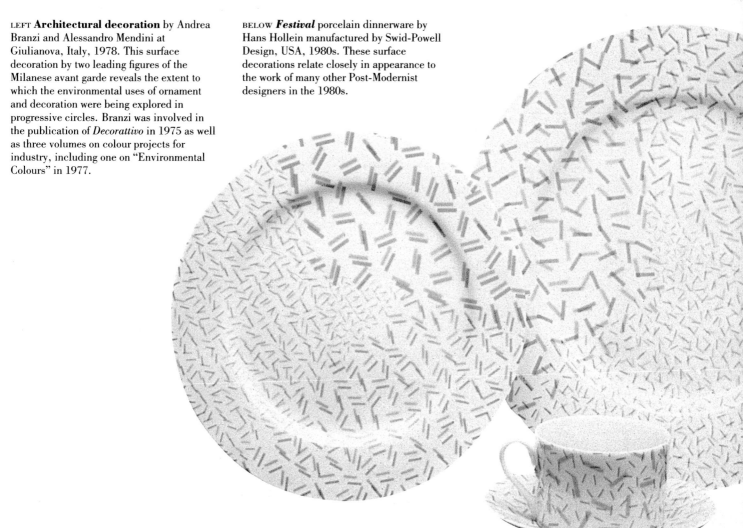

LEFT **Robert Venturi**, Chippendale chairs from the Venturi Collection, manufactured by Knoll International, USA, 1980s. These chairs, laminated with Venturi's *Grandmother* floral pattern, play with references to the past and reflect his efforts both to enhance the language of design with a richer vocabulary and to debunk the cultural reverence with which the past is endowed.

BELOW **Aldo Rossi**, *Il Rilievo* table in black Marquinia marble, white Carrara marble and blue Veneto marble, manufactured by Up & Up, Italy, 1980s. This design relies for its effect on the use of an unexpected material—marble rather than wood—to transform the character of a traditional design. This endows it with the element of wit favoured by many Post-Modernist designers.

LEFT **John Outram**, *Confucius* chest, manufactured in batch production by Alma, Britain, 1980s. This piece, with its references to the classical orders and variety of decorative surface effects, is full of ironic references to the past.

BELOW **Piero Fornasetti**, decorated bicycle, Italy, 1984. Fornasetti had been producing highly decorated surfaces on a wide range of products over several decades. This design blended easily with the decorative concerns of many of his compatriots at this time.

RIGHT **Tadanori Yokoo**, *Science Fiction Movies* poster, Japan, 1975. This poster shows Yokoo's plundering of all kinds of images drawn from science fiction films since the 1920s.

BELOW **James Dyson**, *G-Force Cyclonic Vacuum Cleaner*, designed in Britain in 1979, manufactured by Apex Inc. of Tokyo, 1986. This sculptural, high tech product has an unexpected quality for something with an everyday domestic function, owing to the pink and mauve colour scheme. Use of colour for all kinds of utilitarian products was a feature of 1980s design.

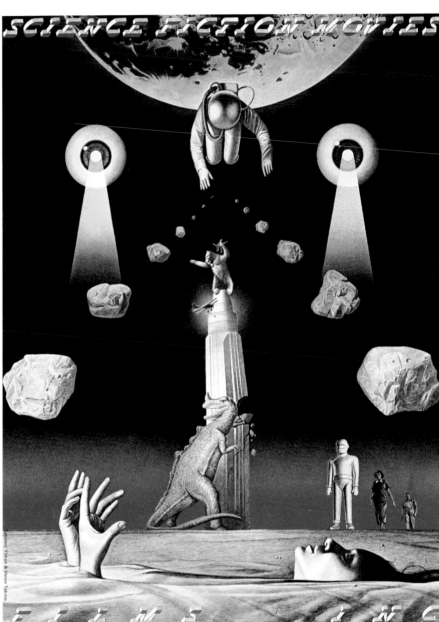

RIGHT **Fred Baier**, *Robot* desk in the style of the *Forbidden Planet*, 1987. The 1980s witnessed the plundering of all kinds of sources and periods for decorative impact: this imposing piece owes something of its inspiration to a 1950s science fiction film.

LEFT **Renzo Piano and Richard Rogers**, Centre Georges Pompidou, Paris. When it opened in the mid 1970s this building did much to bring the High Tech style to public attention. The building's mechanical services were clearly signalled on the outside through the use of a range of colours on the constituent parts, and throughout it explored an emphatically technological aesthetic.

BELOW *Metro* stacking system, designed and made in Chicago for industrial and catering storage in the 1930s, and in continuous production since then. These examples, drawn from the 1980s, typify the fashionable interest in High Tech style for domestic furnishings from the late 1970s. The term was said to derive from a fusion of "high style" and "technology". Aiming to appropriate into a domestic context goods which were originally destined for industrial purposes, the style was popularized in London by Astrohome Ltd which first imported the *Metro* units to Britain in March 1981. It soon found widespread currency in many other outlets, including Conran's Habitat, although the products sold there were generally manufactured only for the style market.

LEFT **David Mercatali and Paolo Pedrizetti**, *Selz* cutlery in nylon and stainless steel, manufactured by Case Casa-Industrie Casalinghi Mari, Italy, 1980s. These pieces rely on proportion and shape: in this instance their status as fashionable objects is emphasized by setting them against the textured background so fashionable in "designer" interiors of the 1970s and 1980s.

BELOW **Matteo Thun**, table lamps from the *Stillight* collection, manufactured by Bieffeplast, Italy, 1980s. The *Stillight* range of table and reading lamps has a strong architectural flavour and, in keeping with many other contemporary designs, draws on a wide range of cultural references for interest and effect.

RIGHT **Cassina**, reissue of Charles Rennie Mackintosh sideboard 328, originally designed in 1918. The Milan-based Cassina company has concentrated its focus on commissioning works from leading modern designers. However, to complement such contemporary "classics", the company from 1965 introduced a range of past classics from the late nineteenth and early twentieth centuries, commencing with an armchair by Le Corbusier. A considerable number of pieces by Mackintosh have been reproduced, alongside works by Rietveld, Frank Lloyd Wright and others.

BELOW **Marcello Morandini**, *Corner* unit, manufactured by Rosenthal, West Germany, 1980s. In keeping with the 1980s tendency to draw on references to past styles, Morandini's corner unit has resonances of 1920s decorative trends as well as the more obvious allusions to De Stijl in the brightly coloured inset.

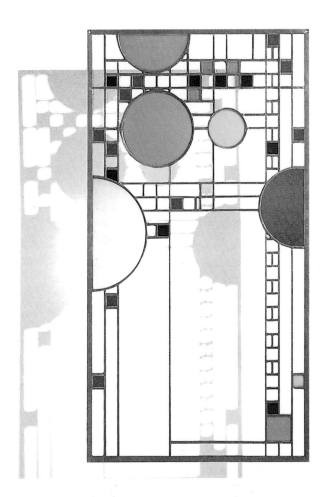

ABOVE **Frank Lloyd Wright**, *Clerestory No 2* window (originally designed in 1911 for the Coonley Playhouse, Riverside, Illinois), manufactured in the 1980s by Oakbrook Esser Studios, USA. One of a number of Wright glass designs reproduced by the studios, it reflects the interest in past design classics in the eclectic 1980s, paralleling the practice of the Milanese furniture firm Cassina in whose "Masters" series Wright also features.

LEFT **Peret**, *Soviets* rug, manufactured by Nani Marquina, Spain, 1980s. Like so many other essays in what might loosely be termed Post-Modernism, this rug design draws on history for many of its modernist-derived decorative motifs. There are clear references to Kazimir Malevich's Suprematism and Wassily Kandinsky's abstract works of the 1920s, as well as to the more decorative designs of Sonia Delaunay.

LEFT **Eduardo Paolozzi**, decorative murals
for Tottenham Court Road underground
station, London, mid 1980s. Paolozzi's
decorative essay is one of a large number
commissioned by London Transport from a
number of artists and designers to improve
the aesthetic environment of London's
underground stations.

BELOW *Neos* collection of clocks, by Nathalie
Du Pasquier and George Sowden,
manufactured by Lorenz, Italy, 1980s.

BELOW **Swatch watches**, late 1980s. Aimed at a young market, these highly decorative watches are conspicuous elements of personal ornament, their potential extended by a number of alternative watch straps. Since quartz crystals and liquid crystal displays have displaced traditional mechanisms, increasingly designers have paid attention to the "packaging".

LEFT **Richard Rogers Partnership**, Centre Commercial, St Herblain, Nantes, France, 1986–7. This detail reveals the extent to which colour was used in the 1980s in order to articulate the component parts of buildings in the High Tech mould, lending the whole something of a decorative aspect.

RIGHT **John and Penny Smith**, *Duet* table setting, manufactured by Design in the Round, Tasmania, Australia, 1980s. This ornamental setting, which involves a wide range of materials, finishes and strong colours, reveals the close interplay between the crafts and design during the 1980s. The room for experimentation in the crafts context often provided fresh sources of inspiration and ideas for decorative designs produced on a larger scale.

LEFT **Ron Arad**, *Italian Fish* chair, manufactured from welded sheet steel and stainless steel, late 1980s. Fabricated in the One Off workshops, Arad's design crosses the boundary between "art" and "design" and is economically geared to an audience of collectors and galleries. Removed from the architecturally charged ambience of the "designer" interior of the early 1980s, Arad's recent work is located within what one critic has described as the "design as culture" lobby.

RIGHT **James Stirling and Michael Wilford Associates**, façade detail from the WZB Building (Government Social Science Research Centre), Berlin, designed in 1979 and completed in 1987. The elegant yet decorative impact of this detail is provided by the use of self-coloured stucco, separated by deep grooves, with window surrounds in red-brown sandstone. Such detailing, with the richness afforded by hand-finishing of the coloured surfaces, fulfilled the architects' intention to create "a friendly unbureaucratic place—the opposite of an 'institutional' environment." The stucco technique was taught to those working on the WZB Building by two men who were seen repairing the stucco on the ancient Charlottenburg Palace.

LEFT **Fumikho Maki**, Spiral Building, Tokyo, 1985. This detail shows Maki's interest in rational modularized elements. This is in marked contrast to the subtle use of colour, shape and decorative textures seen in Isozaki's MOCA and Stirling's WZB buildings.

RIGHT **Arata Isozaki**, Museum of Contemporary Art (MOCA), Los Angeles, 1980s. The use of contrasting materials, including sandstone, concrete, glass and dark-green aluminium panels set in a pink grid, provides this view of the complex with an austere yet decorative ethos.

LEFT **Coca-Cola Tin**, decorated with Edwardian woman drinking Coca-Cola with the Coca-Cola logo, late 1980s, marketed by Virojanglor, Paris. From the 1980s onwards Coca-Cola introduced promotional items to increase sales: calendars, clocks, trays, tins and other items. Many of these featured beautiful women holding Coca-Cola bottles, as in this 1980s reproduction. The motifs embody notions of nostalgia that have played an important part in the swift-changing values of the 1980s as well as the increasing tendency of consumers to pay for the conspicuous consumption of brand names.

RIGHT **Coca-Cola sweatshirt and Colman's Mustard mug**, late 1980s. Historically distinctive advertising images have become desirable consumer items, whether in the marketing of British heritage or American consumerist imperialism.

BELOW **Drinking glasses** decorated with Walt Disney cartoon characters, late 1980s. The Disney empire, known worldwide through its animated characters for over half a century, holds a dominant place in Western culture, sustained by a large film and comic output, Disneyland and the proliferation of innumerable accessories manufactured under licence. With the recent stock market flotation of the projected European Disneyland in France, branded decorative items such as drinking glasses not only provide innocent amusement for children but help to sustain interest in Disney as a leading corporation in the global leisure industry.

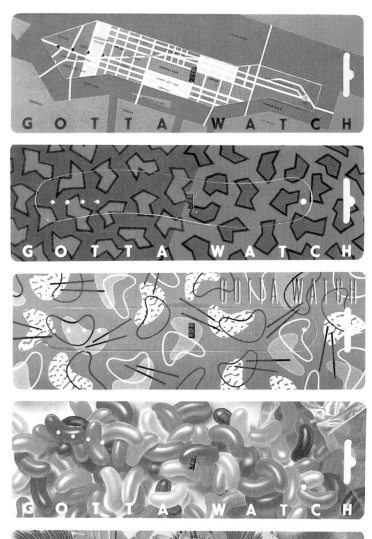

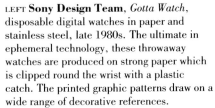

LEFT **Sony Design Team**, *Gotta Watch*, disposable digital watches in paper and stainless steel, late 1980s. The ultimate in ephemeral technology, these throwaway watches are produced on strong paper which is clipped round the wrist with a plastic catch. The printed graphic patterns draw on a wide range of decorative references.

RIGHT **Page** from *Le Livre de Table*, catalogue of Galeries Lafayette, Paris, 1989. The products shown here reflect 1980s *chic* and show that in many of the "architect" and "designer" interiors for which they are destined there is still considerable antipathy to any heavily ornamented surface. However, as with many modernist products of the 1920s and 1930s, there is still a distinctive, albeit highly restrained, ornamental aesthetic.

La modernité

L'œuf

ARZBERG. *2 tasses et soucoupes "Expresso," en porcelaine, 173 F.*

☙ *Seltmann Weiden*

GALERIES LAFAYETTE SÉLECTION. SELTMANN WEIDEN. *Porcelaine, 44 pièces, 3800 F.*

LAVAZZA. *Cafetière "Carmencita," 2 tasses, inox 18/10ᵉ, 300 F.*

GIEN. *Faïence, décor "Angle," design J.P. Caillères. Assiette plate, 145 F. Assiette à dessert, 110 F.*

ALESSI. *Cafetière expresso "La Conica" design Aldo Rossi, acier 18/10ᵉ, 6 tasses, 1050 F.*

QUARTZ. *Assiette en verre, décor "Mer Bleue." 24 x 24 cm, 170 F. 20 x 20 cm, 140 F.*

KOSTA BODA. *Vase en verre soufflé, "Mezzo," 14,5 cm, 350 F. 20 cm, 480 F.*

BODUM. *Bouilloire, design C. Jorgensen, inox 18/10ᵉ, cuivre et bois, 850 F.*

Gien
FRANCE

GIEN. *Faïence, décor "Point noir ou blanc" Vase/bougeoir, 809 F.*

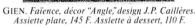

GALERIES LAFAYETTE SÉLECTION. *"Limpide," manche acrylique. Cuillère, fourchette ou couteau, 22 F.*

GALERIES LAFAYETTE SÉLECTION. *Porcelaine, décor "Quintett bleu." Assiette plate, Ø 27 cm, 125 F. Ø 19 cm, 65 F.*

SALINS. *Faïence, décor "Espace." Assiette plate carrée ou triangulaire, existe en 7 coloris, 115 F.*

SOLA FRANCE. *Porcelaine, décor "Turkos," théière, 870 F. Sucrier, 490 F. Pot à lait, 240 F. Cafetière, 790 F. Tasse et soucoupe à thé, 175 F.*

MELIOR. *Cafetière "Boulevard," 3 tasses, rhodium, 340 F.*

GALERIES Lafayette

Design, couleurs mode, voici la table moderne. Scandinave, par Arzberg, Ittala Finland, Kosta Boda, Sola France. Créative avec Bodum, Cacharel, D. Hechter, Guzzini, Salins. D'avant-garde pour J.-M. Patois, M. Graves, N. Perkal, P. Casenove.

8

The Marketing of "Individual" Taste Into the 1990s

Ornament is very much a dominant part of everyday life in the late 1980s, whether in terms of personal adornment, domestic interiors, the design of retailing outlets, the forms and decoration of major architectural commissions, or many other aspects of the environment. Transportation systems, in particular underground networks in London or Stockholm and overground in airports such as London Heathrow or San Francisco International, have provided opportunities for major artistic commissions which enrich the traveller's visual surroundings. On a less elevated level, graffiti art has developed from a simple staking-out of territory and the promotion of identity by spraying "tags" or signatures into a much more dynamic and sophisticated pictorial art form, evident in murals in many large towns and cities throughout Europe and the United States, and perhaps most strikingly seen on the New York subway system. By the 1970s and 1980s subway trains frequently featured highly developed and proficient sprayed images, with a multiplicity of subjects drawn either from imagination or popular culture, and often prepared from preliminary sketches.

Clothing, hairstyles and make-up have for centuries

LEFT **Mural**, New York. In the 1970s and 1980s there have been many ways in which non-commercial design has manifested itself in the environment, whether in the values promoted in community art mural schemes—in which neighbourhoods and pressure groups participate— or in spray painting, which was transformed from being a crude means by which street gangs staked territorial "ownership" to an art form which required high levels of skill and planning. Danny Jenkins' individualistic painted clothing (see page 316) similarly reflects the vibrant interests of street culture. Despite many such fresh initiatives these have generally been hijacked by commercial interests or designers who have rendered anodyne any layers of meaning which such objects originally may have expressed.

provided opportunities for individual or corporate ornamental expression. However, the pace of social and economic change over the past thirty years has witnessed a dramatic increase in scope in these fields. Jewellery has also extended its repertoire, whether in terms of new relationships between body and ornament as in the work of Emmy van Leersum and Gijs Bakker in Holland, the experimentation with acrylics and other materials of Claus Bury and Gerd Rothmann in West Germany, or the use of other new forms and materials by Caroline Broadhead and Susanna Heron in Britain.

T-shirt art is another more everyday medium for communication. The development of its decorative potential has taken vast strides since the late 1940s when the faces of famous individuals began to appear, accompanied by slogans such as "Dew It With Dewey" in the 1948 American Presidential Elections. Plastic-inks technology in the 1950s and the use of photolithography in the 1960s encouraged further self-expression; used since then to promote rock bands, politics, lifestyles or even brandnames, shirts have become, as Gillo Dorfles described them, "sematophors" or bearers of significant signs.[1] However, the very multiplicity of messages about self, society or culture raises an important question about ornament and decorative motifs in a world which has freed itself from the apparent constraints and relative austerity of a Modernist-inherited creed. This relates to the extent to which decorative and ornamental forms seen on buildings, in magazines, advertisements, interior design, furniture and industrial design are genuine bearers of Dorfles's "significant signs" or are simply the end products of the mass-marketing of style. The sub-Descartian epithet "I consume, therefore I am" is

perhaps the most fitting maxim for today's style-conscious consumer, who can draw on an almost inexhaustible fund of decoration and ornament in order to make a "personal statement" about lifestyle and beliefs.

In many Westernized and industrialized countries the concept of design has become increasingly dominated by the forces of marketing and advertising. It has been seen as a commodity which, by mere word association in advertising copy, provides a route to increased sales. The Post-Modernists were looking to enrich the lingua franca of design and decorative ornament through the use of symbol, metaphor, irony and wit. However, the extent to which new freedoms and experimentation have fruitfully contributed to that reality, rather than providing a mere source-book for readily applied, fashionable products, is open to question.

ABOVE **New York** subway train with graffiti, 1970s.

LEFT **Danny Jenkins**, painted leather coat and beret, Bristol, 1989.

NOTES

CHAPTER ONE
Progressive Design and Historical Inspiration 1900 to 1914

1. For an indication of the widespread nature of the movement see N. Pevsner and J. M. Richards, *The Anti-Rationalists: Art Nouveau Architecture and Design*, Architectural Press, London 1973.
2. See, for example E. F. Seckler, "Mackintosh and Vienna," *Architectural Review*, December 1968.
3. Initially the classes were run by Madame Sérusier, wife of the French Symbolist artist, Paul Sérusier, but soon gave way to a much more experiential and experimental approach.
4. The "Martines" designed everything in the shop except the furniture, which was designed by Pierre Fauconnet.
5. He went to Vienna again in 1911 when he met Klimt, Hoffmann and others connected with the Wiener Werkstätte, and many textiles by Hoffmann and Wimmer were used in Parisian fashion accessories in the following year. He also visited the Palais Stoclet in 1912 and commissioned Hoffmann to build him a palace in Paris.
6. This exhibition has perhaps been undervalued as an area of study since it was the platform upon which the foundations of the Deutscher Werkbund were laid. John Heskett presents a full and interesting discussion in Chapter 10, "The Third German Applied Arts Exhibition," *Design in Germany 1870–1918*, Trefoil, London 1986.
7. See J. Campbell, *The German Werkbund*, Princeton University Press, Princeton 1978, pp. 24 and 26.
8. Ibid., Appendix IV.
9. Particularly the Yearbooks which began publication in 1912, containing photographs of members' work, articles, conference addresses and other useful material.
10. Design historians have also placed considerable emphasis on a limited number of architectural contributions by Walter Gropius (the Model Factory and Administration Building), Van de Velde (the Theatre) and others.
11. The vast majority of immigrants, however, travelled third class or steerage and did not enjoy the fruits of design debates.
12. Karl Schmidt had succeeded in involving the Dresdener Werkstätte in ship-fitting design for the German Imperial Navy in 1903.
13. Although the company had gone into American ownership, the *Olympic* still flew the British flag.
14. The *Daily Mail* Ideal Home Exhibitions were instituted in 1908 and continue today. They provide important indicators of popular aspirations for design connected with the home.
15. A remodelled school building originally designed by McKim, Mead & White.
16. W. C. Kidney, *The Architecture of Choice*, George Braziller, New York 1974, p. 106, n. 104 draws attention to a number of guides, catalogues, periodicals and books of the period. These include the *Illustrated Catalogue of Plastic Ornaments* issued by the Decorators' Supply Company, Chicago, around 1903, and *New York Plaisance*, issued as an annual by the Henry Erkins Studios, decorators and decorative supply manufacturers, New York, in 1908.

CHAPTER TWO
From Historicism to Art Deco 1910 to 1940

1. Ministry of Reconstruction, *Reconstruction Problems 17: Art and Industry*, HMSO, London 10 March 1919, p. 6.
2. "The Plain Song of Decoration," *According to Plan*, Design and Industries Association, 1926, p. 4. This is a small compendium of essays reprinted from the British *Manchester Weekly Guardian* in sympathy with the relatively austere aesthetic of the DIA.
3. P. Nash, *Room and Book*, Soncino Press, London 1932, p. 37.
4. The exhibition was re-opened in 1925, the same year as the Exposition des Arts Décoratifs et Industriels in Paris, and still attracted a further ten million visitors. By comparison, the Paris Exposition attracted less than six million. The comparative reluctance of British manufacturers to exhibit at Paris may have had a great deal to do with their projected markets, which were imperial rather than European.

5. *The Times*, 6 May 1924.
6. For an interesting discussion of these and other antecedents of the style see Y. Brunhammer, *1925*, Paris 1976, produced in conjunction with the "Exposition Cinquantenaire de l'Exposition de 1925," organized by the Musée des Arts Décoratifs.
7. R. Banham, *Theory and Design in the First Machine Age*, Architectural Press, London (1960) 1977, p. 248.
8. D. Todd and R. Mortimer, *The New Interior Decoration: an Introduction to its Principles, and International Survey of its Methods*, Batsford, London 1929, p. 22.
9. It is usually alleged that the reason for American non-participation was that there were insufficient products conforming to the exhibition requirements of "modern inspiration" and "real originality."

CHAPTER THREE
Modernism: Opposition to Decoration 1918 to the late 1930s

1. R. Banham, *Theory and Design in the First Machine Age*, Architectural Press, London (1960) 1977, Chapter 14.
2. The Bauhaus was an effective propagandist for its own cause, especially through the *Bauhausbücher*, fourteen of which were published between 1925 and 1930 and explained the Bauhaus aims and objectives. The setting up of the Bauhaus Archive in 1961 further encouraged research into the history and ideology of the institution. There is also a political dimension to this aspect of historical interpretation, which stemmed from the opposition of many leading figures associated with the Bauhaus to the oppressive politics of the right (ultimately represented by the National Socialists). Modernism became more widely disseminated with the emigration of many of its leading proponents to the rest of Europe and the United States. For a long period after the end of the

Second World War historians still tended to focus their researches on notions of a progressive machine aesthetic rather than the ideologically questionable output of artists, architects and designers under the Third Reich.
3. These include studies as diverse as J. Willett, *The New Sobriety: Art and Politics in the Weimar Period 1917–1933*, Thames and Hudson, London 1978; J. Campbell, *The German Werkbund: The Politics of Reform in the Applied Arts*, Princeton 1978; G. Berghaus, "Girlkultur—Feminism, Americanism, and Popular Entertainment in Weimar Germany," *Journal of Design History*, Vol. 1, Nos. 3/4, 1988, p. 193 ff., and N. Bullock, "First the Kitchen—then the Façade," *AA Files*, May 1984.
4. H. Wingler, *The Bauhaus*, MIT, Massachusetts 1969, p. 310.
5. Including John E. Bowlt in his introduction to I. Yasinskaya, *Soviet Textile Design of the Revolutionary Period*, Thames and Hudson, London 1983.
6. E. O'Brian, *The Dance of the Machines: the American Short Story and the Industrial Age*, Jonathan Cape, London 1929.
7. Although critics pointed to the way in which the organization was developing an original school of American design, Jeffrey Meikle, in *Twentieth Century Limited: Industrial Design in America 1925–1939*, Temple University Press, Philadelphia 1979, p. 27, draws attention to the large number of immigrant designers involved and the fact that AUDAC often conducted meetings in German.
8. Including K. C. Plummer, "The Streamlined Moderne," *Art in America*, January/February 1974, pp. 46–54, and D. Gebhard, "The Moderne in the US 1920–1941," *Architectural Association Quarterly*, July 1970.
9. The National Research Council was also involved in the 1939 New York World's Fair.

10. It makes an interesting comparison to the "House of the Future" at the 1928 Ideal Home Exhibition at Olympia in London, which had a garage-hangar for an "aerocar," disposable cardboard "crockery" and pneumatic furniture. The American "House of Tomorrow" was far more closely geared to industrial and prototype promotion.
11. Although it must be remembered that it was open for two seasons, in comparison with the Paris 1931 Colonial and 1937 International Exhibitions which attracted thirty-three and thirty-four million visitors respectively in the six months in which they were open.
12. W. D. Teague, "Building the World of Tomorrow: the New York World's Fair," *Art and Industry*, April 1939, p. 133.
13. Ibid. p. 126.
14. These ideas, like those in Dreyfuss' *Democracity*, looked to earlier propositions such as Ebenezer Howard's notions of the Garden City, Hugh Ferris' *Metropolis of Tomorrow* of 1929, Thomas Adams' *Regional Plan of New York and its Environs* of 1931, and others.

CHAPTER FOUR
Design and Ornament in a Totalitarian Climate 1920 to 1940

1. It has been suggested that this internationalist outlook may have been a contributory cause to the ultimate failure of the Italian Rationalist movement to establish itself as the official style.
2. E. Shapiro, "The Emergence of Italian Rationalism," *Architectural Design*, 1/2, 1981, p. 5 ff.
3. G. Minucci and A. Libera, *La Prima Esposizione dell' Architettura Razionale*, Milan 1928, as cited in E. Shapiro, op. cit., p. 7.
4. R. Banham, *Theory and Design in the First Machine Age*, Architectural Press, London (1960) 1977, p. 193.
5. As quoted in J. Campbell, *The German Werkbund: The Politics of*

Reform and the Applied Arts,
Princeton University Press,
Princeton 1978.

6. Although in recent years this balance
   has been redressed in a number of
   articles and publications including
   Hinz, Mittig, Schäche, Schönberger
   (eds.), *Die Dekoration der Gewalt:
   Kunst und Medien im Faschismus*,
   Geissen 1979.

7. As translated by I. Falk, in H. B.
   Chipp, *Theories of Modern Art: A
   Source Book by Artists and Critics*,
   University of California Press, 1969,
   pp. 476–8.

8. The public building programme was
   also an important economic
   consideration, as seen in B. Hinz,
   Art in the Third Reich, Blackwell,
   Oxford 1979, Chapter 7:
   "Architecture, Arms, Industry and
   War."

9. The First Five Year Plan became a
   Four Year Plan.

CHAPTER FIVE
*From Austerity to Affluence
1940 to 1960*

1. According to the Geffrye Museum
   Catalogue, *Utility Furniture and
   Fashion 1941–51*, ILEA, London
   1974, p. 30, this was at least as
   much to do with reducing the amount
   of administrative paperwork as any
   aesthetically motivated decision.

2. "Utility or Austerity," *Architectural
   Review*, 1942, p. 5.

3. The most important of these
   produced the *Report of the Committee
   on the Constitution of the British
   Standards Institution*, HMSO,
   London 1950 (the Cunliffe Report)
   and the *Report of the Purchase Tax/
   Utility Committee*, HMSO, London
   1952 (the Douglas Committee).

4. Bevis Hillier, *Austerity/Binge*, Studio
   Vista, London 1971.

5. A. P. Sloan, *My Years with General
   Motors* (1963), Penguin Books,

Harmondsworth 1986, p. 277.

6. J. McHale, "Technology and the
   Home," *Ark* (Royal College of Art,
   London), 19, p. 26.

7. Recalling also Hugo Gernsback's
   science-fiction maxim of the interwar
   years, "Science Fiction Today—Cold
   Fact Tomorrow" or the Pullman *City
   of Salina* train of 1934 promoted as
   "Tomorrow's Train Today."

8. R. Banham, *Los Angeles: The
   Architecture of Four Ecologies* (1971),
   Penguin Books, Harmondsworth
   1978, p. 124.

9. R. Banham, "The Style: Flimsy . . .
   Effeminate," M. Banham and B.
   Hillier (eds.), *A Tonic to the Nation:
   The Festival of Britain*, Thames and
   Hudson, London 1976, p. 190.

10. M. Frayn, "Festival," *The Age of
    Austerity 1945–54*, Penguin Books,
    Harmondsworth 1964, p. 331.

11. E. Kaufmann, *What is Modern
    Design?*, Museum of Modern Art,
    New York 1950, p. 8.

12. J. Mashek, "Embalmed Objects:
    Design at the Modern," *Artforum*,
    February 1975, p. 53.

13. E. Kaufmann, "Borax, or the
    Chromium-plated Calf,"
    Architectural Review, August 1948,
    pp. 88–93.

14. For a useful, yet concise, discussion
    of this "Spectre of Americanization"
    see D. Hebdige, "Towards a
    Cartography of Taste: 1935–1962,"
    Block, 4, 1981, p. 39 ff.

15. J. E. Blake, "Space for Decoration,"
    Design, 1954.

CHAPTER SIX
Pop and Post-Pop 1960 to 1975

1. N. Whiteley, *Pop Design: Modernism
   to Mod*, Design Council, London
   1987.

2. M. Duckett, "Are We Suffering from
   Psychedelic Fatigue?" *Design*,
   January 1968.

3. A. Benn, "The Quality of Life,"
   Architectural Association Quarterly,

April/June 1975, pp. 20–27. This
was an elaboration of ideas which he
had expressed in 1968.

4. D. Hebdige, *Subculture: the Meaning
   of Style*, Methuen, London 1979,
   p. 65.

5. See, for example, C. McDermott,
   Street Style: British Design in the 80s,
   Design Council, London 1987.

6. D. Hebdige, op. cit., p. 114.

CHAPTER SEVEN
*Ornament and Post-Modernism
1975 to the 1980s*

1. R. Venturi, *Complexity and
   Contradiction in Architecture*,
   Museum of Modern Art, New York
   1966.

2. Ibid.

3. Barbara Radice, in her book
   *Memphis: Research, Experiences,
   Results, Failures and Successes of
   New Design*, Thames and Hudson,
   London 1985, p. 25, saw its origins
   in a series of meetings in December
   1980. She also recounted that the
   name derived from a line in a 1966
   Bob Dylan song which was playing
   repeatedly at one of those early
   meetings.

4. B. Radice, op. cit., p. 141.

5. J. Kron, S. Slesin, *High Tech: the
   Industrial Style and Source Book for
   the Home*, Allen Lane,
   Harmondsworth 1979.

6. *Habitat Catalogue 1980/81*, London
   p. 6.

7. S. Games, "High Tech and the
   Fashion Scene—A Sense of Déjà-
   vu," *Journal of the RIBA*, September
   1979.

CHAPTER EIGHT
*The Marketing of "Individual"
Taste: into the 1990s*

1. G. Dorfles, "T-Shirts as Mass-
   Media," in *T-Shirt Show*, Electra,
   London 1984.

DESIGNERS AND DESIGN ORGANIZATIONS

The following is by no means a comprehensive list of all designers who have played a formative role in the creation of a twentieth-century ornamental vocabulary. It reflects the tendency of design-historical literature to concentrate on design celebrities rather than the vast array of essentially anonymous (at least in readily accessible published sources) designers who have exerted a major impact on the ornamental tendencies of everyday twentieth-century life.

Archigram

British. Architectural and design group. Formed in Britain in 1961, the group sought to ally Pop with the latest technological developments, whether concerned with audio-visual and propaganda techniques or the exploration of space. Obsolescence, change and expendability were embraced as signs of a healthy society and many of their ideas were presented in a comic-strip derived format. Exerting a strong visual presence, they had a significant effect on Italian radical designers of the 1960s.

Ashley, Laura

British. The company began in the early 1950s, marketing fabric prints to Laura Ashley's designs. After years of steady development, by the 1970s it had become concerned with marketing "a way of life" through products which epitomized "a British country setting." By the end of the decade this increasingly involved the marketing of co-ordinated fabrics, wallpapers and paints. Small, delicate floral motifs characterizing a "country look" became an international success, and the company expanded with outlets across the world, from Britain to Australia, Japan to the United States. Readily identifiable association with a "cottage and chintz" style was consolidated in the *Laura Ashley Book of Interior Decoration* of 1983 as well as in the annual catalogues. In the late 1980s the company began to market furniture reflecting a similar ethos.

Atelier, Martine

See PAUL POIRET.

Baillie Scott, Hugh (1865–1945)

British. Architect and designer. Involved with the Arts and Crafts in Britain through *Studio* magazine; his work became widely known on the Continent, particularly in Germany and Austria.

Bakst, Léon (1866–1924)

Russian. Stage and graphic designer. Widely known for his strikingly exotic and colourful costumes and sets for Diaghilev's Ballets Russes, particularly in the years leading up to the First World War. His designs were highly influential in Paris and London and made a distinct impression on both fashionable dress and interior design.

Barron, Phyliss (1890–1964)

British. Textile designer. Well known for her geometrical and floral designs of the 1920s and '30s, she worked in close conjunction with Dorothy Larcher (1884–1952). Both were leading hand-block printers of fabrics of the period, selling through Footprints in Beauchamp Place, London.

Bauhaus

German. School of art, architecture and design founded in Weimar in 1919 under the directorship of WALTER GROPIUS. Although generally associated with Modern Movement ideals and an experimentation with an abstract, machine age aesthetic, the institution went through a number of distinct phases. The early years exhibited a strongly Expressionist flavour, with a great emphasis on the handicrafts. This was largely due to the influential role played by Johannes Itten until his departure in 1923, when the influences of Russian Constructivism, DE STIJL and other avant-garde tendencies began to make themselves felt. Politically, the position of the School became increasingly difficult in Weimar, forcing it to move in 1925 to Dessau, a much more industrialized centre. Here the Modernist aesthetic, with its dominance of form over ornament, was fully asserted. After Gropius left the Bauhaus in 1928, there were several changes in the academic hierarchy, as well as in the wider national political climate, which forced the Bauhaus to move to Berlin in 1932. It finally closed the following year.

Behrens, Peter (1869–1940)

German. Architect, designer and painter whose early work embraced flowing Art Nouveau motifs. At the Art Colony at Darmstadt in 1901 he designed his own house complete with furnishings and equipment in this style. He is best known for his work for the electrical company AEG, with which he was associated as designer from 1906 until the First World War, and for which his work reflected a much greater commitment to the relation of art and design to industrial production. His standardized, geometrically based outlook was applied to all aspects of the corporate image of AEG, an industrial counterpart to the all-embracing curvilinear motifs and forms associated with Darmstadt. He was a member of the Deutscher Werkbund from its foundation in 1907.

Bel Geddes, Norman (1893–1958)

American. Designer. Once dubbed the "Barnum and Bailey" of industrial design, his visions of a streamlined utopian future as portrayed in his book *Horizons* of 1932 epitomized the importance of technologically derived imagery for many American consumer goods of the 1930s: electric toasters, cookers, pencil sharpeners, cameras, furniture and automobiles were but a few of the products that embraced the forms and ornamental motifs concerned with speed and progress. His "Futurama" display for General Motors at the New York World's Fair of 1939 developed such ideas on a far larger scale.

Bell, Vanessa (1879–1961)

British. Artist and designer. She was a coordinator of the OMEGA WORKSHOPS between 1913 and 1919. In the 1930s she collaborated with DUNCAN GRANT on a range of decorative interior schemes, including those for her home at Charleston Manor in Sussex. She also worked on designs for textiles, rugs, tableware and ballet sets.

Berlage, H. P. (1856–1934)

Dutch. Architect and designer. His Amsterdam Stock Exchange building, begun in 1897, for which he also designed the furniture and many fittings, was highly influential. He was an important figure behind the promotion of the American architect-designers Louis Sullivan and FRANK LLOYD WRIGHT. His outlook influenced both the work of the expressionist Amsterdam School and the more austere appearance of DE STIJL.

Bernard, Oliver (1881–1939)

British. Designer. After a background in theatrical scenery design he came to prominence in the 1920s and '30s. He produced a number of decorative schemes for the British Empire Exhibition at Wembley of 1924 and was involved as technical director to the British exhibit in the Paris Exhibition of the following year. He was well-known for his Deco-inspired interior design work for Lyons Corner Houses, and the chrome and glass entrance and interiors of the Strand Palace and Regent Palace Hotels.

Brandt, Edgar (1880–1960)

French. Designer. Highly influential metalworker whose contributions to the 1925 Paris Exhibition made his work popular with a wide audience on both sides of the Atlantic.

Brangwyn, Frank (1867–1956)

British. Painter and designer. Having worked for William Morris in the 1880s, his designs were very much in the Arts and Crafts style. He produced designs for tableware and rugs, but is perhaps best known for his murals, which include his contribution to the Rockefeller Center, New York.

Branzi, Andrea (b. 1939)

Italian. Architect, designer and writer. Since the early 1970s he has been at the forefront of many aspects of avant-garde tendencies in Italian design, including Archizoom Associati and STUDIO ALCHYMIA. He was a member of Milan Design Consultants (CDM) with whom he published two volumes of research into environmental decoration entitled *Decorattivo*.

Brody, Neville (b. 1957)

British. Graphic designer. Arguably one of the more influential breed of New Wave British graphic designers, who has worked on record sleeves, posters, book and magazine design. His work for *The Face* magazine has made a major impact on mainstream commercial graphics in Britain, drawing on a range of imagery and layouts visually associated with the Modern Movement, particularly Russian Constructivism.

Calder, Alexander (1898–1976)

American. Fine artist and designer. His abstract metal sculptures and mobiles exerted a considerable influence on many designers of the 1950s. The wiry, linear motifs associated with many of his works derived from Paul Klee and Joan Miró.

Chermayeff, Serge (b. 1900)

Russian. Architect and designer. A leading exponent of Modernism in Britain in the 1920s and '30s, with something of the geometric, decorative tendencies associated with French work of the period. He is well-known for his interior designs for the BBC in London and Birmingham, the Cambridge Theatre, London, and his role as director of Waring and Gillow's Modern Art Studio, London, between 1928 and 1931. He has also designed furniture, radios, carpets and other products. He emigrated to the United States in 1939, pursuing a career in architecture, planning and education.

Cliff, Clarice (1899–1972)

British. Ceramic designer. Well-known for her striking Art Deco patterns, particularly for the *Bizarre* range for the Stoke-on-Trent firm of A. J. Wilkinson, for whom she worked between 1918 and 1963; the range also included work by VANESSA BELL and Laura Knight.

Colefax, Sybil (d. 1950)

British. Decorator. The interior decoration firm of Colefax and Fowler was formed in London in 1934 and specialized in producing for a wealthy clientele, often drawn from owners of country houses.

Coles, George (1884–1963)

British. Architect. A highly prolific cinema designer, employing a wide range of styles including Egyptian, Chinese, Art Deco and Neo-Classical.

Conran, Terence (b. 1931)

British. Designer and entrepreneur. Although trained as a textile designer, Conran is perhaps known most widely as the founder of the Habitat stores group, the first of which opened in the Fulham Road, London, in 1964. More recently he has sought to influence wider markets through his company Storehouse plc, which includes British Home Stores, Mothercare and Heal's.

Corbusier, Le (1887–1965)

Swiss. Architect and designer. After working in August Perret's office in France he worked under PETER BEHRENS in Germany in 1910. The rather austere machine aesthetic for which he is most widely known developed from an interest in Greek architecture, Purism (itself deriving from Cubism, a movement which he launched in 1917 with Amedée Ozenfant) and technology. He published his influential book *Vers Une Architecture* in 1923 and caused considerable controversy with his "Pavillon de L'Esprit Nouveau" at the 1925 Paris Exhibition, which implicitly undermined the highly decorative, richly ornamented and luxurious flavour widely promoted elsewhere on the site. In the late 1920s he designed furniture with Charlotte Perriand that explored the possibilities of tubular steel in keeping with the mechanistic tendencies of the contemporary avant garde. In the 1950s he began to explore a more expressive vocabulary.

Day, Lucienne (b. 1917)

British. Textile designer. Well-known for her wallpaper, fabric and carpet designs produced in Britain and abroad. Her *Calyx* design for the 1951 Festival of Britain, with its wiry lines set against abstract geometric shapes, was an archetypal image of 1950s British textile design. In the 1950s and '60s she also produced ceramic designs for Rosenthal porcelain, moving towards a more craft-orientated outlook in the 1970s.

Delaunay, Sonia (1885–1979)

Russian. Designer and artist. She worked in many design media including fashion, stage, textiles, posters and stained glass. Her work was characterized by bright colours and geometrical forms, an idiom which derived from collaboration on colour theory with her painter husband Robert in the years leading up to the First World War.

De Lucchi, Michele (b. 1951)

Italian. Designer and architect. He has worked for STUDIO ALCHYMIA and MEMPHIS, experimenting with the linguistic and expressive possibilities of form and decoration. He has also designed shops for FIORUCCI throughout Europe.

Deskey, Donald (b. 1894)

American. Designer. He was one of the first generation of design consultants in the United States. Heavily influenced by Art Deco, which he had seen at first hand at the 1925 Paris Exhibition, much of his work had a strong, geometric feel. One of his most striking achievements was the co-ordination of the Radio City Music Hall in the Rockefeller Center, New York.

De Stijl

Dutch. Group of designers, architects and fine artists. Founded in 1917 in Leyden by Theo van Doesburg. Many of the visual characteristics of their output derived from the paintings of the Dutch artist Piet Mondrian. It was felt important to establish a new, universal aesthetic, compatible with modern life and technology. Non-representational in form, their work was characterized by flat, geometric planes of colour (red, blue and yellow) set within a matrix of vertical and horizontal (later diagonal) lines. These ideas were applied to textiles, interior design, furniture, architecture, graphics and other design media, and were an important ingredient of European avant-garde design in the 1920s. *De Stijl* magazine was published between 1917 and 1928.

Deutscher Werkbund

German. This association was founded in 1907 with the aim of uniting art and industry and raising the standards of German design. In the years before the First World War there was increasing tension between those who believed in the importance of individual creativity in design and those who advocated the tenets of mass production. Generally, standardized rather than highly expressive ornamental forms were to represent the association's dominant ideology. In the 1920s the Werkbund again became an important propagandist for modern design in everyday life, although its views were suppressed with the rise of Nazism in the early 1930s, leading to its demise in 1934. It was revived in 1947.

Doesburg, Theo van (1883–1931)

Dutch. Designer, architect and painter. See DE STIJL.

Dorn, Marion (1899–1964)

American. Designer. Well-known for her Modernist textile and carpet designs, commissioned by a number of British manufacturers in the 1930s. They often exhibited a strong geometric feel in their flat, bold configurations.

Dufrène, Maurice (1876–1955)

French. Designer. A leading designer of wallpapers, textiles, furniture, interiors, ceramics, glass and other media. From 1921 he was the Studio Director for the Parisian store Galeries Lafayette and was an important exponent of Art Deco.

Dufy, Raoul (1877–1953)

French. Fine artist and designer. He designed textiles for Paul Poiret from 1911, his early work reflecting the contemporary fine arts in France, particularly the brightly coloured paintings of Matisse and the Fauves with whom he was associated. His work for the Lyon firm of Bianchini-Férier, executed from 1912 until the late 1920s, are among his best-known designs. In the early 1930s he also designed printed textiles for the New York firm of Onondaga.

Du Pasquier, Nathalie (b. 1957)

French. Designer. She is well-known for her textile design work for MEMPHIS and Studio Rainbow, and has been involved with design for FIORUCCI.

Earl, Harley (1893–1969)

American. Automobile designer. After joining General Motors in 1925 Earl was placed in charge of the company's Art and Color Section which sought to stimulate sales through annual styling changes. He was a dominant figure in the styling of automobiles after the Second World War, deriving their form and ornamentation from the iconography of rocketry and space, a theme which dominated many products of the decade.

Festival Pattern Group

British. Design project initiated by the British Council of Industrial Design for the Festival of Britain of 1951. Manufacturers were encouraged to produce decorative designs derived from crystallographic structures, a field in which Britain was a world leader in the 1940s. Twenty-six manufacturers from a wide range of design fields participated.

Fiorucci, Elio (b. 1935)

Italian. Entrepreneur. Inspired by the Pop culture of 1960s London, Fiorucci opened his first fashion store in Milan in 1967. The business expanded rapidly and remains geared to the more adventurous trends in youth culture.

Fornasetti, Piero (b. 1913)

Italian. Designer. Perhaps most widely known for his interior and decorative design, produced in collaboration with Giò Ponti. Much of his work is surreal, with *trompe l'oeil* motifs being applied to mass-produced products.

Fraser, Claud Lovat (1890–1921)

British. Designer. Well-known as an illustrator and designer for the theatre and for advertising, as well as for textiles for the London firm of William Foxton & Co.

Gaudí, Antonio (1852–1926)

Spanish. Architect and designer celebrated for his idiosyncratic work in the Art Nouveau style in Barcelona, particularly the Güell Park and Palace. His architecture, interior and furniture designs are strongly organic in their form and ornamentation.

Gentleman, David (b. 1930)

British. Designer and muralist. Known for wallpaper, postage stamp and book illustrations, his most widely seen works are his 1980s mural designs for stations of the London Underground.

Girard, Alexander (b. 1907)

American. Architect and designer. Has worked for a number of companies including General Motors and the Herman Miller furniture company. His textiles are characterized by simple abstract designs, drawn from both contemporary and more primitive sources.

Grant, Duncan (1885–1978)

British. Fine artist and designer, influenced early in his career by the bright colours of Matisse and the Fauves. After meeting the critic Roger Fry he became, from 1912, involved with ceramic, textile and furniture decoration for the OMEGA WORKSHOPS. From 1916 he lived with VANESSA BELL and worked with her on a number of decorative schemes. Later in his career he was involved with graphic, textile, mural and ceramic design, often using striking colours laid in flat fields with an overlay of decorative motifs of flowers and garlands.

Graves, Michael (b. 1934)

American. Architect and designer. Designed interiors for Sunar from 1979 and has since designed furniture for MEMPHIS and metalware for Alessi. Drawing on a wide range of references, from ancient Rome to the 1930s, he has been prominent among Post-Modernists since the completion of the Public Services Building in Portland, Oregon, in 1982.

Gropius, Walter (1883–1969)

German. Architect and designer. Director of the BAUHAUS from its foundation in Weimar in 1919 and then in Dessau until 1928. He was an important advocate of Modernism in architecture and design, and sought to reconcile art and industry through his close association with the DEUTSCHER WERKBUND and through his teachings. After a spell in Britain in the 1930s he emigrated to the United States where he became a renowned advocate of the Modern Movement.

Hoffmann, Josef (1870–1956)

Austrian. Architect and designer. With Koloman Moser he was a founder member of the WIENER WERKSTÄTTE in 1903 and was influenced by the outlook of the late Arts and Crafts designers in Britain as well as by the work of the Scottish designer and architect CHARLES RENNIE MACKINTOSH. Many of his Werkstätte designs exhibited a marked geometricity. His most successful design was the Palais Stoclet, Brussels (1905–11), where he produced a highly decorative integrated environment. He was an important figure at the Vienna School of Applied Arts, where he held the post of Professor of Architecture from 1899 to 1941.

Hollein, Hans (b. 1934)

Austrian. Architect and designer. He established his office in Vienna in 1964 and has become known for his arresting Post-Modern designs. He worked for MEMPHIS in 1981 and Alessi in 1983, and has also designed furniture for Poltranova.

Lalique, René (1860–1945)

French. Designer. A leading figure in French jewellery and glass design, with early work based on the flowing organic forms associated with Art Nouveau. He was well-known for his contributions to international exhibitions and also had a pavilion at the 1925 Paris Exhibition, working in a more geometrically orientated Art Deco style. In 1932 he produced a wide range of designs in glass for the prestigious liner *Normandie*.

Larcher, Dorothy

See PHYLLIS BARRON.

Lissitzky, El (1890–1941)

Russian. Architect and designer. A leading figure in Russian design and education in the years following the 1917 Revolution, he was also highly active on an international front during the 1920s, forging links with German and Dutch avant-garde groups. Working in a largely Constructivist style he experimented with a wide range of design media: furniture, typography, photography, exhibitions and propaganda, graphics and book design.

Loewy, Raymond (1893–1986)

French/naturalized American. Designer. After an early background in electrical engineering he turned to window display and fashion illustration after moving to New York in 1919. In the 1930s he became one of America's leading figures in industrial design, his streamlined designs for cars, refrigerators, railway locomotives and Greyhound buses exerting a strong influence on the styling of many contemporary products. His firm built up a significant international practice and worked on products in almost all design fields, from postage stamps to NASA's Skylab.

Loos, Adolph (1870–1933)

Austrian. Architect, designer and writer. An admirer of Neo-Classicism, he was antipathetic to what he considered an inappropriate use of ornament, as typified by the output of the WIENER WERKSTÄTTE, which was attacked in his famous article of 1908 entitled "Ornament and Crime," although it was not as widely known then as it has subsequently become.

Mackintosh, Charles Rennie (1868–1928)

British. Architect and designer. Mackintosh was influenced by a wide variety of sources including the Arts and Crafts movement and the Celtic Revival. There was a pronounced organic Art Nouveau flavour to much of his work, which covered a range of design media in the

1890s. It received favourable attention in Continental Europe through the pages of *Studio* magazine, particularly in Vienna where his work had an undoubted impact on the WIENER WERKSTÄTTE. Among his major works in Britain were the School of Art and Mrs Cranston's Tea-rooms, both in Glasgow. The more geometric aspects of his work of the early 1900s have been linked to Art Deco.

Malevich, Kasimir (1878–1935)

Russian. Fine artist and designer. After working under the influence of Impressionism, Cubism, Futurism and indigenous Russian art, he developed a form of abstract art entitled Suprematism, in which geometric forms set against light grounds were intended to convey sensations such as falling, ascending and floating. He produced key designs for theatre sets and costumes, architectural projects and ceramics, and in the years following the 1917 Revolution was also significantly involved in education. His book *The Non-Objective World* was published by the BAUHAUS as one of a series exploring progressive aesthetic ideas, following a visit he made there in 1927.

Mallet-Stevens, Robert (1886–1945)

French. Architect and designer. His early designs reflected the influence of the Austrian JOSEF HOFFMANN, who designed the Palais Stoclet for his uncle. He is strongly associated with the Modern Movement of the 1920s and 1930s, although much of his output has a distinctly ornamental flavour. He was also a designer of film sets.

Mare, André (1887–1932)

French. Designer. In the years immediately preceding the First World War, Mare became known for his furniture, wallpaper and bookbinding designs. In 1919 he became a partner to the architect LOUIS SÜE and founded the Compagnie des Arts Français, better known as Süe et Mare. Their work was strongly Art Deco in feel, with floral motifs and swags providing favoured decorative motifs.

Marimekko

Finnish. Retail outlet founded in Helsinki in 1951. The very bright, colourful patterns which typified many of the commissioned designs made an immediate impact, blending Modernism with Finnish folk-art. Marimekko products have been licensed worldwide since the late 1960s.

Marx, Enid (b. 1902)

British. Designer. Known for her textile design and book illustration, often favouring small-scale, abstract motifs. Her most widely known work was produced for the London Underground and the Wartime Utility Schemes.

Maugham, Syrie (1879–1955)

British. Interior designer. After opening a decorator's shop in London in 1924 she soon became a successful and highly fashionable designer of interiors for the wealthy, and was well-known for her use of white with mirrors, and for blending antiques with modern art and design.

Memphis (1981–1989)

Italian. Design group. Based in Milan, the Memphis Group designed textiles, lighting, furniture, metalware, laminates, glass and interiors. Drawing on a wide range of references from ancient Egypt to American consumerism, their rich and varied vocabulary explored the resonances of juxtaposing expensive and everyday materials. The group's impact was international and they were widely imitated; contributors were drawn from Italy, America, Britain, France and Japan.

Mendini, Alessandro (b. 1931)

Italian. Designer, architect and writer. He played an important role in the promotion of progressive design thinking in Italy through his editorship of *Casabella* (1970–76) and *Domus* (1979–85). He has produced work for Nizzoli Associates, STUDIO ALCHYMIA and Alessi.

Moser, Koloman (1868–1918)

Austrian. Painter and designer. A founder of the WIENER WERKSTÄTTE in 1903 with JOSEF HOFFMANN, Moser produced work in many fields of design including furniture, graphics, glass and ceramics.

Muthesius, Hermann (1861–1927)

German. Architect and designer. Muthesius was appointed Technical Attaché at the German Embassy in London in 1895, where he studied developments in the British Arts and Crafts which influenced him heavily in his own work and thoughts. This led to his celebrated publication of *Das Englische Haus* in 1904–5 in which he gave a thorough account of English architecture and design. From 1904 he was an important figure in the reform of Prussian schools of design and sought to promote better standards of design in German industry. This led to his position as one of the founders of the DEUTSCHER WERKBUND in 1907, where he became a strong advocate of standardization.

Omega Workshops (1913–1921)

British. Design group. Launched by the critic Roger Fry, Omega sought to establish a new movement in the decorative arts in Britain. Designers included Fry, VANESSA BELL, Wyndham Lewis, Gaudier-Brzeska and DUNCAN GRANT. The prevailing style owed much to the more decorative tendencies of Cubism and Fauvism.

Paolozzi, Eduardo (b. 1924)

British. Artist and designer. An important figure in the introduction of the imagery of American mass consumerism into the arts in Britain in the 1950s. A member of the Independent Group at the Institute of Contemporary Arts in London which, at its meetings in the early 1950s, looked at themes such as automobile styling, science fiction, popular culture and advertising. He was a leading figure among British Pop artists, and since the 1950s has been involved in textile, fine art and ceramic education in Britain and Germany. He designed the mosaic decorations for Tottenham Court Road Underground station, London, in 1984.

Peche, Dagobert (1887–1923)

Austrian. Designer. Best known for his period as Director of the WIENER WERK-

STÄTTE between 1917 and 1923. His designs were far more effervescent and exuberant than others associated with the early years of the Werkstätte: he drew heavily on Rococo as a source of inspiration.

Poiret, Paul (1877–1934)

French. Designer. A leading couturier and tastemaker of the 1910s and 1920s, Poiret launched the "Atelier Martine" in 1911, a design school for working-class girls. The designs were recognizable by their colourful, flat, often florally based motifs, and extended to textiles, wallpapers, carpets, rugs and interior design. Poiret also started a shop to sell their products which became highly fashionable, but influence waned with the economic depression of the late 1920s.

Pond, Edward (b. 1929)

British. Designer. A leading figure in British textile design since the late 1950s, he has designed for many leading textile and wallpaper manufacturers in Britain and elsewhere. He was responsible for both Pop- and Op-inspired designs in the 1960s, as well as a number of patterns which embraced stylistic revivals. Since establishing Edward Pond Associates in 1976 he has been involved with design consultancy of all kinds.

Popova, Liubov (1889–1924)

Russian. Designer and artist. Although he worked in graphic design, he is best remembered for his Constructivist fabrics and textiles which exhibited strong geometric motifs.

Reeves, Ruth (1892–1966)

American. Designer. After studying at the Pratt Institute in Brooklyn, she worked in Paris 1920–27 under Fernand Léger. She became well known for her textile designs, which showed a strong Cubist influence.

Reid, Jamie (b. 1940)

British. Graphic designer. His 1970s art work for the Punk band, The Sex Pistols, was characterized by directness and

crudity, derived from the ethos of cheap advertising and graffiti. This had a significant impact on the cult of the Punk fanzines.

Rietveld, Gerrit (1888–1964)

Dutch. Designer and architect. After an apprenticeship in cabinet-making Rietveld opened his own furniture business in Utrecht in 1911. He became a member of the DE STIJL group which was founded in 1917. His "Red/Blue Chair" of 1918 and the Schroeder house of 1924 are perhaps the most widely known examples of the De Stijl aesthetic, which explored the geometric vocabulary of forms and primary colours.

Rodchenko, Alexander (1891–1956)

Russian. Designer and artist. One of the leading names of the post-Revolutionary era, he worked in a wide range of media including photography, posters and packaging, clothing, theatre sets and furniture. His Constructivist leanings became heavily geared towards utilitarian art forms.

Ruhlmann, Jacques-Emile (1879–1933)

French. Furniture designer. His work typified the luxury end of the market and explored the potential of expensive materials such as mahogany and ivory. After the First World War he founded his own firm to produce designs which drew both on eighteenth-century precedents and contemporary developments. His work, often associated with the more lavish expressions of Art Deco, attracted considerable attention at the 1925 Paris Exhibition where it could be seen in his "Hotel d'Un Collectionneur".

Sottsass, Ettore (b. 1917)

Italian. Architect and designer. One of the most important Italian designers since the Second World War, working as a consultant to firms such as Olivetti and as a key figure in the "anti-design" arena. His interest in Pop imagery was reflected in his furniture designs for Poltranova in 1966; he also drew on aspects of Eastern mysticism as a source for ceramic designs of the same period. In 1979 he worked with the avant-garde group STUDIO ALCHYMIA, and emerged as the key figure in the formation of the MEMPHIS group.

Stepanova, Varvara (1864–1958)

Russian. Designer. Working in a wide range of design media including graphics and the theatre, she was most widely known for her Constructivist textile designs. She worked with LIUBOV POPOVA at the Tsindel Works in Moscow and was an important figure in the revival of Russian textile design in the 1920s. Many of her designs drew on the imagery of technology.

Studio Alchymia

Italian. Design group. Founded in Milan in the late 1970s, it explored notions of kitsch and the banal as a means of extending the possibilities of a design vocabulary. The "Bau Haus 1" and "Bau Haus 2" exhibitions of 1979 caused considerable controversy in Milan which, despite its importance as a centre for avant-garde design, was more receptive to style-conscious trends.

Süe, Louis (1875–1968)

French. Designer and decorator. In 1919 in partnership with ANDRÉ MARE he founded the Compagnie des Arts Français. With other designers they produced a wide range of furniture and furnishings, many of which were characteristically Art Deco in style.

Tatlin, Vladimir (1885–1953)

Russian. Fine artist and designer. Prior to the 1917 Revolution he was heavily influenced by Futurism and Cubism. Subsequently he became concerned with design of a more utilitarian nature.

Velde, Henry Van de (1863–1957)

Belgian. Architect and designer. After training as a fine artist he was inspired by the English Arts and Crafts Movement and became an important figure in the development of Art Nouveau design from the 1890s. His work was particularly well received in Germany where he enjoyed a wide range of commissions prior to the outbreak of war in 1914. He was a member of the DEUTSCHER WERKBUND from its foundation in 1907, and was Director of the Weimar School of Arts and Crafts from 1908. His commitment to individual expression and creativity in design set him in opposition to HERMANN MUTHESIUS.

Venturi, Robert (b. 1925)

American. Architect, designer and writer. Venturi's ideas have had a profound impact on architecture and design since the 1960s, largely through two books, *Complexity and Contradiction in Architecture* (1966) and *Learning From Las Vegas*, written with Denise Scott Brown and Stephen Izenour (1972). A leading Post-Modernist, he has designed furniture for Knoll and metalware for Alessi.

Wiener Werkstätte (1903–1933)

Austrian. Design Co-operative. Founded by KOLOMAN MOSER and JOSEF HOFFMANN in 1903; early influences were those of C. R. Ashbee and CHARLES RENNIE MACKINTOSH, the former on account of the outlook and practice of his Guild and School of Handicrafts in London, the latter in terms of design style. Initially many of the designs exhibited a strong geometric quality but after about 1915, with the involvement of DAGOBERT PECHE and others, a more florid and free approach characterized much of the workshop's output. After the end of the First World War women designers played an increasingly dominant role and many male detractors unfairly blamed them for the eventual demise of the organization.

Wright, Frank Lloyd (1869–1959)

American. Architect and designer. One of the major influences on twentieth-century architecture and design, he worked for Louis Sullivan in Chicago from 1888 to 1893. He was committed to an Arts and Crafts outlook, designing furniture, metalwork and stained glass within its compass and was involved in the foundation of the Chicago Arts and Crafts Society. He was also interested in Japanese design and, in 1915, went to Tokyo to complete work on the New Imperial Hotel. His work interested many leading architects and designers, exerting a considerable impact on those associated with DE STIJL, particularly after his visit to Europe 1909–10.

FURTHER READING

This outline bibliography is intended to give a flavour of the source material available for the study of twentieth-century ornament. Items have been selected for inclusion which draw on both specialist and popular material in order to indicate the spread of available textual and illustrative publication.

CHAPTER ONE
Progressive Design and Historical Inspiration 1900 to 1914

ANSCOMBE, A., *Omega and After: Bloomsbury and the Decorative Arts*, Thames and Hudson, London, 1981.

ARCHITECTURAL ASSOCIATION, *Czech Functionalism 1918–38*, Architectural Association, London, 1987.

BANHAM, R., *Theory and Design in the First Machine Age*, Architectural Press, London, 1960.

BARONI, D. and D'AURIA, A., *Koloman Moser: Graphic Artist and Designer*, Rizzoli, New York, 1986.

BILLCLIFFE, R., *Charles Rennie Mackintosh—The Complete Furniture Drawings and Interior Design*, Murray, London, 1986.

BURCKHARDT, L., *The Werkbund*, Design Council, London, 1980.

CAMPBELL, J., *The German Werkbund: The Politics of Reform in the Applied Arts*, Princeton University Press, Princeton, 1978.

CORK, R., *Art Beyond the Gallery in Early Twentieth-Century England*, Yale University Press, New Haven and London, 1985.

DARLING, S., *Chicago Furniture: Art, Craft and Industry 1833–1933*, The Chicago Historical Society, Norton, New York and London, 1984.

FISCHER FINE ART, *The Wiener Werkstätte and their Associates 1903–1932*, Fischer Fine Art, London, 1982.

FUCHS, H. and BURKHARDT, F., *Product–Design–History: German Design from 1820 down to the Present Era*, Institute of Foreign Cultural Relations, Stuttgart, 1985.

GLASSTONE, V., *Victorian and Edwardian Theatres*, Thames and Hudson, London, 1975.

GRIGG, J., *Charles Rennie Mackintosh*, Richard Drew, Glasgow, 1987.

HAYWARD GALLERY, *Homage to Barcelona: The City and Its Art 1888–1936*, Arts Council, London, 1985.

HESKETT, J., *Design in Germany 1870–1918*, Trefoil, London, 1986.

KALLIR, J., *Viennese Design and the Wiener Werkstätte*, Thames and Hudson, London, 1986.

KIDNEY, W. C., *The Architecture of Choice: Eclecticism in America 1880–1930*, George Braziller, New York, 1974.

LYNN, C., *Wallpaper in America from the Seventeenth Century to World War 1*, Barra Foundation/Cooper-Hewitt Museum, New York, 1980.

POSENER, J., "Muthesius in England," in *From Schinkel to the Bauhaus*, Architectural Association, London, 1972.

SERVICE, A., *Edwardian Architecture: a Handbook to Building Design in Britain 1890–1914*, Thames and Hudson, London, 1977.

Edwardian Architecture and its Origins, Architectural Press, London, 1975.

Edwardian Interiors: Inside the Homes of the Poor, the Average and the Wealthy, Barrie and Jenkins, London, 1982.

SCHWEIGER, W. J., *Wiener Werkstätte: Design in Vienna 1903–1932*, Thames and Hudson, London, 1984.

STERN, R. A. M., GILMARTIN, G. and MASSENGALE, J., *New York 1900: Metropolitan Architecture and Urbanism 1890–1915*, Rizzoli, New York, 1983.

VERGO, P., *Art in Vienna 1898–1918*, Phaidon, Oxford, 1975.

WALKER, B. (ed.), *Frank Matcham*, Blackstaff, Belfast, 1980.

WOODS, C. (ed.), *Sanderson 1860–1985* (exhibition catalogue), Arthur Sanderson and Sons Ltd, London, 1985.

WILSON, R. G., *McKim, Mead & White, Architects*, Rizzoli, New York, 1983.

CHAPTER TWO
From Historicism to Art Deco 1910 to 1940

ARWAS, V., *Art Deco*, Abrams, New York, 1980.

ATWELL, D., *Cathedrals of the Movies*, Architectural Press, London, 1980.

BATTERSBY, M., *The Decorative Twenties*, Studio Vista, London, 1971; rev. edn. Garner, P. (ed.), The Herbert Press, London, 1988.

The Decorative Thirties, Studio Vista, London, 1969; rev. edn. Garner, P. (ed.), The Herbert Press, London, 1988.

BAUDOT, J.-C., *Arcadia: Slot Machines of Europe and America*, Costello, Tunbridge Wells, 1988.

BRUNHAMMER, Y., *The Nineteen Twenties Style*, Paul Hamlyn, London, 1969.

CERWINSKE, L., *Tropical Deco: the Architecture and Design of Old Miami Beach*, Rizzoli, New York, 1981.

COHEN, A. A., *Sonia Delaunay*, Abrams, London, 1975.

DAVIES, K., *At Home in Manhattan: Modern Decorative Arts, 1925 to the Depression*, Yale University Art Gallery, New Haven, Connecticut, 1983.

DESHOULIÈRES, D., et al., *Robert Mallet-Stevens Architecte*, Archives d'Architecture Moderne, Brussels, 1980.

DUNCAN, A., *American Art Deco*, Thames and Hudson, London, 1986.

GLEYE, P., *The Architecture of Los Angeles*, Rosebud Books, Los Angeles, 1981.

HEIMANN, J. and GEORGES, R., *California Crazy: Roadside Vernacular Architecture*, Chronicle, San Francisco, 1980.

HILLIER, B., *Art Deco*, Studio Vista, London, 1968.

KIMURA, K., *Art Deco Package Collection*, Rikuyo-sha, Tokyo, 1985.

MENTEN, T., *The Art Deco Style in Household Objects, Architecture, Sculpture, Jewelry*, Dover, New York, 1972.

MOURON, H., *Cassandre*, Rizzoli, New York, 1985.

PACKER, W., *The Art of Vogue Covers 1919–1940*, Bonanza, New York, 1980.

ROBINSON, C. and BLETTER, R. H., *Skyscraper Style: Art Deco New York*, Oxford University Press, New York, 1975.

SCARLETT, F. and TOWNLEY, M., *Arts Décoratifs*, Academy Editions, London, 1975.

THAMES TELEVISION, *The Art of Hollywood*, Thames Television, London, 1979.

VERONESI, G., *Style and Design, 1909–29*, Braziller, New York, 1968.

WILSON, R. G., et al., *The Machine Age in America 1918–41*, Abrams, New York, 1986.

CHAPTER THREE
Modernism: Opposition to Decoration 1918 to the late 1930s

ADES, D., *The Twentieth-Century Poster: Design of the Avant Garde*, Abbeville, New York, 1986.

ANIKST, M. (ed.), *Soviet Commercial Design of the Twenties*, Thames and Hudson/Alexandria Press, London, 1987.

ARCHITECTURAL ASSOCIATION, *Czech Functionalism 1918–38*, Architectural Association, London, 1987.

BEL GEDDES, N., *Horizons*, Dover, New York, 1932, repr. 1977.

BUSH, D., *The Streamlined Decade*, Braziller, New York, 1968.

DAVIES, K., *At Home in Manhattan: Modern Decorative Arts, 1925 to the Depression*, Yale University Art Gallery, New Haven, Connecticut, 1983.

ELLIOTT, D., *Art into Production: Soviet Textiles, Fashion and Ceramics 1917–35*, Museum of Modern Art, Oxford, 1984.
New Worlds: Russian Art and Society, Thames and Hudson, London, 1986.

FANELLI, G. and R., *Il Tessuto Art Deco e Anni Trenta*, Cantini, Florence, 1986.

GLEYE, P., *The Architecture of Los Angeles*, Rosebud Books, Los Angeles, 1981.

GRIEF, M., *Depression Modern: the Thirties Style in America*, Universe, New York, 1977.

GUTMAN, R. J. S. and KAUFFMAN, E., *American Diner*, Harper and Row, New York, 1979.

HANKS, D., *Designs of Frank Lloyd Wright*, Studio Vista, London, 1979.

JACKSON, A., *Semi-Detached London: Suburban Life and Transport 1900–1939*, Allen and Unwin, London, 1973.

JAFFÉ, H., *De Stijl 1917–31: Visions of Utopia*, Phaidon, Oxford, 1982.

KHAN-MAGOMEDOV, S. O., *Alexander Rodchenko: the Complete Work*, MIT, Cambridge, Massachusetts, 1987.

LEIDELMEIJER, F., et al., *Art Nouveau en Art Deco in Nederland*, Meulenhoff/Landshoff, Amsterdam, 1983.

LOEWY, R., *Industrial Design*, Overlook, Woodstock, New York, 1979.

MARCHAND, R., *Advertising the American Drdam: Making Way for Modernity 1920–40*, University of California at Los Angeles, Berkeley, 1985.

MEIKLE, J. L., *Twentieth Century Limited: Industrial Design in America*, Temple University Press, Philadelphia, 1979.

NAYLOR, D., *American Picture Palaces: the Architecture of Fantasy*, Van Nostrand Reinhold, New York, 1981.

NAYLOR, G., *The Bauhaus Re-Assessed: Sources and Design Theory*, Herbert Press, London, 1985.

OLIVER, P., et al., *Dunroamin: the Suburban Semi and its Enemies*, Barrie and Jenkins, London, 1981.

SEMBACH, K.-J., *Into the Thirties: Style and Design 1927–1934*, Thames and Hudson, London, 1972.

SHARP, D., *The Picture Palace*, Thames and Hudson, London, 1969.

STEDELIJK MUSEUM, *Malevich*, Stedelijk Museum, Amsterdam, 1989.

TROY, N., *The De Stijl Environment*, MIT, Cambridge, Massachusetts, 1983.

WHITE, S., *The Bolshevik Poster*, Yale University Press, London and New Haven, 1988.

WILSON, R. G., et al., *The Machine Age in America 1918–41*, Abrams, New York, 1986.

WINGLER, H. M., *The Bauhaus: Weimar, Dessau, Berlin, Chicago*, MIT, Cambridge, Massachusetts, 1969.

WIRZ, H. and STRINER, R., *Washington Deco: Art Deco in the Nation's Capital*, Smithsonian Institution Press, Washington, 1984.

WRIGHT, G., *Building the Dream: a Social History of Housing in America*, Pantheon, New York, 1981.

WURTZ, R., *The New York World's Fair 1939/40*, Dover, New York, 1977.

YASINSKAYA, I., *Soviet Textile Design of the Revolutionary Period*, Thames and Hudson, London, 1983.

CHAPTER FOUR
Design and Ornament in a Totalitarian Climate 1920 to 1940

CAMPBELL, J., *The German Werkbund: the Politics of Reform in the Applied Arts*, Princeton University Press, Princeton, 1978.

COMMUNE DI MILANO, *Annitrenta: Arte e Cultura in Italia*, Mazzotta, Milan, 1982.

DANESI, S. and PATTETA, L., *1919–1943: Rationalisme et Architecture en Italie*, Electa, Paris, 1976.

ELLIOTT, D., *Art into Production: Soviet Textiles, Fashion and Ceramics 1917–35*, Museum of Modern Art, Oxford, 1984.
  New Worlds: Russian Art and Society, Thames and Hudson, London, 1986.

FABBRI EDITORI, *Fiat 1899–1989: an Industrial Revolution*, Science Museum, London, 1988.

FANELLI, G. and R., *Il Tessuto Art Deco e Anni Trenta*, Cantini, Florence, 1986.

FUCHS, H. and BURKHARDT, F., *Product–Design–History: German Design from 1820 down to the Present Era*, Institute for Foreign Cultural Relations, Stuttgart, 1985.

HESKETT, J., "Modernism and Archaism in Design in the Third Reich," *Block*, Middlesex Polytechnic, London, No. 3, 1980, pp. 17–20.

HINZ, B., *Art in the Third Reich*, Blackwell, Oxford, 1979.

MILLER-LANE, B., *Architecture and Politics in Germany 1918–1945*, Harvard, Cambridge, Massachusetts, 1968.

YASINSKAYA, I., *Soviet Textile Design of the Revolutionary Period*, Thames and Hudson, London, 1983.

CHAPTER FIVE
From Austerity to Affluence 1940 to 1960

BANHAM, M. and HILLIER, B. (eds.), *A Tonic to the Nation*, Thames and Hudson, London, 1986.

BANHAM, R. (ed. Sparke, P.), *Design By Choice*, Academy Editions, London, 1981.

Los Angeles: the Architecture of Four Ecologies, Penguin, Harmondsworth, repr. 1978.

BAYLEY, S., *Harley Earl and the Dream Machine*, Weidenfeld and Nicolson, London, 1989.

BRADBURY, M. et al., *Fifty Penguin Years*, Penguin, Harmondsworth, 1985.

BRANZI, A. and DE LUCCHI, M., *Il Design Italiano degli Anni '50*, IGIS Edizioni, Milan, 1981.

CARRINGTON, N., *Design and Decoration in the Home*, Batsford, London, 1952.

CENTRE GEORGES POMPIDOU, *Les Années 50*, Centre Georges Pompidou, Paris, 1988.

CONWAY, H., *Ernest Race*, Design Council, London, 1982.

GEFFRYE MUSEUM, *Utility Furniture and Fashion*, ILEA, London, 1974.

FARR, M., *Design in British Industry—a Mid-Century Survey*, Cambridge University Press, Cambridge, 1955.

FESTIVAL COUNCIL, *The Story of the Festival of Britain*, HMSO, London, 1952.

FOSSATI, P., *Il Design in Italia 1945–72*, Einaudi, Turin, 1972.

HESS, A., *Googie: Fifties Coffee Shop Architecture*, Chronicle, San Francisco, 1985.

HIESINGER, K. B. and MARCUS, G. H. (eds.), *Design Since 1945*, Philadelphia Museum of Art, Philadelphia, 1980.

HILLIER, B., *Austerity/Binge: the Decorative Arts of the Forties and Fifties*, Studio Vista, London, 1971.

HINE, T., *Populuxe*, Alfred A. Knopf, New York, 1986.
  Images of an Era: the American Poster 1945–1975, MIT, Cambridge, Massachusetts, 1975.

LARRABEE, L. and VIGNELLI, M., *Knoll Design*, Abrams, New York, 1981.

MacCARTHY, F., *A History of British Design 1830–1970*, Allen and Unwin, London, 1979.

McFADDEN, D. R., *Scandinavian Modern Design 1880–1980*, Abrams, New York, 1982.

PHILLIPS, L., *High Styles: Twentieth-Century American Design*, Whitney Museum, New York, 1985.

PULOS, A. J., *The American Design Adventure: 1940–1975*, MIT, Cambridge, Massachusetts, 1988.

ROYAL COLLEGE OF ART, *Ark*, Royal College of Art, London, No. 19, 1956.

SCHOESER, M., *Marion Straub*, Design Council, London, 1984.

SLOAN, A. P., *My Years with General Motors*, Penguin, Harmondsworth, repr. 1986.

SPARKE, P. (ed.), *Did Britain Make It? British Design in Context 1946–86*, Design Council, London, 1986.

STAAL, G. and WOLTERS, H., *Holland in Norm—Dutch Design 1945–87*, CIP–Gegevens Kononklijke Bibliotheek, The Hague, 1987.

WIGHT GALLERY, FREDERICK S., *Design Process Olivetti 1908–1978*, University of California, Los Angeles, 1979.

CHAPTER SIX
Pop and Post-Pop 1960 to 1975

AMBASZ, E. (ed.), *Italy: the New Domestic Landscape*, Museum of Modern Art, New York, 1972.

BRAKE, M., *The Sociology of Youth Culture and Youth Subcultures*, Routledge and Kegan Paul, London, 1980.

CENTRE GEORGES POMPIDOU, *Design Français 1960–1990*, APCI/Centre Georges Pompidou, Paris, 1988.

COOK, P. (ed.), *Archigram*, Studio Vista, London, 1972.

DORFLES, G. (ed.), *Kitsch: the World of Bad Taste*, Studio Vista, London, 1969.

ERRIGO, A. and LEANING, S., *The Illustrated History of the Rock Album Cover*, Octopus, London, 1979.

HEBDIGE, D., *Subculture: the Meaning of Style*, Methuen, London, 1979.

HENDERSON, S. and LANDAU, R., *Billboard Art*, Chronicle, San Francisco, 1979.

KEEN, G. and LA RUE, M. (eds.), *Underground Graphics*, Academy Editions, London, 1970.

LIPPARD, L., *Pop Art*, Thames and Hudson, London, 3rd edn 1976.

MASTERS, R. E. L. and HOUSTON, J., *Psychedelic Art*, Grove, New York, 1968.

MELLY, G., *Revolt into Style*, Penguin, Harmondsworth, 1967.

"ROLLING STONE," *The Sixties*, Rolling Stone, New York, 1977.

SPARKE, P., *Ettore Sottsass Jnr*, Design Council, London, 1982.

WHEEN, F., *The Sixties*, Channel Four/Century, London, 1982.

WHITELEY, N., *Pop Design: from Modernism to Mod*, Design Council, London, 1987.

WOLFE, T., *The Kandy-Kolored Tangerine-Flake Streamline Baby*, Mayflower, London, 1965.

CHAPTER SEVEN
Ornament and Post-Modernism 1975 to the 1980s

BRANZI, A., *The Hot House*, Thames and Hudson, London, 1984.

DORMER, P. and TURNER, R., *The New Jewelry: Trends and Traditions*, Thames and Hudson, London, 1985.

HEWISON, R., *The Heritage Industry*, Methuen, London, 1987.

HORN, R., *Memphis: Objects, Furniture and Patterns*, Quarto, New York, 1986.

INSTITUTE OF CONTEMPORARY ARTS, *Graphic Rap*, ICA, London, 1982–3.

JENCKS, C., *The Language of Post-Modern Architecture*, Academy, London, 1977.
Post-Modern Classicism, Academy, London, 1980.

JENSEN, R. and CONWAY, P., *Ornamentalism: the New Decorativeness in Architecture and Design*, Allen Lane, Harmondsworth, 1983.

KRON, S. and SLESIN, S., *High Tech: the Industrial Style and Source Book for the Home*, Allen Lane, Harmondsworth, 1978.

MORGAN, A. L. (ed.), *Contemporary Designers*, Macmillan, London, 1984.

RADICE, B., *Memphis: Research, Experiences, Results, Failures and Successes of New Design*, Thames and Hudson, London, 1984.

SARTAGO. P., *Italian Re-Evolution: Design in Italian Society in the Eighties*, Museum of Contemporary Art, La Jolla, California, 1986.

SUDJIC, D., *Cult Objects*, Paladin, London, 1985.

THACKARA, J. and JANE, S., *New British Design*, Thames and Hudson, London, 1986.

VENTURI, R., SCOTT BROWN, D. and IZENOUR, S., *Learning from Las Vegas*, MIT, Cambridge, Massachusetts, 1972.

WILLIAMSON, J., *Consuming Passions: the Dynamics of Popular Culture*, Marion Boyars, London, 1985.

WOLFE, T., *From Bauhaus to Our House*, Cape, London, 1982.

WRIGHT, P., *On Living in an Old Country: the National Past in Contemporary Britain*, Verso, London, 1985.

YORK, P., *Style Wars*, Sidgwick and Jackson, London, 1980.

CHAPTER EIGHT
The Marketing of "Individual" Taste: into the 1990s

ALDERSLEY-WILLIAMS, H., *New American Design: Products and Graphics for a Post-Industrial Age*, Rizzoli, New York, 1988.

CAMUFFO, G., *Pacific Wave: California Graphic Design*, Magnus Edizione, 1987.

COOPER, M. and CHALFANT, H., *Subway Art*, Thames and Hudson, London, 1984.

DORFLES, G., "T-Shirts as Mass Media," in *T-Shirt Show*, Electra, London, 1984.

McDERMOTT, C., *Street Style: British Design in the 80s*, Design Council, London, 1987.

THACKARA, J. (ed.), *Design After Modernism: Beyond the Object*, Thames and Hudson, London, 1988.

Magazines and Periodicals

For the study of changing attitudes to ornament, style and design, especially of the more recent past, much of the most useful material is to be found in contemporary magazines. A wide range of magazines has been in evidence throughout the century, although they have proliferated enormously over the past two decades or so. For an indication of the scope of the current design press see *Design and Applied Arts Index* (Design Documentation, Burwash, England, from 1987) which indexes over 200 journals. Furthermore, many of the books listed above have full bibliographies with extensive historical periodical references. For a wider study of everyday attitudes to ornament, however, it is necessary to look at a cross-section of wider circulation magazines.

INDEX

PICTURE CREDITS

The author and publishers would like to thank the following:

Pat Albeck, London: 248 top. Isabelle Anscombe, *Omega and After: Bloomsbury & the Decorative Arts* (Thames & Hudson): 26, 46 right; Howard Grey 46 all, 47. © Apple Corps: 252 top. Ron Arad, London: 305 bottom. Arcaid, London: Richard Bryant 304, 306 both, 307. Architectural Association, London: 128 bottom, 284; S. Brandolini 298 left; Bob Vickery 126; Yerbury Collection 82 bottom, 85 top, 88, 91, 147 centre, 170. Architectural Press, London: 157. Astrohome Ltd, London: 298 right. Backnumbers, London: 241. Fred Baier, Pewsey: 297. Mrs Zita Mosca Baldessari, Milan: 178. Estate of Giacomo Balla, Rome: 173 bottom. Barnaby's Picture Library, London: 68, 107 bottom, 133 bottom, 175, 186 bottom, 244, 266 right. Bauhaus-Archiv, Berlin: 43 top, 115, 130 top left, 130 top right, 130 bottom left, 133 top, 134 both, 135 both. Bianchini-Férier, Lyon: 20 (archives number 295). Branson Coates, London: Edward Valentine Hames 276–7. Andrea Branzi, Milan: 265. Braun Electric (UK) Ltd: 259. The Brewers Society, London: 81 bottom, 221, 223 top. Brionvega, Milan: A. Ballo 258 top. British Film Institute, London: 72, 89 top, 98 top. British Home Stores plc, London: 281 bottom. Eric Brockway, Warmley: 229 bottom right. The Brooklyn Museum, New York: 101 top (The H. Randolph Lever Fund), 150 top. Cameron Books, London: 232. Casnell Ltd, London: Robin Beeche, 282. Centre de Création Industrielle, Centre G. Pompidou, Paris: Planchet 216 right. Henry Chalfont, New York: 314–15. Chicago Historical Society: 144 both, 151 bottom. Christie's South Kensington: 156. Cinémathèque Française, Paris: 128 top left, 195. Paul Clark, Brighton: 229 bottom left. The Coca-Cola Company Archives, Atlanta, Georgia: 63, 147 bottom. Columbus Association for the Performing Arts, Ohio: 73. Compagnie Générale Maritime: Agence Le Havre 37 both. Cooper-Hewitt Museum, New York: 148 top. Giancarlo Costa, Milan: 177. The Courtauld Institute, London: 162. Shirley Craven, London: 255 left. Estate of Sonia Delaunay, Paris: Monique Schneider Maunoury 78 bottom left, 85 bottom. © Fortunato Depero/DACS: 172 bottom. Design Museum, London: 262 right. Alistair Duncan, New York: 149 (collection: John Axelrod, Boston). Dyson Research Design Development, Bath: 296 left. Edifice, London: 57, 146 top. M. Ekstein & I. J. M. Mazure, London: 139 bottom. English Eccentrics: 288. English Ironstone Tableware Ltd, Stoke-on-Trent: 280. Fashion Institute of Technology, New York: Irving E. Solero 219 (accession # X318). Fiat, London: 176 top. Finarte Casa d'Aste SpA, Milan: 179 right. Ford, Dearborn, Michigan: 225. Formica Ltd: 222 top, 223 bottom left & centre. Fornasetti Srl, Milan: 179 left, 295 bottom. Bibliothèque Forney, Paris: 70 top. Lynne Franks Ltd, London: 303 bottom. Philippe Garner, London: 12–13 & jacket, 16, 17, 18, 31, 32 top left, 44 all, 60, 71, 83 bottom right, 84 bottom, 86 top, 87 bottom, 100 top right, 117 right, 129, 158 top, 210 top, 211, 222 bottom, 230 bottom, 231 all, 249 top, 253, 254 left, 258 bottom, 260 top, 263 left. Gemeentearchief Amsterdam: 127 bottom. General Motors Design, Warren, Michigan: 143 top. Denis Gifford Collection, London: 142 bottom. Milton Glaser Inc., New York: 255 right. Michael Graves, New Jersey: 273. Greater London Photo Library: 66, 216 bottom left, 220. © Greeff Fabrics Inc.: 6 top, 11. Sally & Richard Greenhill, London: 267. Richard & Kellie Gutman Collection, West Roxbury, Massachusetts: 124. Claus Hansmann, Munich: 34 (Österreichisches Museum für Angewandte Kunst, Vienna), 39 (Bayerisches Nationalmuseum, Munich), 42 bottom (private collection), 42 top, 43 bottom and 183 bottom (all Die Neue Sammlung, Munich). Robert Harding Associates, London: 213. Hedrich-Blessing, Chicago: 96 bottom, 146 bottom. Alan Hess, Googie: *Fifties Coffee Shop Architecture* (Chronicle Books, 1985): 202. Historisches Museum der Stadt Wien, Vienna: 33 bottom. The Holburne Museum and Crafts Study Centre, Bath: 158 bottom left. Bernard Holdaway, Rochester, Kent: 236, 247 bottom. Hans Hollein, Vienna: Jerzy Surwillo 285. Angelo Hornak, London: 52, 62, 79, 90, 92, 94, 95 right, 97, title page & 108, 93 both. Hulton-Deutsch, London: 208 top. Ironbridge Gorge Museum Trust: 104 top right. Johnson Wax, Racine: 147 top. Jan & Lily Juffermans, Utrecht, The Netherlands: 129 top. Badisches Landesmuseum, Karlsruhe: 137 bottom right. Knoll International, New York: 197. The Kobal Collection, London: 98 bottom. Historical Archive Friedrich Krupp, Essen: 182 bottom. Larsen Design Studio, New York: 289 bottom right. Laura Ashley, London: 270. Leeds Russian Archive, University of Leeds: 118 (MS783/24 © 1988 Heirs of E. C. Hayes). Liberty, London: 257. The Library of Congress, Washington DC: 109 top (Theodor Horydczak collection neg. # LC-H8-1951-6). The University of Liverpool, University Archives: 36. London Transport Museum: 158 bottom right, 165, 246 left, 302 left. Lufthansa, Cologne: 182 top. Nicholas Lynn, The Winter Palace, London: 139 top, 140 top, 141 top. J. Lyons & Company Ltd, London: 65. Magnum Photos Limited, London: David Hurn 238–9, Leonard Freed 312. Bildarchiv Foto Marburg: 32–3, 113. Kirsty McLaren, London: 14, 99. Alessandro Mendini, Milan: 292. Metropolitan Museum of Art, New York: 100 top left (Gift of Mrs R. C. Jacobsen 1954 [54.14.2ab]), 101 bottom (Gift of Theodore R. Gamble [1983.228.31]). Alan Moss, New York: 96 top, 145 top right, 148 bottom. Musée de Strasbourg: 128 top right. Museo del Tessuto, Prato: 174 middle & bottom. Museum of the City of New York: 28, 50 both, 51 bottom, 143 bottom right & left. Kazumasa Nagai, Tokyo: 303 top. The Newark Museum, New Jersey: 82 top (Purchase 1930), 107 top (Herman E. E. & Paul C. Jaehne Collection, 1939). Robert Opie Collection, London: 104 centre left, 177 middle. Orrefors Sweden: 247 top. Pastoe, Utrecht: 223 bottom right. Philadelphia Museum of Art: 120, 217. G. A. Platz, *Die Baukunst der Neuesten Ziet* (Berlin, 1927): 132 both. Ploegstoffen, Eindhoven: 214 top. Popperfoto, London: 74, 75 both, 189 bottom, 210 bottom, 224 bottom left, 245, 256. Harry Ransom Humanities Research Center, The University of Texas at Austin: 54 (Theater Arts Collection), 100 bottom, 142 top, 151 top (all Norman Bel Geddes Collection). Rath & Doodeheefver B. V. Rijen, The Netherlands: 230 top. Reading Museum & Art Gallery: 78 top. Retrograph Archive Collection, London: 46, 51 top, 70 bottom, 83 top right, 86 bottom, 117 left, 174 top, 181, 216 top, 233, 218. Rex Features Ltd, London: 188, 234, 249 bottom, 252 bottom, 254 right, 261, 266 left. Rijksdienst Beeldende Kunst, The Hague: 110. Roger-Viollet, Paris: 45. Royal Commission on the Ancient & Historical Monuments of Scotland, Edinburgh: 30. Royal Doulton, Stoke-on-Trent: 10 bottom. Arthur Sanderson & Sons Ltd, Uxbridge: 56, 76. Scala, Florence: 137 top, 137 bottom left, 138, 141 bottom, 160, 190, 191. Science Museum, London: 150 left. John & Penny Smith, Tasmania: 305 top. *The Studio*: 35 bottom (1904), 77 (1924). *The Studio Year Book of Decorative Art*: 38 (1914), 40 both (1910), 22 (1912), 67 (1933), 83 left (1937), 102 top & 103 top (1914). Svenskt Tenn, Stockholm: 226, 227. Syracuse University: IDSA Archives, Arents Research Library 229 centre left. Today Interiors, Grantham, Lincolnshire: 281 bottom. Tombrock Corporation, Stamford, Connecticut: 154–5. Topham Picture Source, Edenbridge, Kent: 246–7 centre bottom, 248 bottom, 250–1. By Courtesy of the Board & Trustees of the Victoria & Albert Museum, London: 102 bottom, 104 bottom, 106, 152 both, 158 middle, 159, 199, 204, 205, 208 bottom, 210 middle; Library: 180 left (R. Aloi, *L'Arradamento Moderno*, 1934), 183 top & 186 top (*Innen-Dekoration*, Darmstadt, 1938), 184 bottom (*Innen-Dekoration*, 1939), 184 top (*Kunst im Dritten Reich*, Berlin, 1938), 185 (*Kunst im Dritten Reich*, 1939), 187 (*Kunst im Dritten Reich*, 1937), 189 top (*La Manufacture d'Etat de Porcelaine Lomonosov*). Volkswagen AG, Wolfsburg: 192. Warner Archives, Braintree, Essex: 215 left. © Warner Fabrics plc: 10 top, 153, 214 bottom, 262 left, 264 top, 278–9, 283. © Warner Fabrics plc/Eddie Squires: 263 right. By Courtesy of the Wedgwood Museum Trustees, Barlaston, Stoke-on-Trent, Staffordshire: 6 bottom, 9, 242, 260 bottom, 279. The Wolfsonian Foundation, Miami Beach, Florida: 145 bottom. Jonathan M. Woodham, Brighton, Sussex: 80, 105 right, 196–7, 212 both. The Frank Lloyd Wright Foundation, Arizona: 109 bottom. Tadanori Yokoo, Tokyo: 296 right.

Uncredited pictures are from the John Calmann and King Archives.